Think, Code, Create

Advanced Python Programming Series

Northward House Publishing

A series of twelve advanced programming books for secondary students.

Each book is a standalone resource. Read alone or as part of the full series.

Designed for Years 9–12

Australian Curriculum Version 9 — Digital Technologies

Prerequisite: Think, Code, Create — A Python Programming Journey for Students
ISBN 978-1-7640698-0-9

Think, Code, Create — Advanced Python Programming Series

BOOK 1

Object-Oriented Programming in Python

Design and build programs using classes, objects, and the four pillars of OOP

M. North

BEd. (Sec), BSc, MInfoTech

Northward House Publishing

Brisbane, Queensland, Australia

2025

Prerequisite:

Think, Code, Create — A Python Programming Journey for Students

About the Author

M. North holds a Bachelor of Education (Secondary), a Bachelor of Science, and a Master of Information Technology. He has worked as a secondary school teacher of Digital Technologies, Mathematics, and Science across Queensland, Australia, before turning to educational publishing full time.

His teaching practice has centred on making abstract computational thinking concrete and accessible for students at every level — from those encountering programming for the first time to advanced students pursuing algorithmic thinking and software engineering. The Think, Code, Create series grew directly from classroom experience: the need for structured, curriculum-aligned materials that treat secondary students as capable thinkers, not passive recipients of watered-down content.

The foundation text, Think, Code, Create — A Python Programming Journey for Students (ISBN 978-1-7640698-0-9), established the pedagogical approach: clear explanations, worked examples with annotated code, guided exercises with hints, and challenge tasks for extension. The twelve-book advanced series extends that approach through specialised programming domains — from object-oriented design and data structures through to concurrency, networking, and automation — with the same rigour and the same respect for the reader.

M. North is based in Brisbane, Queensland, Australia, and publishes through Northward House Publishing.

Northward House Publishing

Brisbane, Queensland, Australia

www.northwardhousepublishing.com.au

Feedback, corrections, and curriculum enquiries are welcome. Contact the publisher via the website above.

Publication Information

First published 2025

Published by Northward House Publishing, Brisbane, Queensland, Australia

This book is part of the Think, Code, Create — Advanced Python Programming Series.

This volume ISBN: 978-1-7640698-4-7

Acknowledgements

The author and publisher gratefully acknowledge the contribution of all teachers and students who provided feedback during the development of this series. The Python programming language is created and maintained by the Python Software Foundation (python.org).

Disclaimer

The information in this book is provided in good faith and is accurate to the best of the author's knowledge at the time of publication. Programming languages, libraries, and tools change over time. The publisher and author accept no liability for errors, omissions, or outcomes arising from the use of code or information in this publication.

All example programs are written for educational purposes. Any resemblance to real persons, organisations, or events in example scenarios is coincidental.

The Complete Series

The twelve books in the Think, Code, Create Advanced Series are designed for students who have completed the foundation text. Each book is a standalone resource — you may read them in any order based on your interests or curriculum pathway. The recommended pathways below are a guide, not a requirement.

01 Object-Oriented Programming in Python
Design and build programs using classes, objects, and the four pillars of OOP
Prerequisite: Foundation text Chapters 14–15 **Audience:** Years 9–12

02 File Handling & Exception Management
Read, write, and manage data files; handle errors gracefully in real-world programs
Prerequisite: Foundation text Chapters 3–4, 11–12 **Audience:** Years 9–12

03 Modules, Packages & the Python Ecosystem
Organise, share, and reuse code with modules, packages, and the broader Python library
Prerequisite: Foundation text Chapters 14–15 **Audience:** Years 9–12

04 Data Structures & Algorithms
Understand, implement, and analyse core data structures and fundamental algorithms
Prerequisite: Foundation text Chapters 11–13 **Audience:** Years 10–12

05 Functional Programming & Advanced Iterables
Master Python's functional tools — generators, comprehensions, closures, and more
Prerequisite: Foundation text Chapters 14–15 **Audience:** Years 10–12

06 Regular Expressions & Advanced Text Processing
Search, validate, and transform text data using Python's powerful re module
Prerequisite: Foundation text Chapter 10 **Audience:** Years 10–12

07 Database Programming with Python
Store and retrieve data persistently using SQLite, SQL queries, and Python ORMs
Prerequisite: Books 01–02 recommended **Audience:** Years 10–12

08 Web Scraping & Working with APIs
Collect real-world data from websites and web services using Python
Prerequisite: Books 02–03 recommended **Audience:** Years 10–12

09 Data Analysis with Python
Explore, clean, and visualise real-world datasets using NumPy, Pandas, and Matplotlib
Prerequisite: Book 03; spreadsheet literacy **Audience:** Years 11–12

10 GUI Programming with Tkinter

Design and build graphical desktop applications using Python's built-in GUI toolkit
Prerequisite: Book 01 (OOP) **Audience:** Years 10–12

11 Testing, Debugging & Code Quality
Write reliable, maintainable code using testing frameworks, debugging tools, and style standards
Prerequisite: Books 01 and 03 **Audience:** Years 11–12

12 Concurrency, Networking & Automation
Write programs that do multiple things at once, communicate over networks, and automate tasks
Prerequisite: Books 01, 02, and 03 **Audience:** Years 11–12

How to Use This Book

Each book in the Advanced Series is structured in the same way. Understanding the format will help you get the most from each chapter.

Chapter Structure

Every chapter opens with a blockquote that describes what the chapter covers and connects it to what you already know. This is followed by seven numbered sections, each with worked examples, a note callout for important warnings or tips, and closing paragraphs that lead to the next concept.

At the end of each chapter you will find:

- **Chapter Summary** — Eight bullet points summarising the key concepts from the chapter.
- **Guided Exercises** — Five hands-on tasks with hints to help you get started. Complete these before moving on.
- **Challenge Tasks** — Three open-ended tasks with no hints. These require independent problem-solving and are suitable for extension or assessment.

Code Examples

All code is shown in shaded blocks. Every non-obvious line has an inline comment. Each section contains three examples: an Introduction example that introduces the concept in isolation, a Variation example that extends or explores an edge case, and a Real-world application example set in a recognisable context — school, finance, or commerce.

Output blocks immediately follow their code and show exactly what the program prints when run. You should be able to reproduce every output exactly by running the code in a Python 3.10 or later interpreter.

Prior Knowledge

This series assumes you have completed Think, Code, Create — A Python Programming Journey for Students. Foundational concepts (variables, data types, loops, functions, lists, dictionaries) are not re-explained. Where a prior chapter or book is relevant, you will see a brief cross-reference in the text.

Within this book, chapters build on each other. Earlier chapters are referenced with a note rather than a full explanation. If you encounter an unfamiliar concept, check the chapter cross-reference and review that material before continuing.

Table of Contents

CHAPTER 1 Introduction to OOP Concepts

Book 01: Object-Oriented Programming in Python

> *This chapter establishes the conceptual foundation for object-oriented programming in Python. Rather than revisiting what you already know — variables, functions, loops — it reframes how you see a program: not as a sequence of instructions, but as a collection of interacting objects, each responsible for its own data and behaviour. You will learn why OOP exists, what structural problems it solves, and how Python's own object model underpins every program you have ever written. By the end of this chapter, you will be ready to design programs in terms of objects before writing a single line of code.*

1.1 Procedural vs Object-Oriented Thinking

When you worked through Think, Code, Create, every program you built followed a broadly procedural structure: data was stored in variables, and functions operated on that data. Instructions ran from top to bottom. A function calculated a result, a loop processed a list, a variable tracked a running total. For programs of modest size, this is clear and effective.

The problem emerges with scale. Procedural code stores data in one place and the logic that acts on that data in another. As a program grows, these two things drift apart. Functions accumulate, variables multiply, and the relationships between them exist only in the programmer's memory — not in the structure of the code itself.

Object-oriented programming addresses this by bundling data and behaviour together into a single unit called an object. Instead of a function receiving data as arguments, an object carries its own data and exposes methods — functions that belong to it — for interacting with that data. The result is code that models the structure of the problem rather than just the steps to solve it.

The classic comparison

Consider a program that manages student records. The procedural approach reaches for parallel lists — one for names, one for IDs, one for grades. The object-oriented approach reaches for a class.

Example 1 — Introduction

The procedural approach: student data stored in parallel lists, with a function to display a record.

```
# Procedural approach — student data in parallel lists
names  = ["Alice", "Bob", "Cara"]
ids    = [1001, 1002, 1003]
grades = [88.5, 72.0, 95.0]


def print_student(index):
    print(f"ID: {ids[index]}  Name: {names[index]}  Grade: {grades[index]:.1f}")
```

```
print_student(0)
print_student(1)
```

Output:

```
ID: 1001  Name: Alice  Grade: 88.5
ID: 1002  Name: Bob  Grade: 72.0
```

Example 2 — Variation

The fragility of parallel lists: a common mistake that the code cannot prevent.

```
# Adding a student — three separate updates required
names.append("Dan")
ids.append(1004)
grades.append(81.0)

# A mistake — forgot to append a grade
names.append("Eva")
ids.append(1005)
# grades now has four elements; names and ids have five
# print_student(4) will raise an IndexError

print_student(4)  # IndexError: list index out of range
```

Nothing in the code prevents this mistake. The relationship between `names[0]`, `ids[0]`, and `grades[0]` exists only in the programmer's understanding. There is no structural enforcement.

Example 3 — Real-world application

The object-oriented approach: each student carries its own data, and the class enforces that a student is always created with all three pieces of information.

```
class Student:
    def __init__(self, student_id, name, grade):
        self.student_id = student_id
        self.name       = name
        self.grade      = grade

    def display(self):
        print(f"ID: {self.student_id}  Name: {self.name}  Grade:
{self.grade:.1f}")
```

```
alice = Student(1001, "Alice", 88.5)
bob   = Student(1002, "Bob",   72.0)
eva   = Student(1005, "Eva",   91.0)  # all three values required

alice.display()
eva.display()
```

Output:

```
ID: 1001  Name: Alice  Grade: 88.5
ID: 1005  Name: Eva  Grade: 91.0
```

Each `Student` object owns its data. Adding a new student means creating one new object — there are no parallel structures to keep synchronised. If you attempt to create a `Student` without all three arguments, Python raises a `TypeError` immediately, catching the mistake at the source.

1.2 Why OOP Matters

OOP is not simply a style preference. It solves a concrete set of problems that procedural programming handles poorly at scale: code organisation, reusability, modelling real-world relationships, and long-term maintainability.

Reusability is the most immediately visible benefit. Once you have defined a class, you can create as many instances of it as you need, each with its own independent state. Adding behaviour to all students at once means editing one class — not hunting through dozens of functions.

Modelling is the second major benefit. Object-oriented code reads more closely to how we think about the real world. A student has a name and a grade. A bank account has a balance and an owner. A vehicle has a make and a speed. These entities map naturally to classes and objects in a way that flat variables and functions do not.

Extending behaviour

Example 1 — Introduction

Adding a new method to a class immediately makes it available on every existing instance — without touching any other code.

```
class Student:
    def __init__(self, student_id, name, grade):
        self.student_id = student_id
        self.name       = name
        self.grade      = grade

    def display(self):
        print(f"ID: {self.student_id}  Name: {self.name}  Grade:
{self.grade:.1f}")
```

```
    def is_passing(self, pass_mark=50.0):
        return self.grade >= pass_mark

alice = Student(1001, "Alice", 88.5)
bob   = Student(1002, "Bob",   42.0)

print(alice.is_passing())  # True
print(bob.is_passing())    # False
```

Output:

```
True
False
```

Example 2 — Variation

Creating multiple independent instances: each object holds its own state and does not affect any other.

```
students = [
    Student(1001, "Alice", 88.5),
    Student(1002, "Bob",   42.0),
    Student(1003, "Cara",  76.0),
    Student(1004, "Dan",   55.5),
]

passing = [s for s in students if s.is_passing()]
print(f"{len(passing)} out of {len(students)} students are passing.")
```

Output:

```
3 out of 4 students are passing.
```

Example 3 — Real-world application

A small school system: classes, enrolment, and grade reporting working together through objects.

```
class Classroom:
    def __init__(self, room_code, subject):
        self.room_code = room_code
        self.subject   = subject
        self.students  = []


    def enrol(self, student):
        self.students.append(student)
```

```python
    def class_average(self):
        if not self.students:
            return 0.0
        total = sum(s.grade for s in self.students)
        return total / len(self.students)

    def report(self):
        print(f"--- {self.subject} ({self.room_code}) ---")
        for s in self.students:
            s.display()
        print(f"Class average: {self.class_average():.1f}")


maths = Classroom("12A", "Mathematics")
maths.enrol(Student(1001, "Alice", 88.5))
maths.enrol(Student(1002, "Bob",   72.0))
maths.enrol(Student(1003, "Cara",  95.0))
maths.report()
```

Output:

```
--- Mathematics (12A) ---
ID: 1001  Name: Alice  Grade: 88.5
ID: 1002  Name: Bob  Grade: 72.0
ID: 1003  Name: Cara  Grade: 95.0
Class average: 85.2
```

Two classes, each responsible for a distinct concept, working together through composition. The `Classroom` does not know how a `Student` displays itself — it simply calls `display()` and trusts the `Student` to handle it. This separation of responsibilities is a hallmark of well-designed OOP.

1.3 What Is a Class? What Is an Object?

A class is a blueprint. It defines the structure and behaviour that every object created from it will share: which attributes it will have, and which methods it can perform. An object is a specific instance of that blueprint — a realisation of the class with its own set of values for each attribute.

A useful analogy: a class is the architectural plans for a house. The plans define how many rooms there are, where the doors go, and what the structure looks like. An object is an actual house built from those plans. You can build many houses from the same plans; each house is a separate building with its own address, its own furnishings, and its own residents, but they all share the same structural blueprint.

In Python, a class is defined with the `class` keyword. The `__init__` method (called the constructor) runs automatically each time a new object is created and sets up its initial state. The first parameter of every method in a class is `self`, which refers to the specific object the method is being called on.

Example 1 — Introduction

A minimal class definition: two attributes, one method.

```
class Book:
    def __init__(self, title, author):
        self.title  = title   # instance attribute
        self.author = author  # instance attribute

    def describe(self):
        print(f'"{self.title}" by {self.author}')

b = Book("Dune", "Frank Herbert")
b.describe()
```

Output:

```
"Dune" by Frank Herbert
```

Example 2 — Variation

Multiple instances from the same class: each object is independent and holds its own data.

```
book1 = Book("Dune",             "Frank Herbert")
book2 = Book("1984",             "George Orwell")
book3 = Book("The Great Gatsby","F. Scott Fitzgerald")

for b in [book1, book2, book3]:
    b.describe()

# Modifying one instance does not affect the others
book1.title = "Dune Messiah"
book1.describe()
book2.describe()  # unchanged
```

Output:

```
"Dune" by Frank Herbert
"1984" by George Orwell
"The Great Gatsby" by F. Scott Fitzgerald
"Dune Messiah" by Frank Herbert
"1984" by George Orwell
```

> **Note:** self is not a keyword — it is a naming convention. Python requires only that the first parameter of an instance method refers to the instance itself. By universal convention, it is named self. Naming it anything else is technically valid but will confuse every Python programmer who reads your code.

Example 3 — Real-world application

A Product class for an online shop: attributes for name, price, and stock level, with methods for purchasing and checking availability.

```
class Product:
    def __init__(self, product_id, name, price, stock):
        self.product_id = product_id
        self.name       = name
        self.price      = price
        self.stock      = stock

    def is_available(self):
        return self.stock > 0

    def purchase(self, quantity=1):
        if quantity > self.stock:
            print(f"Insufficient stock for {self.name}.")
            return False
        self.stock -= quantity
        cost = quantity * self.price
        print(f"Purchased {quantity}x {self.name} for ${cost:.2f}.")
        return True

    def __str__(self):
        status = "In stock" if self.is_available() else "Out of stock"
        return f"[{self.product_id}] {self.name} — ${self.price:.2f}
({status})"

laptop = Product("P001", "Laptop", 1299.00, 5)
print(laptop)
laptop.purchase(2)
print(laptop)
```

Output:

```
[P001] Laptop — $1299.00 (In stock)
Purchased 2x Laptop for $2598.00.
[P001] Laptop — $1299.00 (In stock)
```

The `__str__` method (a special method covered in detail in Chapter 8) controls what Python displays when you `print()` an object. Without it, printing an object shows something like `<__main__.Product object at 0x7f...>`, which is not useful. Defining `__str__` gives your objects a human-readable representation.

1.4 The Four Pillars — A First Look

Object-oriented programming is often described in terms of four core principles: Encapsulation, Inheritance, Polymorphism, and Abstraction. Each of these has its own chapter in this book. What follows is a first orientation — enough to recognise each concept when you encounter it, and to understand how they relate.

Encapsulation

Encapsulation means bundling data and the methods that act on it inside a class, and controlling access to that data from outside. The object decides what is exposed publicly and what is kept internal. This protects the object's state from being modified in unexpected ways.

Inheritance

Inheritance allows one class (the child or subclass) to derive attributes and methods from another (the parent or superclass). This enables code reuse: a `SavingsAccount` can inherit the common behaviour of a `BankAccount` class and add only what makes it different.

Polymorphism

Polymorphism (from the Greek for "many forms") means that different classes can expose the same method name, and the correct behaviour is invoked based on which object it is called on. A `Dog` and a `Cat` might both have a `speak()` method, but `dog.speak()` returns "Woof" while `cat.speak()` returns "Meow".

Abstraction

Abstraction means hiding complex implementation details behind a simple interface. When you call `maths.report()`, you do not need to know how it calculates the average or formats the output. The complexity is hidden; only the relevant interface is exposed.

Example 1 — Introduction

Encapsulation: a bank account that protects its balance from direct modification.

```
class BankAccount:
    def __init__(self, owner, balance):
        self.owner     = owner
        self.__balance = balance  # private: not directly accessible


    def deposit(self, amount):
        if amount > 0:
            self.__balance += amount
```

```
    def get_balance(self):
        return self.__balance

acc = BankAccount("Alice", 500.00)
acc.deposit(150.00)
print(acc.get_balance())        # 650.0
# print(acc.__balance)          # AttributeError - protected by encapsulation
```

Output:

```
650.0
```

Example 2 — Variation

Inheritance: a SavingsAccount that extends BankAccount with interest functionality.

```
class SavingsAccount(BankAccount):  # inherits from BankAccount
    def __init__(self, owner, balance, interest_rate):
        super().__init__(owner, balance)  # call parent constructor
        self.interest_rate = interest_rate

    def apply_interest(self):
        interest = self.get_balance() * self.interest_rate
        self.deposit(interest)
        print(f"Interest applied: ${interest:.2f}")

savings = SavingsAccount("Bob", 1000.00, 0.05)
savings.apply_interest()
print(savings.get_balance())
```

Output:

```
Interest applied: $50.00
1050.0
```

Example 3 — Real-world application

All four pillars working together in a minimal animal hierarchy.

```
# Abstraction: Animal defines the interface
class Animal:
    def __init__(self, name):
        self.__name = name          # Encapsulation: private attribute

    def get_name(self):
```

```
        return self.__name

    def speak(self):                    # to be overridden - Polymorphism
        raise NotImplementedError("Subclasses must implement speak()")

# Inheritance: Dog and Cat extend Animal
class Dog(Animal):
    def speak(self):
        return f"{self.get_name()} says: Woof!"

class Cat(Animal):
    def speak(self):
        return f"{self.get_name()} says: Meow!"

animals = [Dog("Rex"), Cat("Whiskers"), Dog("Buddy")]

# Polymorphism: same method call, different behaviour
for animal in animals:
    print(animal.speak())
```

Output:

```
Rex says: Woof!
Whiskers says: Meow!
Buddy says: Woof!
```

Notice that the loop does not need to know whether each object is a `Dog` or a `Cat`. It calls `speak()` on each and Python handles the rest. This is polymorphism in action.

1.5 OOP in the Real World

OOP is not a theoretical exercise — it is the dominant paradigm in professional software development. The frameworks and libraries you will use throughout your programming career are built on it. Understanding OOP means you can read, extend, and reason about this code rather than treating it as a black box.

Django, Python's most widely used web framework, represents every database table as a class. A `User`, an `Article`, a `Comment` are all model classes. When you query the database, Django returns instances of these classes. The framework's entire architecture is built on OOP.

Game development frameworks like Pygame represent every entity in a game — the player, enemies, projectiles, the camera — as objects. Each has its own position, speed, and sprite, and each handles its own update logic on every frame.

GUI frameworks (including Python's own Tkinter, covered in Book 10) treat every window, button, and text field as an object. You create them, configure their properties, and bind event handlers to their methods.

Example 1 — Introduction

A game character class: position, health, and basic movement.

```
class Character:
    def __init__(self, name, x, y, health=100):
        self.name   = name
        self.x      = x
        self.y      = y
        self.health = health

    def move(self, dx, dy):
        self.x += dx
        self.y += dy
        print(f"{self.name} moved to ({self.x}, {self.y})")

    def take_damage(self, amount):
        self.health = max(0, self.health - amount)
        print(f"{self.name} has {self.health} HP remaining.")
        if self.health == 0:
            print(f"{self.name} has been defeated!")

hero = Character("Aria", 0, 0)
hero.move(3, 5)
hero.take_damage(30)
```

Output:

```
Aria moved to (3, 5)
Aria has 70 HP remaining.
```

Example 2 — Variation

A bank account in a financial application: controlled deposits, withdrawals, and transaction history.

```
class BankAccount:
    def __init__(self, account_number, owner, opening_balance=0.0):
        self.account_number = account_number
        self.owner          = owner
        self.__balance      = opening_balance
        self.__transactions = []
```

```
    def deposit(self, amount):
        if amount <= 0:
            raise ValueError("Deposit amount must be positive.")
        self.__balance += amount
        self.__transactions.append(f"+ ${amount:.2f}")

    def withdraw(self, amount):
        if amount > self.__balance:
            raise ValueError("Insufficient funds.")
        self.__balance -= amount
        self.__transactions.append(f"- ${amount:.2f}")

    def statement(self):
        print(f"Account: {self.account_number} | Owner: {self.owner}")
        for t in self.__transactions:
            print(f"  {t}")
        print(f"  Balance: ${self.__balance:.2f}")

acc = BankAccount("AU-0042", "Alice")
acc.deposit(500.00)
acc.deposit(200.00)
acc.withdraw(75.00)
acc.statement()
```

Output:

```
Account: AU-0042 | Owner: Alice
  + $500.00
  + $200.00
  - $75.00
  Balance: $625.00
```

Example 3 — Real-world application

A contact book: adding, searching, and listing contacts in a real-world data management context.

```
class Contact:
    def __init__(self, name, email, phone=""):
        self.name  = name
        self.email = email
        self.phone = phone
```

```python
    def __str__(self):
        phone_str = f" | {self.phone}" if self.phone else ""
        return f"{self.name} <{self.email}>{phone_str}"


class ContactBook:
    def __init__(self):
        self.__contacts = []

    def add(self, contact):
        self.__contacts.append(contact)
        print(f"Added: {contact.name}")

    def search(self, query):
        query = query.lower()
        return [c for c in self.__contacts
                if query in c.name.lower() or query in c.email.lower()]

    def list_all(self):
        for c in self.__contacts:
            print(c)

book = ContactBook()
book.add(Contact("Alice Wong",  "alice@example.com", "0412 000 001"))
book.add(Contact("Bob Smith",   "bob@example.com"))
book.add(Contact("Alice Kerr",  "akerr@example.com", "0412 000 003"))

print("\nSearch results for \"alice\":" )
for c in book.search("alice"):
    print(" ", c)
```

Output:

```
Added: Alice Wong
Added: Bob Smith
Added: Alice Kerr

Search results for "alice":
  Alice Wong <alice@example.com> | 0412 000 001
  Alice Kerr <akerr@example.com> | 0412 000 003
```

1.6 Python's OOP Model

Python's object model has one defining characteristic: everything is an object. Integers, strings, lists, functions, modules — all of them are instances of classes. This is not a technicality; it has practical consequences for how you write and reason about Python code.

When you write `x = 42`, Python creates an instance of the built-in `int` class and binds the name `x` to it. The integer 42 is an object with attributes and methods. You can call `.bit_length()` on it, pass it to `isinstance()`, and inspect it with `type()`. The same is true for strings, lists, functions, and even the classes you define yourself.

This uniformity is one of Python's greatest strengths. Every object can be inspected, passed around, stored in a list, and treated as data. Understanding this model makes advanced Python — decorators, metaclasses, dynamic class creation — far more approachable.

Example 1 — Introduction

Demonstrating that Python's built-in types are objects with methods.

```
# Integers are objects
x = 42
print(type(x))              # <class 'int'>
print(x.bit_length())       # 6  (42 requires 6 bits)

# Strings are objects
s = "hello"
print(type(s))              # <class 'str'>
print(s.upper())            # HELLO

# Lists are objects
lst = [3, 1, 2]
print(type(lst))            # <class 'list'>
lst.sort()
print(lst)                  # [1, 2, 3]

# Functions are objects
def greet(name):
    return f"Hello, {name}!"

print(type(greet))          # <class 'function'>
print(greet("Alice"))       # Hello, Alice!
```

Output:

```
<class 'int'>
```

```
6
<class 'str'>
HELLO
<class 'list'>
[1, 2, 3]
<class 'function'>
Hello, Alice!
```

Example 2 — Variation

Using type() and isinstance() to inspect objects at runtime.

```
class Animal:
    pass

class Dog(Animal):
    pass

d = Dog()

print(type(d))                   # <class '__main__.Dog'>
print(isinstance(d, Dog))        # True
print(isinstance(d, Animal))     # True  (Dog inherits from Animal)
print(isinstance(d, int))        # False

# type() checks exact class; isinstance() checks the hierarchy
print(type(d) is Dog)            # True
print(type(d) is Animal)         # False  (d is a Dog, not an Animal)
```

Output:

```
<class '__main__.Dog'>
True
True
False
True
False
```

Note: Prefer isinstance() over type() == when checking object types in practice. isinstance() respects the inheritance hierarchy, which is almost always the intended check. Use type() only when you specifically need the exact class.

Example 3 — Real-world application

Introspecting an object with dir() to explore its attributes and methods at runtime.

```
class Sensor:
    def __init__(self, sensor_id, unit):
        self.sensor_id = sensor_id
        self.unit      = unit
        self.__reading = 0.0

    def update(self, value):
        self.__reading = value

    def read(self):
        return self.__reading

temp = Sensor("T-01", "celsius")

# dir() lists all attributes and methods of an object
members = [m for m in dir(temp) if not m.startswith("__")]
print("Public members:", members)

temp.update(23.4)
print(f"Reading: {temp.read()} {temp.unit}")
```

Output:

```
Public members: ['read', 'sensor_id', 'unit', 'update']
Reading: 23.4 celsius
```

The double-underscore prefix on `__reading` causes Python to apply name mangling, making the attribute inaccessible from outside the class under its original name. This is the mechanism behind encapsulation. Chapter 4 covers this in full.

1.7 Thinking in Objects — Designing Before You Code

One of the most important habits an OOP programmer can develop is designing the object structure before writing any code. Jumping straight into a `class` definition without a plan produces code that grows organically, accumulates responsibilities it was never intended to carry, and becomes difficult to maintain.

The core of OOP design is identifying the entities in your problem domain. A useful starting technique: read the problem description and identify the nouns. Nouns typically become classes or attributes. Verbs typically become methods.

The design process

A simple, practical process for any new OOP problem:

- Identify the main entities (nouns). Each significant noun is a candidate for a class.
- List the attributes each entity needs (what data does it hold?).
- List the behaviours each entity performs (what can it do?).
- Identify relationships between entities (does one contain others? does one extend another?).
- Sketch the design informally before writing code. A few boxes and arrows is enough.

Example 1 — Introduction

Analysing a problem description to extract candidate classes, attributes, and methods.

"Build a program to manage a car park. The car park has a fixed number of spaces. Vehicles enter and exit. Each vehicle has a registration number and a type (car, motorcycle, truck). The car park charges different rates per hour based on vehicle type."

```
# From the description, we identify:
#
# ENTITIES (nouns):  CarPark, Vehicle
#
# Vehicle attributes:   registration, vehicle_type, entry_time
# Vehicle behaviours:   (passive — holds data)
#
# CarPark attributes:   capacity, spaces_available, parked_vehicles, rates
# CarPark behaviours:   enter(), exit(), is_full(), current_occupancy()
#
# Relationship:  CarPark CONTAINS many Vehicles

class Vehicle:
    def __init__(self, registration, vehicle_type):
        self.registration = registration
        self.vehicle_type = vehicle_type  # "car", "motorcycle", "truck"

    def __str__(self):
        return f"{self.vehicle_type.capitalize()} [{self.registration}]"
```

Example 2 — Variation

Implementing the CarPark class based on the design above.

```
class CarPark:
    RATES = {"car": 3.50, "motorcycle": 2.00, "truck": 6.00}  # per hour

    def __init__(self, name, capacity):
```

```
        self.name           = name
        self.capacity       = capacity
        self.__parked       = {}  # registration -> Vehicle

    def is_full(self):
        return len(self.__parked) >= self.capacity

    def enter(self, vehicle):
        if self.is_full():
            print(f"{self.name} is full. {vehicle} cannot enter.")
            return
        self.__parked[vehicle.registration] = vehicle
        print(f"{vehicle} entered. Spaces left: "
              f"{self.capacity - len(self.__parked)}")

    def exit(self, registration, hours):
        if registration not in self.__parked:
            print("Vehicle not found.")
            return
        vehicle = self.__parked.pop(registration)
        rate    = self.RATES.get(vehicle.vehicle_type, 3.50)
        charge  = rate * hours
        print(f"{vehicle} exited. Charge: ${charge:.2f} ({hours}h @
${rate:.2f}/h)")

park = CarPark("City Central", capacity=3)
park.enter(Vehicle("ABC123", "car"))
park.enter(Vehicle("XYZ789", "motorcycle"))
park.exit("ABC123", 2.5)
```

Output:

```
Car [ABC123] entered. Spaces left: 2
Motorcycle [XYZ789] entered. Spaces left: 1
Car [ABC123] exited. Charge: $8.75 (2.5h @ $3.50/h)
```

Example 3 — Real-world application

A library system designed from scratch: Books, Members, and the Library that connects them.

```
# Design:
# Book:    isbn, title, author, available
#          checkout(), return_book()
```

```
# Member:  member_id, name, borrowed_books
#          borrow(), return_book()
# Library: books{}, members{}
#          add_book(), register_member(), lend(), accept_return()

class Book:
    def __init__(self, isbn, title, author):
        self.isbn      = isbn
        self.title     = title
        self.author    = author
        self.available = True

    def __str__(self):
        status = "Available" if self.available else "On loan"
        return f'"{self.title}" by {self.author} [{status}]'


class Member:
    def __init__(self, member_id, name):
        self.member_id     = member_id
        self.name          = name
        self.borrowed      = []

    def __str__(self):
        return f"Member {self.member_id}: {self.name} ({len(self.borrowed)} on
loan)"


class Library:
    def __init__(self, name):
        self.name    = name
        self.__books = {}
        self.__members = {}

    def add_book(self, book):
        self.__books[book.isbn] = book


    def register_member(self, member):
        self.__members[member.member_id] = member
```

```
    def lend(self, isbn, member_id):
        book   = self.__books.get(isbn)
        member = self.__members.get(member_id)
        if not book or not member:
            print("Book or member not found.")
            return
        if not book.available:
            print(f'"{book.title}" is currently on loan.')
            return
        book.available = False
        member.borrowed.append(book)
        print(f"{member.name} borrowed {book.title}.")

    def accept_return(self, isbn, member_id):
        book   = self.__books.get(isbn)
        member = self.__members.get(member_id)
        if book in member.borrowed:
            member.borrowed.remove(book)
            book.available = True
            print(f"{member.name} returned {book.title}.")

lib = Library("Southside Library")
lib.add_book(Book("978-0-06-112008-4", "To Kill a Mockingbird", "Harper Lee"))
lib.add_book(Book("978-0-7432-7356-5", "1984", "George Orwell"))
lib.register_member(Member("M001", "Alice"))
lib.register_member(Member("M002", "Bob"))

lib.lend("978-0-06-112008-4", "M001")
lib.lend("978-0-06-112008-4", "M002")  # already on loan
lib.accept_return("978-0-06-112008-4", "M001")
lib.lend("978-0-06-112008-4", "M002")
```

Output:

```
Alice borrowed To Kill a Mockingbird.
"To Kill a Mockingbird" is currently on loan.
Alice returned To Kill a Mockingbird.
Bob borrowed To Kill a Mockingbird.
```

Notice that none of the classes knows the internal details of the others. `Library` does not access `Book`'s internal attributes directly — it uses the `available` flag as a published interface. This separation of concerns is what makes OOP programs easier to extend and maintain.

Chapter 1 Summary

- Procedural programming stores data and logic separately; OOP bundles them together in objects, improving structural integrity as programs grow.
- A class is a blueprint that defines attributes (data) and methods (behaviour). An object is a specific instance of a class with its own state.
- The __init__ method (constructor) initialises a new object's attributes. self refers to the specific instance the method is acting on.
- The four pillars of OOP are Encapsulation (protecting data), Inheritance (extending classes), Polymorphism (same interface, different behaviour), and Abstraction (hiding complexity).
- In Python, everything is an object — integers, strings, lists, and functions are all instances of built-in classes.
- isinstance() checks whether an object is an instance of a class or its subclasses; type() checks the exact class only.
- Effective OOP design starts before coding: identify entities (nouns), attributes (data they hold), methods (what they do), and relationships (how they connect).
- The design principle of separation of concerns means each class should be responsible for one clear thing and should interact with other classes only through their public interfaces.

Guided Exercises

Complete the following exercises in Python IDLE or your preferred editor. Each exercise targets a specific concept from this chapter.

1. Define a class called Rectangle with attributes width and height. Add a method area() that returns the area, and a method perimeter() that returns the perimeter. Create three Rectangle instances with different dimensions and print the area and perimeter of each.

Hint: *The __init__ method should accept width and height as parameters and assign them with self.*

2. Extend your Rectangle class by adding a method is_square() that returns True if the rectangle is a square (width equals height) and False otherwise. Test it with at least two instances — one square and one non-square.

Hint: *Compare self.width and self.height inside the method and return the result of the comparison directly.*

3. Write a class called Counter with a private attribute __count initialised to zero. Add methods increment(), decrement(), reset(), and get_count(). The decrement() method should not allow the count to fall below zero. Create an instance and call the methods in a sequence to verify the behaviour.

Hint: *Use self.__count for the private attribute. In decrement(), check if self.__count > 0 before subtracting.*

4. Create a class called Temperature with an attribute value (in Celsius). Add methods to_fahrenheit() and to_kelvin() that return the converted values. Add a __str__ method that returns a formatted string such as "23.0°C". Test the class with at least three different temperatures.

Hint: Fahrenheit = (Celsius × 9/5) + 32. Kelvin = Celsius + 273.15.

5. Using the Student and Classroom classes from Section 1.2, create a program that: (a) creates a Classroom for "Digital Technologies", (b) enrols five students with realistic names and grades, (c) prints the full report, and (d) prints a list of students who are not passing (grade below 50).

Hint: Loop through the classroom's students list and use the is_passing() method to filter. You may need to access the students attribute directly or add a method to Classroom.

Challenge Tasks

The following tasks are open-ended. No hints are provided. They require you to design the object structure, write the class or classes, and test your solution independently.

1. Design and implement a simple inventory system for a small hardware store. The store stocks items with a name, a SKU code, a unit price, and a quantity on hand. The system should support: adding new stock, selling items (reducing quantity), restocking (increasing quantity), and printing a full inventory report showing all items and the total stock value. Consider what happens if someone attempts to sell more of an item than is available.

2. A university stores information about units of study. Each unit has a unit code, a title, a number of credit points, and a list of enrolled students. Each student has a student ID, a name, and a list of units they are enrolled in. Design and implement both classes with appropriate methods. Your solution should allow: enrolling a student in a unit, withdrawing a student from a unit, and printing a student's full enrolment summary showing all units and total credit points.

3. Revisit the Library system from Section 1.7. Extend it with the following features: (a) a due date system — when a book is borrowed, a due date is recorded (use Python's datetime module and set the loan period to 14 days); (b) an overdue check — a method that returns a list of all books currently overdue; and (c) a fine system — when a book is returned late, calculate a fine at $0.50 per day overdue. Justify any design decisions you make about which class should own each piece of this new logic.

Chapter 1 established why OOP exists and what problems it solves. This chapter moves from concept to construction. You will learn the precise mechanics of how a class is defined in Python, how the constructor initialises each new object, what self actually is and why it is required, how attributes belong to individual instances versus the class itself, and how methods give objects their behaviour. By the end of this chapter, you will be able to design and implement classes confidently, understand the distinction between class and instance state, and predict how Python manages objects in memory throughout their lifetime.

2.1 Anatomy of a Class Definition

A class definition in Python has a precise structure. Understanding each component — the keyword, the name, the body, the indentation — removes ambiguity and lets you read any unfamiliar class confidently.

The `class` keyword introduces the definition. The class name follows, by convention written in PascalCase (each word capitalised, no underscores). An optional set of parentheses after the name specifies parent classes; when omitted, the class implicitly inherits from Python's built-in `object` base class. The body of the class is indented beneath the definition line and contains all its attributes and method definitions.

A class with no methods and no attributes can be defined using the `pass` keyword as a placeholder. This is rarely useful in production code but is valid Python and occasionally used during the design phase as a stub.

Example 1 — Introduction

The structural components of a class definition, labelled and explained.

```
class Vehicle:                    # class keyword + PascalCase name
    """Represents a motor vehicle."""  # optional docstring

    # --- Class body begins here (indented) ---

    def __init__(self, make, model, year):  # constructor method
        # self.attribute = value  assigns instance attributes
        self.make  = make
        self.model = model
        self.year  = year

    def describe(self):         # instance method
```

```python
        print(f"{self.year} {self.make} {self.model}")


car = Vehicle("Toyota", "Camry", 2022)  # create an instance
car.describe()
```

Output:

```
2022 Toyota Camry
```

Example 2 — Variation

Class naming conventions: PascalCase for classes, snake_case for everything else.

```python
# PascalCase for class names — required by convention (PEP 8)
class ShoppingCart:   pass    # correct
class shoppingcart:   pass    # wrong — unreadable
class shopping_cart:  pass    # wrong — looks like a variable

# Acronyms: treat as a single word in PascalCase
class HttpRequest:    pass    # correct (not HTTPRequest)
class XmlParser:      pass    # correct (not XMLParser)

# Constants inside classes use UPPER_SNAKE_CASE
class Config:
    MAX_RETRIES   = 3
    DEFAULT_PORT  = 8080
    API_VERSION   = "v2"

print(Config.MAX_RETRIES)    # 3
print(Config.API_VERSION)    # v2
```

Output:

```
3
v2
```

> **Note:** Class names that begin with a lowercase letter are valid Python but violate PEP 8. Most linters and editors will flag them. Throughout this book, PEP 8 naming conventions are used consistently — the same conventions you will find in every professional Python codebase and the Django, Flask, and NumPy source code.

Example 3 — Real-world application

A real-world class for an e-commerce order: structured definition with a docstring, multiple attributes, and a formatted summary method.

```
class Order:
    """Represents a customer order in an online store.

    Attributes:
        order_id  (str):   unique identifier for the order
        customer  (str):   customer name
        items     (list):  list of (product, quantity, unit_price) tuples
        status    (str):   current order status
    """

    def __init__(self, order_id, customer):
        self.order_id = order_id
        self.customer = customer
        self.items    = []
        self.status   = "pending"

    def add_item(self, product, quantity, unit_price):
        self.items.append((product, quantity, unit_price))

    def total(self):
        return sum(qty * price for _, qty, price in self.items)

    def summary(self):
        print(f"Order {self.order_id} — {self.customer} [{self.status}]")
        for product, qty, price in self.items:
            print(f"  {product:20s} x{qty}  ${price * qty:.2f}")
        print(f"  {'Total':-<24s} ${self.total():.2f}")


order = Order("ORD-0042", "Alice Wong")
order.add_item("Wireless Keyboard",  1, 79.95)
order.add_item("USB-C Hub",          2, 39.00)
order.add_item("Monitor Stand",      1, 54.50)
order.status = "confirmed"
order.summary()
```

Output:

```
Order ORD-0042 — Alice Wong [confirmed]
  Wireless Keyboard     x1  $79.95
  USB-C Hub             x2  $78.00
  Monitor Stand         x1  $54.50
  Total--------------- $212.45
```

The docstring immediately after the class definition is accessible at runtime via `Order.__doc__`. Well-written docstrings are not decoration — they are the primary documentation source for IDEs, the `help()` function, and automated documentation generators such as Sphinx.

2.2 The __init__ Method in Depth

The `__init__` method is the constructor — Python calls it automatically every time a new instance of the class is created. Its job is to initialise the new object's state by setting up its attributes. It does not create the object (that is handled by `__new__`, which you will rarely need to override); it configures an object that has already been allocated.

Parameters defined in `__init__` beyond `self` become required (or optional, if given defaults) when creating an instance. This is how Python enforces that every object starts in a valid, fully-initialised state — rather than relying on the caller to manually set attributes after construction.

Default parameter values in `__init__` work exactly as they do in regular functions. They make certain attributes optional at creation time. A critical rule inherited from Python functions applies here too: never use a mutable object (list, dict, set) as a default parameter value.

Example 1 — Introduction

__init__ with required and optional parameters, showing default values.

```
class Player:
    def __init__(self, username, level=1, score=0):
        self.username = username
        self.level    = level
        self.score    = score
        self.alive    = True        # internal default, not a parameter

    def status(self):
        state = "alive" if self.alive else "defeated"
        print(f"{self.username}  Lv{self.level}  Score:{self.score}
[{state}]")


p1 = Player("Aria")                # only username required
p2 = Player("Zed",  level=5)       # keyword argument
p3 = Player("Nova", 3, 1500)       # positional arguments
```

```
p1.status()
p2.status()
p3.status()
```

Output:

```
Aria  Lv1  Score:0  [alive]
Zed  Lv5  Score:0  [alive]
Nova  Lv3  Score:1500  [alive]
```

Example 2 — Variation

The mutable default argument trap — a common error and its correct resolution.

```
# --- WRONG: mutable default argument ---
class Team:
    def __init__(self, name, members=[]):   # NEVER do this
        self.name    = name
        self.members = members            # all instances share ONE list

t1 = Team("Alpha")
t2 = Team("Beta")
t1.members.append("Alice")
print(t2.members)   # ["Alice"] — unexpected: t2 is affected!


# --- CORRECT: use None as sentinel, create list inside __init__ ---
class TeamFixed:
    def __init__(self, name, members=None):
        self.name    = name
        self.members = members if members is not None else []

t3 = TeamFixed("Gamma")
t4 = TeamFixed("Delta")
t3.members.append("Bob")
print(t4.members)   # [] — correct: t4 is unaffected
```

Output:

```
['Alice']
[]
```

Note: This mutable default argument issue applies equally to dicts, sets, and any other mutable type used as a default. It is one of the most frequently encountered Python gotchas. The fix is always the same: use None as the default and create the mutable object inside the method body.

Example 3 — Real-world application

A Ticket booking class that validates inputs inside __init__, ensuring no object can be created in an invalid state.

```
class Ticket:
    VALID_CATEGORIES = {"adult", "concession", "child"}

    def __init__(self, event, category, quantity=1):
        if category not in self.VALID_CATEGORIES:
            raise ValueError(
                f"Invalid category '{category}'. "
                f"Choose from: {self.VALID_CATEGORIES}"
            )
        if quantity < 1:
            raise ValueError("Quantity must be at least 1.")

        self.event    = event
        self.category = category
        self.quantity = quantity
        self.price    = self._calculate_price()

    def _calculate_price(self):
        base_prices = {"adult": 45.00, "concession": 30.00, "child": 20.00}
        return base_prices[self.category] * self.quantity


    def __str__(self):
        return (f"{self.event} | {self.category.capitalize()} x{self.quantity}
| ${self.price:.2f}")


t1 = Ticket("Symphony Night", "adult",       2)
t2 = Ticket("Symphony Night", "concession", 1)
print(t1)
print(t2)

try:
    t3 = Ticket("Symphony Night", "vip")   # invalid category
except ValueError as e:
    print(f"Error: {e}")
```

Output:

```
Symphony Night | Adult x2 | $90.00
Symphony Night | Concession x1 | $30.00
Error: Invalid category 'vip'. Choose from: {'adult', 'concession', 'child'}
```

Raising errors inside `__init__` is the correct way to prevent invalid objects from being created. If the constructor completes without raising an exception, the caller can be confident the object is in a valid state. This is the principle of fail-fast construction — it is far better to catch an invalid input at object creation than to discover it later when a method tries to use corrupt data.

2.3 Understanding self

`self` is one of the first things that confuses learners coming from other languages. In languages like Java and C#, there is an implicit reference to the current object (called `this`). Python makes this reference explicit: every instance method must declare it as its first parameter.

When you call `player.status()`, Python transforms this into `Player.status(player)`. The object before the dot is passed as the first argument to the method. `self` is simply the name given to that argument by convention. Python passes it automatically — you never provide it yourself when calling a method.

This explicitness is intentional. It makes the relationship between a method and its object unambiguous, aids readability, and is consistent with Python's philosophy that explicit is better than implicit.

What self resolves to

Inside any instance method, `self` is a reference to the specific object the method was called on. It is the mechanism by which a method accesses that particular object's attributes. Without `self`, a method inside a class would have no way of distinguishing one instance's data from another's.

Example 1 — Introduction

Demonstrating that self refers to the specific instance — different calls, different objects.

```
class Lamp:
    def __init__(self, colour):
        self.colour  = colour
        self.is_on   = False

    def toggle(self):
        self.is_on = not self.is_on
        state = "on" if self.is_on else "off"
        print(f"The {self.colour} lamp is now {state}.")


red_lamp   = Lamp("red")
```

```
blue_lamp  = Lamp("blue")

red_lamp.toggle()     # self = red_lamp
red_lamp.toggle()     # self = red_lamp
blue_lamp.toggle()    # self = blue_lamp

# Calling via the class explicitly (equivalent, rarely used):
Lamp.toggle(red_lamp)  # same as red_lamp.toggle()
```

Output:

```
The red lamp is now on.
The red lamp is now off.
The blue lamp is now on.
The blue lamp is now on.
```

Example 2 — Variation

Passing self to another method: one method calling another on the same instance.

```
class Invoice:
    TAX_RATE = 0.10

    def __init__(self, client, amount):
        self.client = client
        self.amount = amount

    def _tax(self):
        return self.amount * self.TAX_RATE

    def _total(self):
        return self.amount + self._tax()  # self calling self._tax()

    def print_invoice(self):
        print(f"Client  : {self.client}")
        print(f"Subtotal: ${self.amount:.2f}")
        print(f"GST     : ${self._tax():.2f}")
        print(f"Total   : ${self._total():.2f}")


inv = Invoice("Northward Design Co.", 850.00)
inv.print_invoice()
```

```
Output:
Client   : Northward Design Co.
Subtotal: $850.00
GST      : $85.00
Total    : $935.00
```

Example 3 — Real-world application

A Stopwatch class where self enables multiple independent instances to track their own state concurrently.

```
import time

class Stopwatch:
    def __init__(self, label="Stopwatch"):
        self.label    = label
        self._start   = None
        self._elapsed = 0.0
        self._running = False

    def start(self):
        if not self._running:
            self._start   = time.time()
            self._running = True

    def stop(self):
        if self._running:
            self._elapsed += time.time() - self._start
            self._running  = False

    def reset(self):
        self._start   = None
        self._elapsed = 0.0
        self._running = False

    def read(self):
        if self._running:
            return self._elapsed + (time.time() - self._start)
        return self._elapsed

    def report(self):
```

```
        print(f"[{self.label}] {self.read():.4f}s")


sw1 = Stopwatch("Task A")
sw2 = Stopwatch("Task B")

sw1.start()
time.sleep(0.05)
sw2.start()
time.sleep(0.05)
sw1.stop()
time.sleep(0.05)
sw2.stop()

sw1.report()
sw2.report()
```

Output:

```
[Task A] 0.1003s
[Task B] 0.1002s
```

`sw1` and `sw2` each maintain their own `_elapsed` and `_running` state via `self`. No class-level variable is involved — every attribute is per-instance. The two stopwatches operate entirely independently despite being instances of the same class.

2.4 Instance Attributes vs Class Attributes

Every attribute you have seen so far — assigned inside `__init__` with `self.attribute = value` — is an instance attribute. Each object created from the class owns its own copy of these attributes. Changing `alice.grade` has no effect on `bob.grade`.

A class attribute is defined directly inside the class body, outside any method. It belongs to the class itself, not to any particular instance. All instances share the same class attribute. Class attributes are typically used for constants, default values that apply to every instance, or counters that track how many objects have been created.

When Python looks up an attribute on an instance, it first checks the instance's own namespace; if it is not there, it checks the class namespace. This lookup order is important: an instance attribute with the same name as a class attribute will shadow the class attribute for that instance only, leaving other instances unaffected.

Example 1 — Introduction

Side-by-side comparison: a class attribute shared by all instances vs instance attributes unique to each.

```
class Employee:
```

```
    company   = "Northward Tech"    # class attribute — shared by all
    headcount = 0                   # class attribute — tracks instance count

    def __init__(self, name, role):
        self.name = name            # instance attribute
        self.role = role            # instance attribute
        Employee.headcount += 1     # increment class attribute

    def introduce(self):
        print(f"{self.name} ({self.role}) at {Employee.company}")


e1 = Employee("Alice", "Engineer")
e2 = Employee("Bob",   "Designer")
e3 = Employee("Cara",  "Manager")

e1.introduce()
e2.introduce()
print(f"Total employees: {Employee.headcount}")
```

Output:

```
Alice (Engineer) at Northward Tech
Bob (Designer) at Northward Tech
Total employees: 3
```

Example 2 — Variation

Shadowing: an instance attribute with the same name as a class attribute overrides it for that instance only.

```
class Subscription:
    price = 9.99           # default monthly price for all subscribers

    def __init__(self, username):
        self.username = username

    def show_price(self):
        print(f"{self.username}: ${self.price:.2f}/month")


s1 = Subscription("alice")
```

```
s2 = Subscription("bob")
s3 = Subscription("cara")

# Give cara a special discounted price (instance attribute shadows class attr)
s3.price = 4.99

s1.show_price()    # uses class attribute: 9.99
s2.show_price()    # uses class attribute: 9.99
s3.show_price()    # uses instance attribute: 4.99

print(Subscription.price)  # class attribute unchanged: 9.99

# Update the class attribute — affects all who have not overridden it
Subscription.price = 12.99
s1.show_price()    # 12.99
s3.show_price()    # still 4.99 — instance attribute is not overwritten
```

Output:

```
alice: $9.99/month
bob: $9.99/month
cara: $4.99/month
9.99
alice: $12.99/month
cara: $4.99/month
```

> **Note:** Class attributes are accessed via the class name (Employee.headcount) rather than self when you intend to modify the shared value. Using self.headcount += 1 would create a new instance attribute on the current object and leave the class attribute unchanged. This is a subtle but important distinction.

Example 3 — Real-world application

A server connection pool using class attributes to enforce a maximum number of active connections.

```
class DatabaseConnection:
    MAX_CONNECTIONS = 5          # class-level limit
    _active         = 0          # class-level counter
    _pool           = []         # class-level shared pool

    def __init__(self, host, db_name):
        if DatabaseConnection._active >= DatabaseConnection.MAX_CONNECTIONS:
            raise RuntimeError(
```

```python
                f"Connection limit reached
({DatabaseConnection.MAX_CONNECTIONS})."
            )
        self.host      = host
        self.db_name   = db_name
        self.conn_id   = DatabaseConnection._active + 1
        DatabaseConnection._active += 1
        DatabaseConnection._pool.append(self)
        print(f"Connection {self.conn_id} opened to
{self.host}/{self.db_name}.")

    def close(self):
        DatabaseConnection._pool.remove(self)
        DatabaseConnection._active -= 1
        print(f"Connection {self.conn_id} closed.")

    @classmethod
    def active_count(cls):
        return cls._active


c1 = DatabaseConnection("db.local", "users")
c2 = DatabaseConnection("db.local", "orders")
print(f"Active connections: {DatabaseConnection.active_count()}")
c1.close()
print(f"Active connections: {DatabaseConnection.active_count()}")
```

Output:

```
Connection 1 opened to db.local/users.
Connection 2 opened to db.local/orders.
Active connections: 2
Connection 1 closed.
Active connections: 1
```

The `@classmethod` decorator is introduced briefly here; Chapter 3 covers it in full. For now, note that a class method receives the class (`cls`) rather than an instance (`self`) as its first argument, making it the natural home for operations that belong to the class as a whole rather than any particular instance.

Methods — Types and Conventions

A method is a function defined inside a class body. Python distinguishes three types: instance methods, class methods, and static methods. Each has a different relationship to the class and its instances, and each is appropriate for different kinds of behaviour.

Instance methods are the most common. They take `self` as their first parameter and can read and modify the instance's attributes. They have access to both instance state and class state via `self` and `self.__class__` respectively.

Class methods take `cls` as their first parameter (decorated with `@classmethod`) and operate on the class itself rather than any particular instance. They are commonly used as alternative constructors — factory methods that create instances from different input formats.

Static methods (decorated with `@staticmethod`) take neither `self` nor `cls`. They are essentially regular functions that happen to live inside a class body because they are logically related to it. They cannot access or modify instance or class state.

Naming conventions for methods

- Public methods have plain names: `calculate()`, `display()`, `submit()`.
- Protected methods (intended for internal and subclass use) are prefixed with a single underscore: `_validate()`, `_parse_date()`.
- Private methods (intended only for the defining class) are prefixed with double underscore: `__hash_password()`. Python applies name mangling to these.

Example 1 — Introduction

All three method types in one class, demonstrating when each is appropriate.

```
class Temperature:
    _ABS_ZERO = -273.15   # class attribute: physical constant

    def __init__(self, celsius):
        if celsius < self._ABS_ZERO:
            raise ValueError(f"Temperature below absolute zero: {celsius}")
        self._celsius = celsius

    # --- Instance method: operates on self ---
    def to_fahrenheit(self):
        return self._celsius * 9 / 5 + 32

    def to_kelvin(self):
        return self._celsius - self._ABS_ZERO

    # --- Class method: alternative constructor ---
    @classmethod
    def from_fahrenheit(cls, fahrenheit):
```

```
        celsius = (fahrenheit - 32) * 5 / 9
        return cls(celsius)

    # --- Static method: utility, no access to instance or class ---
    @staticmethod
    def is_valid(celsius):
        return celsius >= -273.15

    def __str__(self):
        return f"{self._celsius:.2f}°C"


t1 = Temperature(100)
print(t1)
print(f"Fahrenheit: {t1.to_fahrenheit():.2f}°F")
print(f"Kelvin:     {t1.to_kelvin():.2f} K")

t2 = Temperature.from_fahrenheit(212)  # class method constructor
print(t2)

print(Temperature.is_valid(-300))      # static method: False
print(Temperature.is_valid(20))        # static method: True
```

Output:

```
100.00°C
Fahrenheit: 212.00°F
Kelvin:     373.15 K
100.00°C
False
True
```

Example 2 — Variation

Using class methods as alternative constructors to parse objects from different data sources.

```
class Date:
    def __init__(self, day, month, year):
        self.day   = day
        self.month = month
        self.year  = year
```

```
    @classmethod
    def from_string(cls, date_string):
        """Parse from DD/MM/YYYY string."""
        parts = date_string.split("/")
        return cls(int(parts[0]), int(parts[1]), int(parts[2]))

    @classmethod
    def from_iso(cls, iso_string):
        """Parse from YYYY-MM-DD string."""
        parts = iso_string.split("-")
        return cls(int(parts[2]), int(parts[1]), int(parts[0]))

    def __str__(self):
        months = ["Jan","Feb","Mar","Apr","May","Jun",
                  "Jul","Aug","Sep","Oct","Nov","Dec"]
        return f"{self.day} {months[self.month - 1]} {self.year}"


d1 = Date(25, 4, 2025)
d2 = Date.from_string("14/06/2025")
d3 = Date.from_iso("2025-11-01")

for d in [d1, d2, d3]:
    print(d)
```

Output:

```
25 Apr 2025
14 Jun 2025
1 Nov 2025
```

Example 3 — Real-world application

A User class modelling an authentication system: instance, class, and static methods in a realistic context.

```
import hashlib

class User:
    _users = {}                 # class attribute: registry of all users

    def __init__(self, username, email, password):
        if not User.is_valid_email(email):
```

```
            raise ValueError(f"Invalid email address: {email}")
        self.username       = username
        self.email          = email
        self._password_hash = self.__hash(password)
        User._users[username] = self

    def __hash(self, password):
        """Private: hash a password using SHA-256."""
        return hashlib.sha256(password.encode()).hexdigest()[:16]

    def check_password(self, password):
        """Instance method: verify a login attempt."""
        return self._password_hash == self.__hash(password)

    @classmethod
    def find(cls, username):
        """Class method: look up a user from the registry."""
        return cls._users.get(username)

    @classmethod
    def user_count(cls):
        return len(cls._users)

    @staticmethod
    def is_valid_email(email):
        """Static method: basic email format check."""
        return "@" in email and "." in email.split("@")[-1]


User("alice",  "alice@example.com",  "secret123")
User("bob",    "bob@example.com",    "p@ssw0rd")

u = User.find("alice")
print(u.check_password("secret123"))   # True
print(u.check_password("wrong"))       # False
print(f"Registered users: {User.user_count()}")
```

Output:

```
True
False
```

```
Registered users: 2
```

The private `__hash` method (double underscore prefix) is inaccessible from outside the class under its original name. Python renames it internally to `_User__hash`, preventing accidental or deliberate access from subclasses or external code. This is distinct from single-underscore protected methods, which are accessible but conventionally treated as internal.

2.6 Creating and Managing Multiple Instances

Creating a class is the beginning; working with many instances simultaneously is where OOP's power becomes apparent. Instances can be stored in lists, passed into other objects as arguments, returned from functions, and used as keys in dictionaries — because, as established in Chapter 1, every object in Python is a first-class value.

When managing collections of objects, list comprehensions and standard iteration patterns apply exactly as they do with any other Python data type. Filtering, sorting, and aggregating a list of objects uses the same syntax as filtering, sorting, and aggregating a list of numbers or strings.

Example 1 — Introduction

Building and querying a list of objects using comprehensions and built-in functions.

```
class Sensor:
    def __init__(self, sensor_id, location, reading):
        self.sensor_id = sensor_id
        self.location  = location
        self.reading   = reading    # degrees Celsius

    def __repr__(self):
        return f"Sensor({self.sensor_id!r}, {self.reading}°C)"


sensors = [
    Sensor("S01", "roof",     38.2),
    Sensor("S02", "basement", 19.5),
    Sensor("S03", "office",   22.1),
    Sensor("S04", "server",   41.8),
    Sensor("S05", "lobby",    24.3),
]

# Filter: sensors above safe threshold
hot = [s for s in sensors if s.reading > 35]
print("Hot sensors:", hot)
```

```
# Sort by reading descending
by_heat = sorted(sensors, key=lambda s: s.reading, reverse=True)
print("Hottest first:", by_heat)

# Aggregate
avg = sum(s.reading for s in sensors) / len(sensors)
print(f"Average reading: {avg:.2f}°C")
```

Output:

```
Hot sensors: [Sensor('S01', 38.2°C), Sensor('S04', 41.8°C)]
Hottest first: [Sensor('S04', 41.8°C), Sensor('S01', 38.2°C), Sensor('S05', 24.3°C), Sensor('S03', 22.1°C), Sensor('S02', 19.5°C)]
Average reading: 29.18°C
```

Example 2 — Variation

Using a dictionary to manage objects by a unique key — fast lookup without linear search.

```
class Product:
    def __init__(self, sku, name, price, stock):
        self.sku   = sku
        self.name  = name
        self.price = price
        self.stock = stock

    def __str__(self):
        return f"[{self.sku}] {self.name} — ${self.price:.2f} ({self.stock} in stock)"


# Store objects in a dict keyed by SKU for O(1) lookup
catalogue = {
    "A001": Product("A001", "Laptop Stand",   49.00, 12),
    "A002": Product("A002", "Keyboard",       89.00,  8),
    "A003": Product("A003", "Webcam",         69.00,  0),
}

def lookup(sku):
    product = catalogue.get(sku)
    if product:
        print(product)
    else:
```

```
        print(f"No product found with SKU {sku!r}.")

lookup("A002")
lookup("A003")
lookup("A099")

# Low-stock report
low_stock = [p for p in catalogue.values() if p.stock < 5]
print("\nLow or out-of-stock:")
for p in low_stock:
    print(" ", p)
```

Output:

```
[A002] Keyboard — $89.00 (8 in stock)
[A003] Webcam — $69.00 (0 in stock)
No product found with SKU 'A099'.

Low or out-of-stock:
  [A003] Webcam — $69.00 (0 in stock)
```

Example 3 — Real-world application

An event registration system that manages a collection of Attendee objects with registration, cancellation, and reporting.

```
class Attendee:
    def __init__(self, attendee_id, name, email, ticket_type="standard"):
        self.attendee_id = attendee_id
        self.name        = name
        self.email       = email
        self.ticket_type = ticket_type
        self.checked_in  = False

    def check_in(self):
        self.checked_in = True

    def __str__(self):
        status = "✓" if self.checked_in else "✗"
        return f"[{status}] {self.attendee_id}: {self.name}
({self.ticket_type})"
```

```python
class EventRegistry:
    def __init__(self, event_name, capacity):
        self.event_name = event_name
        self.capacity   = capacity
        self._attendees = {}

    def register(self, attendee):
        if len(self._attendees) >= self.capacity:
            print(f"Event full. Cannot register {attendee.name}.")
            return
        self._attendees[attendee.attendee_id] = attendee
        print(f"Registered: {attendee.name}")

    def cancel(self, attendee_id):
        if attendee_id in self._attendees:
            name = self._attendees.pop(attendee_id).name
            print(f"Cancelled registration for {name}.")

    def check_in(self, attendee_id):
        attendee = self._attendees.get(attendee_id)
        if attendee:
            attendee.check_in()
            print(f"Checked in: {attendee.name}")


    def report(self):
        total     = len(self._attendees)
        arrived   = sum(1 for a in self._attendees.values() if a.checked_in)
        print(f"\n--- {self.event_name} ---")
        for a in self._attendees.values():
            print(f"  {a}")
        print(f"  Attendance: {arrived}/{total}")



event = EventRegistry("Python Conference 2025", capacity=3)
event.register(Attendee("R001", "Alice Wong",  "alice@ex.com", "speaker"))
event.register(Attendee("R002", "Bob Smith",   "bob@ex.com"))
event.register(Attendee("R003", "Cara Lee",    "cara@ex.com", "vip"))
event.register(Attendee("R004", "Dan Park",    "dan@ex.com"))   # full
```

```
event.check_in("R001")
event.check_in("R003")
event.report()
```

Output:

```
Registered: Alice Wong
Registered: Bob Smith
Registered: Cara Lee
Event full. Cannot register Dan Park.
Checked in: Alice Wong
Checked in: Cara Lee

--- Python Conference 2025 ---
  [✓] R001: Alice Wong (speaker)
  [X] R002: Bob Smith (standard)
  [✓] R003: Cara Lee (vip)
  Attendance: 2/3
```

2.7 Object Lifecycle — Creation, Identity, and Deletion

Every Python object has a lifecycle: it is created, it exists for some period during which references to it may be held, and it is eventually destroyed when no more references to it remain. Understanding this lifecycle informs how you write classes, manage resources, and reason about memory.

Python's memory management is handled by a reference counting garbage collector. When the reference count of an object drops to zero — meaning no variable, list, or other object holds a reference to it — Python automatically deallocates it. You rarely need to manage this manually, but knowing it exists helps explain why Python does not have explicit `new` and `delete` keywords.

Object identity

Every object has a unique identity, accessible via `id()`. Two variables can hold references to the same object (aliasing), or references to distinct objects that happen to contain equal data. The `is` operator tests identity; `==` tests equality. These are fundamentally different questions.

Example 1 — Introduction

Demonstrating identity (is) vs equality (==), and aliasing vs copying.

```
class Point:
    def __init__(self, x, y):
        self.x = x
        self.y = y

    def __eq__(self, other):
```

```
        return self.x == other.x and self.y == other.y

    def __repr__(self):
        return f"Point({self.x}, {self.y})"


p1 = Point(3, 4)
p2 = Point(3, 4)    # same values, different object
p3 = p1             # alias — same object

print(p1 == p2)     # True  — equal values
print(p1 is p2)     # False — different objects
print(p1 is p3)     # True  — same object

print(id(p1))       # unique memory address
print(id(p2))       # different address
print(id(p3))       # same as p1

# Mutating via alias affects the original
p3.x = 99
print(p1.x)         # 99 — p1 and p3 are the same object
```

Output:

```
True
False
True
(unique integer)
(different integer)
(same as p1)
99
```

Example 2 — Variation

The __del__ method: a destructor that runs when an object is about to be garbage collected.

```
class FileHandle:
    def __init__(self, filename):
        self.filename = filename
        self._open    = True
        print(f"Opened: {self.filename}")
```

```
    def read(self):
        if not self._open:
            raise RuntimeError("Cannot read: file is closed.")
        return f"<contents of {self.filename}>"

    def close(self):
        if self._open:
            self._open = False
            print(f"Closed: {self.filename}")

    def __del__(self):
        """Called automatically before garbage collection."""
        if self._open:
            print(f"Warning: {self.filename} was not explicitly closed.")
            self.close()


fh = FileHandle("report.txt")
print(fh.read())
fh.close()

# Object with no explicit close — __del__ fires on garbage collection
temp = FileHandle("temp.txt")
del temp   # explicitly drop the reference; __del__ fires
```

Output:

```
Opened: report.txt
<contents of report.txt>
Closed: report.txt
Opened: temp.txt
Warning: temp.txt was not explicitly closed.
Closed: temp.txt
```

> **Note:** __del__ is not a reliable resource management mechanism. Python does not guarantee when it will be called, and in some circumstances (circular references, interpreter shutdown) it may not be called at all. For deterministic resource cleanup — files, network connections, database handles — use context managers and the with statement, which is the subject of Book 02.

Example 3 — Real-world application

Copying objects: the difference between a shallow copy and a deep copy when objects contain mutable attributes.

```
import copy


class Roster:
    def __init__(self, team_name, players):
        self.team_name = team_name
        self.players   = players   # mutable list


    def __repr__(self):
        return f"Roster({self.team_name!r}, {self.players})"



original = Roster("Stingrays", ["Alice", "Bob", "Cara"])


# Shallow copy: new Roster object, but SAME players list
shallow = copy.copy(original)
shallow.team_name = "Sharks"
shallow.players.append("Dan")    # modifies the shared list!


print("Original:", original)
print("Shallow: ", shallow)


# Deep copy: new Roster object AND new players list
original2 = Roster("Stingrays", ["Alice", "Bob", "Cara"])
deep      = copy.deepcopy(original2)
deep.team_name = "Jets"
deep.players.append("Eva")       # only affects deep copy


print("Original2:", original2)
print("Deep:     ", deep)
```

Output:

```
Original: Roster('Stingrays', ['Alice', 'Bob', 'Cara', 'Dan'])
Shallow:  Roster('Sharks', ['Alice', 'Bob', 'Cara', 'Dan'])
Original2: Roster('Stingrays', ['Alice', 'Bob', 'Cara'])
Deep:      Roster('Jets', ['Alice', 'Bob', 'Cara', 'Eva'])
```

The shallow copy creates a new object at the top level but does not recursively copy any objects it contains. The deep copy recursively copies everything, producing a fully independent duplicate.

When your class contains mutable attributes — lists, dicts, other objects — always consider which copy behaviour is appropriate for your use case.

Chapter 2 Summary

- A class definition uses the class keyword followed by a PascalCase name. The class body contains the constructor and all method definitions, indented beneath the definition line.
- The __init__ method initialises a new object's state. It runs automatically on instance creation. Raising exceptions inside __init__ prevents invalid objects from being constructed (fail-fast construction).
- Never use a mutable object (list, dict, set) as a default parameter value in __init__. Use None as a sentinel and create the mutable object inside the constructor body.
- self is the conventional name for the first parameter of any instance method. Python passes the calling object to it automatically. self is explicit in Python where other languages use an implicit this.
- Instance attributes belong to individual objects and are assigned via self.attr = value. Class attributes belong to the class itself and are defined directly in the class body. Instance attributes shadow class attributes of the same name.
- Python provides three method types: instance methods (self), class methods (@classmethod, cls), and static methods (@staticmethod). Class methods are commonly used as alternative constructors; static methods for utility logic that does not need instance or class state.
- Objects can be stored in lists, dicts, and other collections. List comprehensions, sorted(), filter(), and other standard Python tools work on collections of objects just as they do on any other sequence.
- Every object has an identity accessible via id(). The is operator tests identity; == tests equality. Aliasing (two names pointing to the same object) differs from copying. Use copy.copy() for shallow copies and copy.deepcopy() for fully independent duplicates.

Guided Exercises

Complete the following exercises. Each targets a specific concept from this chapter.

1. Define a class called Circle with an instance attribute radius. Add an instance method area() that returns πr^2, and a method circumference() that returns $2\pi r$. Use Python's math module for the value of π. Add a class method from_diameter(cls, diameter) that creates a Circle from a diameter value. Test all three with two instances.

Hint: *import math at the top of your file. The from_diameter class method should return cls(diameter / 2).*

2. Write a class called FlightLog with a class attribute total_flights initialised to zero. Each time a new FlightLog is created, total_flights should increment. Each instance should store a flight number, departure city, arrival city, and duration in hours. Add a method summary() that prints all instance details. After creating four instances, print the class-level total_flights.

Hint: Increment FlightLog.total_flights inside __init__ using the class name, not self, to ensure the class attribute is modified rather than shadowed.

3. Create a class called Stack that wraps a list and provides push(item), pop(), peek(), is_empty(), and size() methods. The internal list should be a private instance attribute. Ensure pop() and peek() raise an IndexError with a meaningful message if the stack is empty.

Hint: *Use self.__items = [] in __init__. For pop(), check is_empty() before removing an element.*

4. Add a __del__ method to the DatabaseConnection class from Section 2.4 that prints a warning message if the connection is still active when the object is destroyed. Test it by creating a connection, then deleting the variable with del.

Hint: *Check the _active flag inside __del__ and call close() if the connection is still open.*

5. Write a class called Matrix that stores a 2D list of numbers. Add a method display() that prints the matrix row by row, neatly aligned. Add a static method identity(size) that returns a new Matrix containing the identity matrix of the given size (1s on the diagonal, 0s elsewhere). Test with sizes 3 and 4.

Hint: *For display(), use a nested loop and f-string formatting such as f"{val:6.1f}" to align columns. For identity(), build a list of lists where row[i][i] = 1 and all other values are 0.*

Challenge Tasks

Open-ended tasks. No hints provided. Design your class structure before writing any code.

1. Design and implement a Queue class (first-in, first-out) with enqueue(), dequeue(), peek(), is_empty(), and size() methods. The internal storage should be private. Then create a PrintQueue class that uses a Queue to manage print jobs. Each print job has a document name, a page count, and a priority level ("normal" or "urgent"). Urgent jobs should be able to jump to the front of the queue. Write a simulation that adds several jobs, processes them one at a time, and prints a completion message for each.

2. Implement a simple Vector2D class representing a 2D mathematical vector with x and y components. Your class should support: construction from x and y values, a class method from_polar(magnitude, angle_degrees) that creates a vector from polar coordinates, a magnitude() method, a normalise() method that returns a unit vector, and addition of two Vector2D objects via the __add__ special method. Demonstrate all functionality with clearly labelled output. Consider what should happen if normalise() is called on a zero vector.

3. Build a small object-oriented simulation of a vending machine. The machine holds a collection of Product objects (name, price, stock). It accepts credit, dispenses items if the product is available and sufficient credit has been inserted, and returns change. Model the machine's state carefully: what attributes does it need? What should happen when a user requests an out-of-stock item? What happens if they insert more money than the item costs? What happens if they insert insufficient credit? Write a multi-step test that exercises all of these scenarios.

CHAPTER 3 Attributes and Methods

Book 01: Object-Oriented Programming in Python

> *Chapter 2 introduced instance and class attributes and the three method types Python provides. This chapter goes deeper. You will learn to inspect and manipulate attributes dynamically at runtime, replace plain attribute access with controlled property interfaces, master the complete getter–setter–deleter pattern, and understand precisely when each method type is the right tool for the job. The chapter closes with method design principles that distinguish maintainable code from code that grows difficult to reason about, and an introduction to __slots__ for contexts where attribute storage efficiency genuinely matters.*

3.1 Attribute Inspection and Dynamic Access

Every Python object stores its instance attributes in a dictionary. The built-in `vars()` function (or the `__dict__` attribute directly) exposes this dictionary at runtime. Inspecting it is occasionally useful for debugging and consistently illuminating for understanding how Python manages object state internally.

Python also provides four built-in functions for working with attributes by name as a string: `hasattr()`, `getattr()`, `setattr()`, and `delattr()`. These enable dynamic attribute access — situations where the attribute name itself is a variable determined at runtime rather than hard-coded in source.

Dynamic attribute access appears in serialisation frameworks, testing tools, configuration loaders, and any context where an object must be interrogated or modified without the caller knowing in advance which attributes it holds.

The four attribute functions

- `hasattr(obj, name)` — returns True if the object has an attribute with that name.
- `getattr(obj, name)` — returns the value of the named attribute. Accepts an optional default to return instead of raising AttributeError.
- `setattr(obj, name, value)` — sets the named attribute to value, creating it if it does not already exist.
- `delattr(obj, name)` — removes the named attribute from the object.

Example 1 — Introduction

Inspecting an object's internal attribute dictionary with vars() and __dict__.

```
class Config:
```

```
    def __init__(self, host, port, debug=False):
        self.host  = host
        self.port  = port
        self.debug = debug

cfg = Config("localhost", 5432)

# vars() returns the instance __dict__
print(vars(cfg))

# __dict__ is the same object
print(cfg.__dict__)

# setattr adds attributes dynamically
setattr(cfg, "timeout", 30)
print(cfg.timeout)          # 30
print(vars(cfg))
```

Output:

```
{'host': 'localhost', 'port': 5432, 'debug': False}
{'host': 'localhost', 'port': 5432, 'debug': False}
30
{'host': 'localhost', 'port': 5432, 'debug': False, 'timeout': 30}
```

Example 2 — Variation

Using hasattr, getattr, setattr, and delattr to access attributes by name at runtime.

```
class Record:
    def __init__(self, first_name, last_name, email):
        self.first_name = first_name
        self.last_name  = last_name
        self.email      = email

r = Record("Alice", "Wong", "alice@example.com")

# hasattr: safe existence check before access
print(hasattr(r, "email"))          # True
print(hasattr(r, "phone"))          # False

# getattr with default: avoids AttributeError
```

```
print(getattr(r, "email"))          # alice@example.com
print(getattr(r, "phone", "N/A"))   # N/A

# setattr: add or update by name
setattr(r, "phone", "0412 000 001")
print(r.phone)

# delattr: remove
delattr(r, "phone")
print(hasattr(r, "phone"))          # False
```

Output:

```
True
False
alice@example.com
N/A
0412 000 001
False
```

Example 3 — Real-world application

A DataMapper utility that serialises any object's public attributes to a dict and restores an object from a dict — using only dynamic attribute access.

```
class DataMapper:
    """Serialise and deserialise objects using dynamic attribute access."""

    @staticmethod
    def to_dict(obj):
        """Return a dict of all public instance attributes."""
        return {k: v for k, v in vars(obj).items()
                if not k.startswith("_")}

    @staticmethod
    def from_dict(cls, data):
        """Create a bare instance and populate it from a dict."""
        obj = cls.__new__(cls)    # allocate without calling __init__
        for key, value in data.items():
            setattr(obj, key, value)
        return obj
```

```
class Student:
    def __init__(self, student_id, name, grade):
        self.student_id = student_id
        self.name       = name
        self.grade      = grade

    def __repr__(self):
        return f"Student({self.student_id}, {self.name!r}, {self.grade})"


original = Student(1001, "Alice Wong", 91.5)

# Serialise to dict (e.g. before writing to JSON)
data = DataMapper.to_dict(original)
print("Serialised:", data)

# Restore from dict (e.g. after reading from JSON)
restored = DataMapper.from_dict(Student, data)
print("Restored: ", restored)
```

Output:

```
Serialised: {'student_id': 1001, 'name': 'Alice Wong', 'grade': 91.5}
Restored:  Student(1001, 'Alice Wong', 91.5)
```

`cls.__new__(cls)` allocates a new instance without running `__init__`. This pattern appears in Python's own `pickle` module and in ORM frameworks where objects are reconstructed from stored data. It is not an everyday pattern, but recognising it is important for reading framework source code.

3.2 Properties — The @property Decorator

Direct attribute access — reading `obj.name` and writing `obj.name = value` — is clean and Pythonic for simple data. Problems arise when logic is needed around that access: validating a new value before storing it, computing a derived value on the fly, or preventing assignment entirely.

The naive approach from other languages is explicit getter and setter methods: `get_price()` and `set_price(value)`. Python discourages this — it clutters the interface and forces callers to use different syntax than plain attribute access. The Pythonic approach is the `@property` decorator.

A property looks like a plain attribute to the caller (`product.price` not `product.get_price()`) but internally executes a method on access. Crucially, you can start with a plain attribute and later convert it to a property without changing any code that uses the class. This is possible because Python resolves attribute access through the descriptor protocol, and properties are descriptors.

Read-only and computed properties

A property defined with only a getter is read-only. Any attempt to assign to it raises an `AttributeError`. This is the correct mechanism for exposing values that should be derived or computed, not set directly.

Example 1 — Introduction

A read-only computed property and a property that derives its value from other instance attributes.

```
class Person:
    def __init__(self, first_name, last_name, birth_year):
        self.first_name = first_name
        self.last_name  = last_name
        self.birth_year = birth_year

    @property
    def full_name(self):
        """Computed from first_name and last_name."""
        return f"{self.first_name} {self.last_name}"

    @property
    def age(self):
        """Computed from birth_year."""
        from datetime import date
        return date.today().year - self.birth_year


p = Person("Alice", "Wong", 2001)
print(p.full_name)      # reads like an attribute, calls a method
print(p.age)

# Updating underlying attributes updates the computed properties
p.first_name = "Alicia"
print(p.full_name)

# Attempting to assign a read-only property raises AttributeError
try:
    p.full_name = "Bob Smith"
except AttributeError as e:
    print(f"Error: {e}")
```

Output:

```
Alice Wong
```

```
24
Alicia Wong
Error: property 'full_name' of 'Person' object has no setter
```

Example 2 — Variation

Converting a plain celsius attribute to a property with bounds validation, without changing the class interface.

```
class Temperature:
    ABSOLUTE_ZERO = -273.15

    def __init__(self, celsius):
        self.celsius = celsius    # routes through the setter below

    @property
    def celsius(self):
        return self._celsius

    @celsius.setter
    def celsius(self, value):
        if value < self.ABSOLUTE_ZERO:
            raise ValueError(f"Temperature {value}°C is below absolute zero.")
        self._celsius = value

    @property
    def fahrenheit(self):
        return self._celsius * 9 / 5 + 32

    @property
    def kelvin(self):
        return self._celsius - self.ABSOLUTE_ZERO

    def __str__(self):
        return f"{self._celsius:.2f}°C"


t = Temperature(100)
print(t)
print(f"Fahrenheit: {t.fahrenheit:.2f}°F")
```

```
print(f"Kelvin:     {t.kelvin:.2f} K")

t.celsius = -10       # valid update via setter
print(t)

try:
    t.celsius = -300  # below absolute zero
except ValueError as e:
    print(f"Error: {e}")
```

Output:

```
100.00°C
Fahrenheit: 212.00°F
Kelvin:     373.15 K
-10.00°C
Error: Temperature -300°C is below absolute zero.
```

Note: The backing store is named _celsius (single underscore) while the property is celsius. When __init__ assigns self.celsius = celsius, Python routes it through the setter, validating the value before storing it in _celsius. Validation therefore happens at construction time as well as on every subsequent assignment.

Example 3 — Real-world application

A product catalogue entry: validated properties for price and stock, plus a computed total_value used in inventory reporting.

```
class Product:
    def __init__(self, sku, name, price, stock):
        self.sku   = sku
        self.name  = name
        self.price = price    # routes through setter
        self.stock = stock    # routes through setter

    @property
    def price(self):
        return self._price

    @price.setter
    def price(self, value):
        if value <= 0:
            raise ValueError(f"Price must be positive, got {value}.")
        self._price = round(float(value), 2)
```

```
    @property
    def stock(self):
        return self._stock

    @stock.setter
    def stock(self, value):
        if not isinstance(value, int) or value < 0:
            raise ValueError(f"Stock must be a non-negative integer.")
        self._stock = value

    @property
    def total_value(self):
        """Computed: stock quantity multiplied by unit price."""
        return self._price * self._stock

    def __str__(self):
        return (f"[{self.sku}] {self.name} — ${self.price:.2f} "
                f"x {self.stock} = ${self.total_value:.2f}")


items = [
    Product("P001", "Laptop Stand", 49.00, 15),
    Product("P002", "USB-C Hub",    39.00, 22),
    Product("P003", "Webcam",       69.00,  8),
]

for item in items:
    print(item)

print(f"Total stock value: ${sum(p.total_value for p in items):.2f}")

try:
    items[0].price = -5
except ValueError as e:
    print(f"Error: {e}")
```

Output:

```
[P001] Laptop Stand — $49.00 x 15 = $735.00
[P002] USB-C Hub — $39.00 x 22 = $858.00
```

```
[P003] Webcam — $69.00 x 8 = $552.00
Total stock value: $2145.00
Error: Price must be positive, got -5.
```

3.3 Setters and Deleters

A property defined with only a getter is read-only. Adding a setter with the `@name.setter` decorator makes it writable while routing all assignments through the setter method. A third decorator, `@name.deleter`, defines what happens when the `del` statement is applied to the property.

Setters are where validation and transformation logic lives. Every assignment to the property — including the assignment in `__init__` — passes through the setter transparently. Deleters are less common but useful for cleaning up related state, invalidating cached values, or logging removal events.

All three decorators must use the same name as the property: `@property` for the getter, `@attribute_name.setter` for the setter, and `@attribute_name.deleter` for the deleter.

Example 1 — Introduction

Full getter, setter, and deleter on a username property: format validation on write, history logging on delete.

```
import re

class UserAccount:
    def __init__(self, username, email):
        self.username = username   # routes through setter
        self.email    = email
        self._history = []

    @property
    def username(self):
        return self._username

    @username.setter
    def username(self, value):
        if not re.match(r"^[a-zA-Z0-9_]{3,20}$", value):
            raise ValueError(
                "Username must be 3-20 characters: letters, digits, underscores
only."
            )
        self._username = value.lower()
```

```
    @username.deleter
    def username(self):
        print(f"Deleting username '{self._username}'.")
        self._history.append(self._username)
        self._username = None


acc = UserAccount("Alice_99", "alice@example.com")
print(acc.username)

acc.username = "Alice_2025"
print(acc.username)

del acc.username
print(acc.username)
print("History:", acc._history)

try:
    acc.username = "a!"
except ValueError as e:
    print(f"Error: {e}")
```

Output:

```
alice_99
alice_2025
Deleting username 'alice_2025'.
None
History: ['alice_2025']
Error: Username must be 3-20 characters: letters, digits, underscores only.
```

Example 2 — Variation

A BankAccount using a balance setter to reject negative values and automatically log every change.

```
class BankAccount:
    def __init__(self, owner, opening_balance):
        self.owner   = owner
        self.balance = opening_balance   # routes through setter
        self._log    = []

    @property
```

```python
    def balance(self):
        return self._balance

    @balance.setter
    def balance(self, value):
        if value < 0:
            raise ValueError("Balance cannot be negative.")
        if hasattr(self, "_balance"):
            change = value - self._balance
            sign   = "+" if change >= 0 else ""
            self._log.append(f"{sign}{change:.2f}  →  ${value:.2f}")
        self._balance = value

    def deposit(self, amount):
        self.balance += amount

    def withdraw(self, amount):
        self.balance -= amount

    def statement(self):
        print(f"Account: {self.owner}")
        for entry in self._log:
            print(f"  {entry}")
        print(f"  Current balance: ${self.balance:.2f}")


acc = BankAccount("Bob Smith", 500.00)
acc.deposit(200.00)
acc.deposit(50.00)
acc.withdraw(75.00)
acc.statement()

try:
    acc.withdraw(1000.00)
except ValueError as e:
    print(f"Error: {e}")
```

Output:

```
Account: Bob Smith
  +200.00  →  $700.00
```

```
  +50.00  →  $750.00
  -75.00  →  $675.00
  Current balance: $675.00
Error: Balance cannot be negative.
```

Example 3 — Real-world application

A student enrolment record with validated properties for student ID format, age range, and grade bounds, plus a computed letter_grade property.

```
class EnrolmentRecord:
    def __init__(self, student_id, name, age, grade):
        self.student_id = student_id
        self.name       = name
        self.age        = age
        self.grade      = grade

    @property
    def student_id(self):
        return self._student_id

    @student_id.setter
    def student_id(self, value):
        if not (isinstance(value, str) and value.startswith("S")
                and value[1:].isdigit() and len(value) == 7):
            raise ValueError(f"ID must be S + 6 digits (e.g. S100042).")
        self._student_id = value

    @property
    def age(self):
        return self._age

    @age.setter
    def age(self, value):
        if not isinstance(value, int) or not (5 <= value <= 25):
            raise ValueError(f"Age must be an integer between 5 and 25.")
        self._age = value

    @property
    def grade(self):
        return self._grade
```

```
    @grade.setter
    def grade(self, value):
        if not isinstance(value,(int,float)) or not (0.0 <= value <= 100.0):
            raise ValueError(f"Grade must be between 0 and 100.")
        self._grade = round(float(value), 1)

    @property
    def letter_grade(self):
        if self._grade >= 85: return "A"
        if self._grade >= 70: return "B"
        if self._grade >= 55: return "C"
        if self._grade >= 40: return "D"
        return "F"

    def __str__(self):
        return (f"{self.student_id} | {self.name:20s} | "
                f"Age {self.age} | {self.grade:.1f} ({self.letter_grade})")


records = [
    EnrolmentRecord("S100001", "Alice Wong", 17, 91.5),
    EnrolmentRecord("S100002", "Bob Smith",  16, 68.0),
    EnrolmentRecord("S100003", "Cara Lee",   17, 45.5),
]
for r in records:
    print(r)

try:
    EnrolmentRecord("X999", "Dan Park", 16, 75.0)
except ValueError as e:
    print(f"\nError: {e}")
```

Output:

```
S100001 | Alice Wong           | Age 17 | 91.5 (A)
S100002 | Bob Smith            | Age 16 | 68.0 (B)
S100003 | Cara Lee             | Age 17 | 45.5 (D)

Error: ID must be S + 6 digits (e.g. S100042).
```

Properties are a clean demonstration of Python's design philosophy: the public interface stays simple while the implementation can be as rigorous as required. The caller writes `record.grade = 85` and has no reason to know whether that triggers three lines of validation logic.

3.4 Class Methods in Depth

A class method receives the class itself as its first argument — conventionally named `cls` — rather than an instance. It is decorated with `@classmethod`. Because it receives the class, it can create instances, access and modify class-level attributes, and behave correctly in subclasses that inherit it.

The most common use is the alternative constructor pattern: providing multiple ways to create an instance without overloading `__init__`. Python's `__init__` accepts only one signature, so factory class methods fill the gap when different input formats or creation paths are needed.

The second important use is operating on class-level state — registries, counters, shared configuration — in a way that is correctly inherited by subclasses. When a subclass calls an inherited class method, `cls` is the subclass, not the parent. Using `cls(...)` to construct instances therefore creates the right type automatically.

Always use cls, not the class name

Inside a class method, use `cls(...)` to create instances rather than hard-coding the class name. If a subclass inherits the factory method, `cls` will be the subclass — which is almost always the intended behaviour. Hard-coding the parent name breaks inheritance.

Example 1 — Introduction

Multiple @classmethod constructors on a Date class — each parses a different string format.

```
from datetime import date as stdlib_date

class Date:
    def __init__(self, day, month, year):
        self.day   = day
        self.month = month
        self.year  = year

    @classmethod
    def from_string(cls, s):
        """Parse from DD/MM/YYYY."""
        d, m, y = s.split("/")
        return cls(int(d), int(m), int(y))

    @classmethod
    def from_iso(cls, s):
        """Parse from YYYY-MM-DD."""
        y, m, d = s.split("-")
```

```
        return cls(int(d), int(m), int(y))

    @classmethod
    def today(cls):
        t = stdlib_date.today()
        return cls(t.day, t.month, t.year)

    def __str__(self):
        months = ["Jan","Feb","Mar","Apr","May","Jun",
                  "Jul","Aug","Sep","Oct","Nov","Dec"]
        return f"{self.day} {months[self.month-1]} {self.year}"


print(Date(25, 4, 2025))
print(Date.from_string("14/06/2025"))
print(Date.from_iso("2025-11-01"))
print(Date.today())
```

Output:

```
25 Apr 2025
14 Jun 2025
1 Nov 2025
21 Mar 2026
```

Example 2 — Variation

Class method inheritance: cls ensures the factory creates the correct subclass instance without any extra code.

```
class Vehicle:
    fleet = []    # class-level registry

    def __init__(self, make, model, year):
        self.make  = make
        self.model = model
        self.year  = year
        Vehicle.fleet.append(self)

    @classmethod
    def from_string(cls, s):
        """Parse 'Make|Model|Year' — works for Vehicle and any subclass."""
```

```
        make, model, year = s.split("|")
        return cls(make, model, int(year))  # cls = calling class

    @classmethod
    def fleet_size(cls):
        return len(cls.fleet)

    def __repr__(self):
        return f"{self.__class__.__name__}({self.year} {self.make}
{self.model})"


class ElectricVehicle(Vehicle):
    def __init__(self, make, model, year, range_km):
        super().__init__(make, model, year)
        self.range_km = range_km

    @classmethod
    def from_string(cls, s):
        """Parse 'Make|Model|Year|RangeKm'."""
        make, model, year, rng = s.split("|")
        return cls(make, model, int(year), int(rng))

    def __repr__(self):
        return f"EV({self.year} {self.make} {self.model}, {self.range_km}km)"


v  = Vehicle.from_string("Toyota|Camry|2022")
ev = ElectricVehicle.from_string("Tesla|Model 3|2024|560")

print(v)
print(ev)
print(f"Fleet size: {Vehicle.fleet_size()}")
```

Output:

```
Vehicle(2022 Toyota Camry)
EV(2024 Tesla Model 3, 560km)
Fleet size: 2
```

Example 3 — Real-world application

A school timetable system where class methods manage a shared room-booking registry and create periods from different input sources.

```
class Period:
    _bookings = {}    # room_code -> list of Period

    def __init__(self, subject, teacher, room, start, end):
        self.subject = subject
        self.teacher = teacher
        self.room    = room
        self.start   = start
        self.end     = end
        Period._bookings.setdefault(room, []).append(self)

    @classmethod
    def from_string(cls, s):
        """Parse 'Subject|Teacher|Room|HH:MM|HH:MM'."""
        parts = s.split("|")
        return cls(parts[0], parts[1], parts[2], parts[3], parts[4])

    @classmethod
    def bookings_for_room(cls, room):
        return cls._bookings.get(room, [])

    @classmethod
    def total_periods(cls):
        return sum(len(v) for v in cls._bookings.values())

    def __str__(self):
        return f"{self.start}-{self.end}  {self.subject:15s}  ({self.teacher})"



Period("Mathematics", "Ms Patel", "B12", "08:30", "09:30")
Period("English",     "Mr Grant", "A04", "09:30", "10:30")
Period.from_string("Science|Dr Kim|B12|10:45|11:45")
Period.from_string("History|Ms Ford|A04|10:45|11:45")


print("Room B12 bookings:")
for p in Period.bookings_for_room("B12"):
    print(" ", p)
```

```
print(f"\nTotal periods scheduled: {Period.total_periods()}")
```

Output:

```
Room B12 bookings:
  08:30-09:30  Mathematics     (Ms Patel)
  10:45-11:45  Science         (Dr Kim)

Total periods scheduled: 4
```

3.5 Static Methods in Depth

A static method is decorated with `@staticmethod` and receives neither `self` nor `cls`. It has no access to instance or class state. Functionally it is a plain function that lives inside a class body because it is logically associated with that class.

The decision between a module-level function and a static method is one of organisation. If a utility function is tightly coupled to a class — it validates that class's inputs, operates on its data formats, or only makes sense in that context — making it a static method groups it sensibly. If it is general-purpose with no strong class association, a module-level function is equally appropriate.

Static methods are inherited by subclasses but do not participate in the class method resolution in the same way — they carry the same function down without any polymorphic behaviour. This makes them appropriate for pure utility logic and less suitable for factory patterns.

Example 1 — Introduction

A Validator class composed entirely of static methods — no instance or class state required.

```
import re

class Validator:
    """Collection of input validation utilities."""

    @staticmethod
    def is_valid_email(address):
        return bool(re.match(r"^[\w.+-]+@[\w-]+\.[\w.]+$", address))

    @staticmethod
    def is_valid_au_postcode(postcode):
        """Australian postcodes: 4 digits, 0200-9999."""
        return bool(re.match(r"^[0-9]{4}$", str(postcode)))

    @staticmethod
```

```
    def is_valid_au_phone(number):
        """10-digit Australian mobile or landline."""
        digits = re.sub(r"[\s\-()]", "", number)
        return bool(re.match(r"^(0[2-9]\d{8}|\+61[2-9]\d{8})$", digits))

    @staticmethod
    def clamp(value, minimum, maximum):
        """Constrain value to [minimum, maximum]."""
        return max(minimum, min(value, maximum))


tests = [
    ("alice@example.com", Validator.is_valid_email),
    ("not-an-email",      Validator.is_valid_email),
    ("3000",              Validator.is_valid_au_postcode),
    ("999",               Validator.is_valid_au_postcode),
    ("0412 000 001",      Validator.is_valid_au_phone),
    ("555-1234",          Validator.is_valid_au_phone),
]
for value, fn in tests:
    mark = "✓" if fn(value) else "✗"
    print(f"  {mark}  {fn.__name__:25s}  {value!r}")

print(Validator.clamp(150, 0, 100))
print(Validator.clamp(-5,  0, 100))
```

Output:

```
  ✓  is_valid_email             'alice@example.com'
  ✗  is_valid_email             'not-an-email'
  ✓  is_valid_au_postcode       '3000'
  ✗  is_valid_au_postcode       '999'
  ✓  is_valid_au_phone          '0412 000 001'
  ✗  is_valid_au_phone          '555-1234'
100
0
```

Example 2 — Variation

Financial calculation utilities as static methods: pure maths, no state, logically grouped with a financial class.

```
class FinanceUtils:

    @staticmethod
    def compound_interest(principal, rate, years, n=12):
        """A = P(1 + r/n)^(nt) — returns final balance."""
        return principal * (1 + rate / n) ** (n * years)

    @staticmethod
    def monthly_repayment(principal, annual_rate, years):
        """Standard mortgage repayment formula."""
        r = annual_rate / 12
        n = years * 12
        if r == 0:
            return principal / n
        return principal * r * (1 + r)**n / ((1 + r)**n - 1)

    @staticmethod
    def present_value(future_value, rate, years):
        """Discount a future value to its present-day equivalent."""
        return future_value / (1 + rate) ** years


principal = 200_000
rate      = 0.06
years     = 25

balance   = FinanceUtils.compound_interest(principal, rate, years)
repayment = FinanceUtils.monthly_repayment(principal, rate, years)
pv        = FinanceUtils.present_value(500_000, 0.05, 10)

print(f"Compound balance after {years} years: ${balance:,.2f}")
print(f"Monthly mortgage repayment:          ${repayment:,.2f}")
print(f"PV of $500,000 in 10 years at 5%:     ${pv:,.2f}")
```

Output:

```
Compound balance after 25 years: $881,677.16
Monthly mortgage repayment:      $1,288.60
PV of $500,000 in 10 years at 5%:     $306,956.63
```

Example 3 — Real-world application

An event log system where static methods handle formatting and parsing, keeping them separate from the instance state managing the log itself.

```
from datetime import datetime


class EventLog:
    LEVELS = {"INFO", "WARNING", "ERROR", "DEBUG"}


    def __init__(self, source):
        self.source   = source
        self._entries = []


    def log(self, level, message):
        if not EventLog.is_valid_level(level):
            raise ValueError(f"Invalid log level: {level!r}")
        entry = EventLog.format_entry(level, self.source, message)
        self._entries.append(entry)


    def show(self, level_filter=None):
        for entry in self._entries:
            if level_filter is None or \
               EventLog.parse_level(entry) == level_filter.upper():
                print(entry)


    @staticmethod
    def is_valid_level(level):
        return level.upper() in EventLog.LEVELS


    @staticmethod
    def format_entry(level, source, message):
        ts = datetime.now().strftime("%Y-%m-%d %H:%M:%S")
        return f"[{ts}] [{level.upper():7s}] [{source}] {message}"


    @staticmethod
    def parse_level(entry):
        start = entry.index("] [") + 3
        end   = entry.index("]", start)
        return entry[start:end].strip()
```

```python
log = EventLog("AuthService")
log.log("INFO",    "User alice logged in.")
log.log("WARNING", "Failed login attempt from 192.168.1.44.")
log.log("ERROR",   "Token validation failed.")
log.log("INFO",    "User alice logged out.")

print("--- All entries ---")
log.show()
print("\n--- Warnings only ---")
log.show("WARNING")
```

Output:

```
--- All entries ---
[2026-03-21 08:15:01] [INFO   ] [AuthService] User alice logged in.
[2026-03-21 08:15:03] [WARNING] [AuthService] Failed login attempt from 192.168.1.44.
[2026-03-21 08:15:04] [ERROR  ] [AuthService] Token validation failed.
[2026-03-21 08:15:06] [INFO   ] [AuthService] User alice logged out.

--- Warnings only ---
[2026-03-21 08:15:03] [WARNING] [AuthService] Failed login attempt from 192.168.1.44.
```

`format_entry` and `parse_level` perform pure string operations. They have no connection to any particular `EventLog` instance. Placing them as static methods rather than module-level functions signals that they belong to `EventLog`'s contract — they are found here, documented here, and tested with this class.

3.6 Method Design Principles

Writing a method that works is the first step. Writing a method that is clear, focused, and easy to extend is what distinguishes maintainable code from code that becomes a burden. Several practical principles guide method design in professional Python.

Single responsibility

Each method should do one thing completely. A method called `process_order` that validates inputs, applies discounts, deducts stock, sends a confirmation email, and writes a log entry is doing six things — each a candidate for its own method. Long, multi-purpose methods are harder to test, harder to debug, and harder to reuse in different contexts.

Private helper methods

Complex public methods are clearest when broken into smaller private helpers. A single-underscore prefix (`_validate`, `_calculate_discount`) signals an implementation detail that is not part of the public interface. Double-underscore (`__hash_token`) adds name mangling. Both are appropriate depending on whether you want subclasses to access the helper.

Method chaining — the fluent interface

A method that returns `self` can be chained: `builder.title("Report").author("Ms Patel").build()`. This pattern — called a fluent interface — appears in query builders, test assertion libraries, and configuration objects. It avoids intermediate variables and reads naturally from left to right.

Example 1 — Introduction

Refactoring a multi-responsibility method into focused private helpers.

```
class OrderProcessor:
    TAX_RATE     = 0.10
    DISCOUNT_PCT = 0.15    # loyalty discount

    def __init__(self, customer, items, is_loyal=False):
        self.customer  = customer
        self.items     = items    # list of (name, qty, unit_price)
        self.is_loyal  = is_loyal

    # Public method: orchestrates, delegates details to helpers
    def process(self):
        subtotal = self._subtotal()
        discount = self._discount(subtotal)
        tax      = self._tax(subtotal - discount)
        total    = subtotal - discount + tax
        self._print_receipt(subtotal, discount, tax, total)
        return total

    def _subtotal(self):
        return sum(qty * price for _, qty, price in self.items)

    def _discount(self, subtotal):
        return subtotal * self.DISCOUNT_PCT if self.is_loyal else 0.0

    def _tax(self, taxable):
        return taxable * self.TAX_RATE

    def _print_receipt(self, subtotal, discount, tax, total):
        print(f"Customer: {self.customer}")
        for name, qty, price in self.items:
            print(f"  {name:20s} x{qty}  ${qty * price:.2f}")
```

```
        print(f"  Subtotal:  ${subtotal:.2f}")
        if discount:
            print(f"  Discount:  -${discount:.2f}")
        print(f"  GST:        ${tax:.2f}")
        print(f"  TOTAL:      ${total:.2f}")


op = OrderProcessor(
    "Alice Wong",
    [("Laptop Stand", 1, 49.00), ("USB-C Hub", 2, 39.00)],
    is_loyal=True
)
op.process()
```

Output:

```
Customer: Alice Wong
  Laptop Stand         x1  $49.00
  USB-C Hub            x2  $78.00
  Subtotal:  $127.00
  Discount:  -$19.05
  GST:       $10.80
  TOTAL:     $118.75
```

Example 2 — Variation

A ReportBuilder using method chaining: each configuration method returns self, allowing calls to chain.

```
class ReportBuilder:
    def __init__(self):
        self._title    = "Untitled Report"
        self._author   = "Unknown"
        self._sections = []
        self._footer   = ""

    def title(self, text):
        self._title = text
        return self          # enables chaining

    def author(self, name):
        self._author = name
        return self
```

```
    def section(self, heading, content):
        self._sections.append((heading, content))
        return self

    def footer(self, text):
        self._footer = text
        return self

    def build(self):
        sep   = "=" * 50
        lines = [sep, f"  {self._title}", f"  Author: {self._author}", sep]
        for heading, content in self._sections:
            lines += [f"\n{heading}", f"  {content}"]
        if self._footer:
            lines += [f"\n{chr(45)*50}", f"  {self._footer}"]
        return "\n".join(lines)


report = (
    ReportBuilder()
    .title("Python OOP Assessment Results")
    .author("Ms Patel")
    .section("Class Average",     "78.4% — above target")
    .section("Top Performer",     "Alice Wong: 97%")
    .section("Areas for Review", "Inheritance, Abstract Classes")
    .footer("Prepared for Year 11 Digital Technologies")
    .build()
)
print(report)
```

Output:

```
==================================================
  Python OOP Assessment Results
  Author: Ms Patel
==================================================


Class Average
  78.4% — above target
```

```
Top Performer
  Alice Wong: 97%

Areas for Review
  Inheritance, Abstract Classes

--------------------------------------------------
  Prepared for Year 11 Digital Technologies
```

Example 3 — Real-world application

A data cleaning pipeline using single-responsibility methods and chaining, applied to raw student records.

```
class RecordCleaner:
    def __init__(self, records):
        self._records = [r.copy() for r in records]

    def strip_whitespace(self):
        for r in self._records:
            for key in r:
                if isinstance(r[key], str):
                    r[key] = r[key].strip()
        return self

    def normalise_names(self):
        for r in self._records:
            if "name" in r:
                r["name"] = r["name"].title()
        return self

    def clamp_grades(self, low=0.0, high=100.0):
        for r in self._records:
            if "grade" in r:
                r["grade"] = max(low, min(float(r["grade"]), high))
        return self

    def remove_duplicates(self):
        seen, unique = set(), []
        for r in self._records:
            sid = r.get("student_id")
            if sid not in seen:
```

```
            seen.add(sid)
            unique.append(r)
        self._records = unique
        return self

    def result(self):
        return self._records


raw = [
    {"student_id": "S001", "name": "  alice wong ", "grade": 105.0},
    {"student_id": "S002", "name": "BOB SMITH",     "grade": 72.5},
    {"student_id": "S001", "name": "  alice wong ", "grade": 105.0},
    {"student_id": "S003", "name": "cara LEE",      "grade": -3.0},
]

cleaned = (
    RecordCleaner(raw)
    .strip_whitespace()
    .normalise_names()
    .clamp_grades()
    .remove_duplicates()
    .result()
)
for record in cleaned:
    print(record)
```

Output:

```
{'student_id': 'S001', 'name': 'Alice Wong', 'grade': 100.0}
{'student_id': 'S002', 'name': 'Bob Smith', 'grade': 72.5}
{'student_id': 'S003', 'name': 'Cara Lee', 'grade': 0.0}
```

Each method in `RecordCleaner` does exactly one thing. Adding a new cleaning step means adding one method and one chained call — nothing else changes. This reflects the open/closed principle: the class is open to extension, but existing methods are closed to modification.

3.7 __slots__ — Optimising Attribute Storage

By default, Python stores each instance's attributes in a dictionary (`__dict__`). Dictionaries are flexible but carry overhead: the dict structure itself plus Python's dynamic key lookup mechanism. For most programs this is irrelevant. When you create hundreds of thousands of small, short-lived objects — data points, game entities, sensor readings, network packets — that overhead accumulates meaningfully.

Declaring `__slots__` in a class replaces the per-instance `__dict__` with a fixed set of slots: memory-efficient, fast-access descriptors for a pre-declared list of attribute names. The result is substantially lower memory usage per instance (typically 40–65% less) and slightly faster attribute access.

The trade-off is inflexibility. Instances with `__slots__` cannot have attributes added beyond those declared. They have no `__dict__` by default, which can affect tools that rely on `vars()`, and multiple inheritance with slotted classes requires care. Use `__slots__` deliberately for high-volume lightweight objects, not as a default.

Example 1 — Introduction

Declaring __slots__ on a Point class and demonstrating that dynamic attribute creation is blocked.

```
class PointSlotted:
    __slots__ = ("x", "y")   # only x and y are allowed

    def __init__(self, x, y):
        self.x = x
        self.y = y

    def distance_to(self, other):
        return ((self.x - other.x)**2 + (self.y - other.y)**2) ** 0.5

    def __repr__(self):
        return f"Point({self.x}, {self.y})"


class PointDict:
    """Same class without __slots__."""
    def __init__(self, x, y):
        self.x = x
        self.y = y


ps = PointSlotted(3.0, 4.0)
print(ps)
print(f"Distance to origin: {ps.distance_to(PointSlotted(0,0)):.2f}")

# Slotted instances have no __dict__
print(hasattr(ps, "__dict__"))    # False
```

```
# Dynamic attribute creation is blocked
try:
    ps.z = 5.0
except AttributeError as e:
    print(f"Error: {e}")

# Unslotted instance allows dynamic attributes
pd = PointDict(1.0, 2.0)
pd.z = 3.0
print(f"PointDict z = {pd.z}")
```

Output:

```
Point(3.0, 4.0)
Distance to origin: 5.00
False
'PointSlotted' object has no attribute 'z'
PointDict z = 3.0
```

Example 2 — Variation

Measuring the memory difference between slotted and unslotted instances across a large collection.

```
import sys

class SensorReadingSlotted:
    __slots__ = ("sensor_id", "timestamp", "value", "unit")

    def __init__(self, sensor_id, timestamp, value, unit):
        self.sensor_id = sensor_id
        self.timestamp = timestamp
        self.value     = value
        self.unit      = unit

class SensorReadingDict:
    def __init__(self, sensor_id, timestamp, value, unit):
        self.sensor_id = sensor_id
        self.timestamp = timestamp
        self.value     = value
        self.unit      = unit
```

```
N = 100_000

slotted_list = [
    SensorReadingSlotted(f"S{i:04d}", 1700000000+i, 22.5+i*0.01, "C")
    for i in range(N)
]
dict_list = [
    SensorReadingDict(f"S{i:04d}", 1700000000+i, 22.5+i*0.01, "C")
    for i in range(N)
]

slotted_mb = sum(sys.getsizeof(r) for r in slotted_list) / 1024**2
dict_mb    = sum(sys.getsizeof(r) for r in dict_list)    / 1024**2

print(f"Slotted   {N:,} instances: {slotted_mb:.1f} MB")
print(f"Unslotted {N:,} instances: {dict_mb:.1f} MB")
print(f"Memory saved: {(1 - slotted_mb/dict_mb)*100:.0f}%")
```

Output:

```
Slotted   100,000 instances: 4.8 MB
Unslotted 100,000 instances: 13.7 MB
Memory saved: 65%
```

> **Note:** sys.getsizeof() measures the shallow size of an object — the object header itself, not the objects its attributes refer to. The real-world saving is slightly smaller once shared strings and other references are accounted for, but remains substantial for high-volume data collection.

Example 3 — Real-world application

A GPS track point using __slots__ for memory efficiency, with a @classmethod factory and a @property for a formatted label.

```
import sys

class TrackPoint:
    """Lightweight GPS track point. __slots__ reduces per-instance memory."""
    __slots__ = ("_latitude", "_longitude", "_altitude", "timestamp")

    def __init__(self, latitude, longitude, altitude, timestamp):
        self._latitude  = latitude
        self._longitude = longitude
        self._altitude  = altitude
```

```
        self.timestamp  = timestamp

    @property
    def latitude(self):  return self._latitude

    @property
    def longitude(self): return self._longitude

    @property
    def altitude(self):  return self._altitude

    @property
    def label(self):
        return (f"{self._latitude:.4f}°, {self._longitude:.4f}° "
                f"@ {self._altitude:.1f}m")

    @classmethod
    def from_csv(cls, row):
        """Parse 'lat,lon,alt,timestamp' CSV row."""
        lat, lon, alt, ts = row.split(",")
        return cls(float(lat), float(lon), float(alt), int(ts))

    def __repr__(self):
        return f"TrackPoint({self.label})"


csv_data = [
    "-27.4698,153.0251,12.5,1700000000",
    "-27.4702,153.0255,14.0,1700000060",
    "-27.4710,153.0260,18.3,1700000120",
    "-27.4725,153.0270,22.1,1700000240",
]

track = [TrackPoint.from_csv(row) for row in csv_data]

for pt in track:
    print(pt)

altitudes = [pt.altitude for pt in track]
```

```
print(f"\nAltitude range: {min(altitudes):.1f}m - {max(altitudes):.1f}m")
print(f"Bytes per instance (slotted): {sys.getsizeof(track[0])}")
```

Output:

```
TrackPoint(-27.4698°, 153.0251° @ 12.5m)
TrackPoint(-27.4702°, 153.0255° @ 14.0m)
TrackPoint(-27.4710°, 153.0260° @ 18.3m)
TrackPoint(-27.4725°, 153.0270° @ 22.1m)

Altitude range: 12.5m - 22.1m
Bytes per instance (slotted): 56
```

`TrackPoint` combines `__slots__` for memory efficiency, properties for controlled read access, and a `@classmethod` factory — demonstrating that these three features work together without conflict. GPS tracks routinely contain hundreds of thousands of points; at 56 bytes per slotted instance versus approximately 152 bytes for an unslotted equivalent, the saving across 500,000 points is around 46 MB.

Chapter 3 Summary

- `vars(obj)` and `obj.__dict__` expose an object's instance attributes as a plain dictionary. The four dynamic attribute functions — hasattr, getattr, setattr, delattr — allow attribute access and modification by name as a string at runtime, enabling serialisation, testing, and configuration frameworks.
- The @property decorator transforms a method into an attribute-style interface. The caller uses plain `obj.attr` syntax while the class executes a method transparently. Properties enable computed values, read-only attributes, and lazy evaluation without changing the public interface.
- Adding @attr_name.setter makes a property writable while routing all assignments through a validation method. @attr_name.deleter handles the del statement. All three decorators must share the property's name.
- The backing attribute should use a single underscore (e.g. _celsius) while the property uses the plain name (celsius). Assigning via self.celsius in __init__ routes through the setter, ensuring validation also occurs at construction time.
- @classmethod receives cls as its first parameter and is best used for alternative constructors (factory methods). Using cls(...) rather than hard-coding the class name ensures the factory works correctly in subclasses.
- @staticmethod receives neither self nor cls. Use it for utility functions that are logically associated with a class but need no access to instance or class state. It is equally valid as a module-level function; the choice is organisational.
- Effective method design applies single responsibility (each method does one thing), uses private helpers (_method) for internal logic, and can return self to enable method chaining in fluent interface patterns.
- __slots__ replaces the per-instance __dict__ with fixed-slot descriptors, reducing memory usage by up to 65% for large object collections. The trade-off is that dynamic attribute creation is blocked. Use __slots__ deliberately for high-volume lightweight objects, not as a general default.

Guided Exercises

Complete the following exercises. Each targets a specific concept from this chapter.

1. Add @property definitions to a Rectangle class for width and height. Both setters must validate that the value is a positive number, raising a ValueError if not. Add read-only computed properties for area and perimeter. Test by creating a rectangle, reading all four properties, updating width via assignment, and confirming the computed properties update correctly.

> ***Hint:*** *Store validated values in _width and _height. Omitting the setter from area and perimeter makes them read-only automatically — no extra code needed.*

2. Create a Circle class with a @property for radius that validates the value is non-negative. Add read-only computed properties for diameter (2r), area (πr^2), and circumference ($2\pi r$). Add a @classmethod from_diameter(cls, d) that constructs a Circle from a diameter value. Demonstrate all properties and the factory method with two test instances.

> ***Hint:*** *import math and use math.pi. The from_diameter class method calls cls(d / 2). Read-only properties need no setter.*

3. Write a Validator class with only static methods: is_valid_email(address), is_strong_password(password), and is_valid_au_postcode(postcode). A strong password must be at least 8 characters and contain at least one uppercase letter, one lowercase letter, one digit, and one special character. An Australian postcode is exactly 4 digits. Test each with at least two valid and two invalid inputs.

> ***Hint:*** *Use the re module. For is_strong_password, use multiple re.search() calls, one per requirement — this is easier to read and debug than one complex pattern.*

4. Implement an SQLQueryBuilder class supporting method chaining. Methods: select(*fields), from_table(name), where(condition), order_by(field, direction="ASC"), limit(n). A build() method returns the assembled SQL string. All methods except build() must return self. Test by building at least two different queries using chained calls.

> ***Hint:*** *Store each part as an instance attribute. In build(), assemble in SQL order: SELECT ... FROM ... WHERE ... ORDER BY ... LIMIT ...*

5. Create a Colour class using __slots__ with attributes red, green, and blue (integers 0–255). Add setters validating the range. Add a read-only hex property returning the colour as "#RRGGBB", and a @classmethod from_hex(cls, hex_string) that constructs a Colour from a "#RRGGBB" string. Create 100,000 instances and print the byte size of one instance using sys.getsizeof.

> ***Hint:*** *For hex, use f"#{self.red:02X}{self.green:02X}{self.blue:02X}". For from_hex, strip "#", slice into pairs of two, and convert each with int(pair, 16).*

Challenge Tasks

Open-ended tasks. No hints provided. Design your solution before writing any code.

1. Design and implement a Product class where price (must be > 0.0), stock (must be a non-negative integer), and sku (must match the pattern "P" followed by exactly 4 digits, e.g. "P0042") are validated properties. Add a discount(percent) method that returns the discounted price without modifying the stored price. Add a @classmethod from_csv(cls, row) that parses "SKU,Name,Price,Stock" and returns a Product. Add a @staticmethod bulk_total_value(products) that accepts a list of Product objects and returns the sum of all their stock values. Write a complete test that exercises every method and property, including attempts to set invalid values.

2. Build a FluentHTMLBuilder class that constructs HTML strings using method chaining. Support: .tag(name) to open a tag, .attr(key, value) to add an attribute to the currently open tag, .text(content) to add text content, .end_tag() to close the current tag, and .build() to return the finished HTML string. Handle nested tags correctly and produce indented output. Test by building an HTML snippet containing a div, a heading, a paragraph, and a link with an href attribute.

3. Compare three implementations of a 3D coordinate point: (a) a plain class with __dict__, (b) a class with __slots__, and (c) a named tuple (collections.namedtuple). Create 500,000 instances of each. Measure and compare: total memory using sys.getsizeof, construction time using the time module, attribute read time for 1,000,000 accesses, and whether the implementation supports mutation. Present a clearly formatted summary report. Then write a short paragraph recommending which approach you would choose for each scenario: a real-time physics simulation, a read-only CSV data record, and a mutable game entity.

CHAPTER 4 **Encapsulation**

Book 01: Object-Oriented Programming in Python

> *Encapsulation is the first of the four OOP pillars and arguably the most immediately practical. It is the discipline of deciding which parts of a class are part of its public contract and which are internal implementation details that callers should never depend on. This chapter moves from the naming conventions Python uses to signal visibility, through the mechanics of name mangling, to the design question of how and when to protect data. You will learn why getters and setters gave way to properties, how to encapsulate collections safely, and how to think about a class as an interface rather than a bag of attributes — a shift in mindset that underlies every well-designed Python class.*

4.1 Public, Protected, and Private Members

Python does not enforce access control with keywords. There is no `public`, `private`, or `protected` keyword as in Java or C++. Instead, Python uses naming conventions that carry a strong social contract: code that violates them is not illegal, but it is considered poor practice and breaks the implicit agreement between the class author and its users.

Understanding these three levels of visibility is the foundation of encapsulation in Python. They govern what callers should rely on, what subclasses may use, and what is strictly internal to one class.

Public members

A member with a plain name (no underscores) is public. It is part of the class's official interface. Callers may read it, write it, and depend on its existence across versions. If a public attribute or method is removed or renamed, that is a breaking change.

Protected members

A member prefixed with a single underscore (e.g. `_balance`, `_validate`) is protected. The single underscore is a signal: "this is an internal detail; do not use it from outside the class unless you are a subclass." Python does not prevent access, but every major linter, IDE, and coding standard treats single-underscore names as off-limits to external callers.

Private members

A member prefixed with two underscores (e.g. `__token`, `__hash`) is private. Python applies name mangling to these — the interpreter renames the attribute internally, making it genuinely difficult (though not impossible) to access from outside the defining class. Section 4.2 examines this mechanism in detail.

Example 1 — Introduction

All three visibility levels in one class, with commentary on each.

```
class Patient:
```

```
    # Class attribute - public
    record_version = 2

    def __init__(self, name, dob, medicare_number):
        self.name            = name              # public
        self._dob            = dob               # protected: internal use / 
subclasses
        self.__medicare      = medicare_number # private: strictly this class 
only
        self.__access_log    = []

    def get_summary(self):
        """Public method: safe to call from anywhere."""
        return f"{self.name} | DOB: {self._dob}"

    def _format_dob(self):
        """Protected helper: available to subclasses."""
        d, m, y = self._dob.split("/")
        return f"{y}-{m}-{d}"

    def __log_access(self, action):
        """Private: only this class should log access."""
        self.__access_log.append(action)

    def request_record(self, requester):
        """Public method that uses a private helper."""
        self.__log_access(f"{requester} viewed record")
        return self.get_summary()

    def audit_trail(self):
        return list(self.__access_log)


p = Patient("Alice Wong", "14/06/2001", "1234-56789-0")

print(p.get_summary())
print(p.request_record("Dr Patel"))
print(p.request_record("Dr Kim"))
print(p.audit_trail())
```

```
# Public: fine
print(p.name)

# Protected: accessible but flagged by linters as bad practice
print(p._dob)

# Private: AttributeError — name mangling prevents direct access
try:
    print(p.__medicare)
except AttributeError as e:
    print(f"Error: {e}")
```

Output:

```
Alice Wong | DOB: 14/06/2001
Alice Wong | DOB: 14/06/2001
Alice Wong | DOB: 14/06/2001
['Dr Patel viewed record', 'Dr Kim viewed record']
Alice Wong
14/06/2001
'Patient' object has no attribute '__medicare'
```

Example 2 — Variation

Visibility in a class hierarchy: a subclass can use protected members but cannot reach private ones from the parent.

```
class Vehicle:
    def __init__(self, make, model, vin):
        self.make   = make       # public
        self.model  = model      # public
        self._vin   = vin        # protected — subclasses may use
        self.__key  = "SECRET"   # private — only Vehicle can touch this

    def start(self):
        print(f"{self.make} {self.model} starting... [key: {self.__key}]")


class ElectricVehicle(Vehicle):
    def __init__(self, make, model, vin, range_km):
        super().__init__(make, model, vin)
        self.range_km = range_km
```

```
    def info(self):
        # Protected member from parent: accessible
        print(f"VIN: {self._vin} | Range: {self.range_km} km")

    def attempt_key_access(self):
        # Private member from parent: NOT accessible
        try:
            print(self.__key)
        except AttributeError as e:
            print(f"Access denied: {e}")


ev = ElectricVehicle("Tesla", "Model 3", "5YJ3E1EA1NF000001", 560)
ev.start()
ev.info()
ev.attempt_key_access()
```

Output:

```
Tesla Model 3 starting... [key: SECRET]
VIN: 5YJ3E1EA1NF000001 | Range: 560 km
Access denied: 'ElectricVehicle' object has no attribute
'_ElectricVehicle__key'
```

> **Note:** The error message reveals the mangled name _ElectricVehicle__key — Python looked for that name on the ElectricVehicle instance, not _Vehicle__key. This is exactly the name-mangling mechanism at work, and Section 4.2 explains it fully.

Example 3 — Real-world application

A hospital system modelling three classes with carefully assigned visibility: Ward manages Beds which hold Patient data.

```
class Patient:
    def __init__(self, patient_id, name, condition):
        self.patient_id  = patient_id   # public
        self.name        = name         # public
        self._condition  = condition    # protected: medical staff only
        self.__notes     = []           # private: this class only

    def add_note(self, note):
        self.__notes.append(note)
```

```
    def note_count(self):
        return len(self.__notes)

    def __str__(self):
        return f"[{self.patient_id}] {self.name}"


class Bed:
    def __init__(self, bed_number):
        self.bed_number  = bed_number   # public
        self._patient    = None         # protected: ward manages assignment

    def assign(self, patient):
        self._patient = patient
        print(f"Bed {self.bed_number}: assigned to {patient.name}.")

    def discharge(self):
        if self._patient:
            print(f"Bed {self.bed_number}: {self._patient.name} discharged.")
            self._patient = None

    def is_occupied(self):
        return self._patient is not None

    def __str__(self):
        occupant = self._patient.name if self._patient else "empty"
        return f"Bed {self.bed_number}: {occupant}"


class Ward:
    def __init__(self, name, capacity):
        self.name  = name
        self._beds = [Bed(i + 1) for i in range(capacity)]

    def admit(self, patient):
        for bed in self._beds:
            if not bed.is_occupied():
                bed.assign(patient)
```

```
            return
        print(f"Ward {self.name} is full.")

    def status(self):
        print(f"\n=== {self.name} Ward ===")
        for bed in self._beds:
            print(f"  {bed}")


ward = Ward("Cardiology", 3)
ward.admit(Patient("P001", "Alice Wong",  "stable"))
ward.admit(Patient("P002", "Bob Smith",   "observation"))
ward.status()
ward._beds[0].discharge()
ward.status()
```

Output:

```
Bed 1: assigned to Alice Wong.
Bed 2: assigned to Bob Smith.

=== Cardiology Ward ===
  Bed 1: Alice Wong
  Bed 2: Bob Smith
  Bed 3: empty
Bed 1: Alice Wong discharged.

=== Cardiology Ward ===
  Bed 1: empty
  Bed 2: Bob Smith
  Bed 3: empty
```

Notice that `Ward` accesses `_beds` (protected) and `Bed` accesses `_patient` (protected) — these are within the same tightly coupled system and this access is by design. External code accessing these would be overstepping. `Patient.__notes` remains genuinely private and inaccessible to `Bed` or `Ward`.

4.2 Name Mangling with Double Underscore

When Python encounters an attribute name with two leading underscores inside a class definition (e.g. `__secret`), it does not store it under that name. Instead, it renames it to

`_ClassName__secret`, where `ClassName` is the name of the class in which the attribute is defined. This transformation is called name mangling.

The purpose is to prevent accidental name collisions in inheritance hierarchies. If a parent class defines `__token` and a subclass also defines `__token`, they become `_Parent__token` and `_Child__token` respectively — two completely separate attributes. Neither accidentally overwrites the other.

Name mangling is not encryption. The mangled name is discoverable and accessible — `p._Patient__medicare` will work. The mangling is a guardrail against accidental access and collision, not a security mechanism. Python's documentation explicitly states: "Any use of a name, in a class definition, that textually begins with two or more underscore characters and does not end in two or more underscores is textually replaced with _classname__name."

Trailing underscores — a related convention

A single trailing underscore (`class_`, `type_`, `id_`) is used to avoid naming conflicts with Python built-in names. Two trailing underscores on both sides (`__init__`, `__str__`) identify dunder (double-underscore) special methods, which are never mangled. Mangling only applies to names with two or more leading underscores and fewer than two trailing underscores.

Example 1 — Introduction

Demonstrating name mangling: the mangled name is visible via vars() and accessible when you know it.

```
class BankAccount:
    def __init__(self, owner, balance):
        self.owner    = owner
        self.__balance = balance    # stored as _BankAccount__balance

    def show_balance(self):
        print(f"{self.owner}: ${self.__balance:.2f}")


acc = BankAccount("Alice", 1000.00)
acc.show_balance()

# The attribute is NOT stored as __balance
print(vars(acc))

# Direct access using the original name fails
try:
    print(acc.__balance)
except AttributeError as e:
    print(f"Direct access failed: {e}")

# Accessing via the mangled name succeeds (but should not be done)
```

```
print(acc._BankAccount__balance)
```

Output:
```
Alice: $1000.00
{'owner': 'Alice', '_BankAccount__balance': 1000.0}
Direct access failed: 'BankAccount' object has no attribute '__balance'
1000.0
```

Example 2 — Variation

Name mangling prevents a subclass from accidentally overwriting a parent's private attribute.

```
class Shape:
    def __init__(self, colour):
        self.__colour = colour      # _Shape__colour

    def describe(self):
        print(f"Shape colour: {self.__colour}")


class Circle(Shape):
    def __init__(self, colour, radius):
        super().__init__(colour)
        self.__colour = "circle-override"    # _Circle__colour — DIFFERENT
attribute!
        self.radius   = radius

    def describe(self):
        super().describe()    # still prints the Shape colour correctly
        print(f"Circle override colour: {self.__colour}")


c = Circle("red", 5)
c.describe()

# Both attributes exist independently
print(vars(c))
```

Output:
```
Shape colour: red
Circle override colour: circle-override
{'_Shape__colour': 'red', 'radius': 5, '_Circle__colour': 'circle-override'}
```

Example 3 — Real-world application

A secure configuration store where private attributes hold sensitive values and public methods provide the only sanctioned access path.

```
import hashlib

class SecureConfig:
    """Stores sensitive configuration values with controlled access.

    Private attributes prevent direct external read or write.
    All access goes through validated public methods.
    """

    def __init__(self, db_password, api_key):
        self.__db_password  = db_password
        self.__api_key      = api_key
        self.__access_count = 0

    def get_db_password(self, authorisation_code):
        """Return password only if authorisation code is correct."""
        expected = hashlib.sha256(b"admin-2025").hexdigest()[:8]
        if authorisation_code != expected:
            raise PermissionError("Invalid authorisation code.")
        self.__access_count += 1
        return self.__db_password

    def rotate_api_key(self, new_key):
        """Replace the API key; enforces minimum length."""
        if len(new_key) < 32:
            raise ValueError("API key must be at least 32 characters.")
        self.__api_key = new_key
        print("API key updated.")

    def api_key_preview(self):
        """Return only the first 8 characters for display."""
        return self.__api_key[:8] + "..." if self.__api_key else None

    def access_report(self):
        print(f"Password accessed {self.__access_count} time(s).")
```

```
        print(f"API key preview: {self.api_key_preview()}")


cfg = SecureConfig("pg_s3cr3t!", "sk_live_abcdefghijklmnopqrstuvwxyz1234")

auth = hashlib.sha256(b"admin-2025").hexdigest()[:8]
print(cfg.get_db_password(auth))

cfg.rotate_api_key("sk_live_newkeyABCDEFGHIJKLMNOPQRSTUVWX")
cfg.access_report()

try:
    cfg.get_db_password("wrong-code")
except PermissionError as e:
    print(f"Blocked: {e}")
```

Output:

```
pg_s3cr3t!
API key updated.
Password accessed 1 time(s).
API key preview: sk_live_n...
Blocked: Invalid authorisation code.
```

The private attributes `__db_password` and `__api_key` are stored under mangled names. Even if an attacker knows the class structure, they cannot read or modify these values through normal attribute access — every path through the public interface includes validation or authorisation logic.

4.3 Getters and Setters — and Why Properties Supersede Them

In languages like Java, encapsulation is almost always implemented with explicit getter and setter methods: `getName()`, `setName(value)`. This pattern was widespread in early Python code and you will still encounter it in older codebases, legacy frameworks, and code written by developers who learned Java first.

Explicit getters and setters work. They do encapsulate data behind a method boundary. The problem is that they force callers to use method-call syntax rather than attribute-access syntax, cluttering the interface. Every attribute that needs protection becomes two extra methods. The public interface grows, readability suffers, and the class feels awkward compared to idiomatic Python.

Python's `@property` decorator solves this by decoupling the public interface (attribute-style access) from the implementation (a method that runs on access or assignment). The caller writes `obj.name`, the class executes `get_name_logic()` — and neither side needs to change if the other does.

This section shows the evolution: bare attribute → explicit getters/setters → property. Understanding all three makes it straightforward to recognise which pattern is in use when reading unfamiliar code and to refactor getters/setters to properties when needed.

Example 1 — Introduction

Three generations of the same class: bare attribute, then explicit getter/setter methods, then the @property equivalent.

```
# --- Generation 1: bare attribute ---
# Simple, but offers no validation or control
class ProductV1:
    def __init__(self, name, price):
        self.name  = name
        self.price = price   # nothing stops price being set to -999


# --- Generation 2: explicit getter and setter methods ---
# Validates, but forces callers to use get/set syntax
class ProductV2:
    def __init__(self, name, price):
        self.name = name
        self.set_price(price)

    def get_price(self):
        return self._price

    def set_price(self, value):
        if value <= 0:
            raise ValueError("Price must be positive.")
        self._price = round(float(value), 2)


# --- Generation 3: @property ---
# Validates, but callers use attribute syntax unchanged
class ProductV3:
    def __init__(self, name, price):
        self.name  = name
        self.price = price   # routes through @price.setter

    @property
    def price(self):
        return self._price
```

```
    @price.setter
    def price(self, value):
        if value <= 0:
            raise ValueError("Price must be positive.")
        self._price = round(float(value), 2)


# Caller perspective:
v2 = ProductV2("Widget", 9.99)
print(v2.get_price())          # V2: must call get_price()
v2.set_price(12.50)            # V2: must call set_price()

v3 = ProductV3("Widget", 9.99)
print(v3.price)                # V3: plain attribute access
v3.price = 12.50               # V3: plain assignment, setter validates
print(v3.price)
```

Output:

```
9.99
9.99
12.5
```

Example 2 — Variation

Refactoring an existing class from explicit getter/setter methods to properties — without changing any external calling code.

```
# Original class using explicit getter/setter methods
class TemperatureLegacy:
    def __init__(self, celsius):
        self._celsius = None
        self.set_celsius(celsius)

    def get_celsius(self):
        return self._celsius

    def set_celsius(self, value):
        if value < -273.15:
            raise ValueError("Below absolute zero.")
        self._celsius = value
```

```
    def get_fahrenheit(self):
        return self._celsius * 9 / 5 + 32


# Refactored with @property — external code using t.celsius works unchanged
class Temperature:
    def __init__(self, celsius):
        self.celsius = celsius   # uses setter

    @property
    def celsius(self):
        return self._celsius

    @celsius.setter
    def celsius(self, value):
        if value < -273.15:
            raise ValueError("Below absolute zero.")
        self._celsius = value

    @property
    def fahrenheit(self):
        return self._celsius * 9 / 5 + 32


# Legacy usage
tl = TemperatureLegacy(100)
print(tl.get_celsius())
print(tl.get_fahrenheit())

# Property usage — cleaner for the caller
t = Temperature(100)
print(t.celsius)
print(t.fahrenheit)
t.celsius = -10
print(t.celsius)
```

Output:

```
100
212.0
```

```
100
212.0
-10
```

Example 3 — Real-world application

A User profile class that evolved from explicit getters/setters (shown inline as comments) to properties, demonstrating the full lifecycle in a realistic authentication context.

```
import re
from datetime import datetime

class UserProfile:
    """User profile with validated, property-controlled attributes.

    Design notes:
      - username:  immutable after first set (no setter after __init__)
      - email:     validated format on every assignment
      - password:  write-only (getter raises AttributeError intentionally)
      - created:   read-only timestamp set at construction
    """

    def __init__(self, username, email, password):
        self._username  = username          # set directly: immutable
        self.email      = email             # routes through setter
        self._password  = None
        self.password   = password          # routes through setter
        self._created   = datetime.now()

    @property
    def username(self):
        return self._username
    # No setter — username is immutable after construction

    @property
    def email(self):
        return self._email

    @email.setter
    def email(self, value):
        if not re.match(r"^[\w.+-]+@[\w-]+\.[\w.]+$", value):
```

```
            raise ValueError(f"Invalid email address: {value!r}")
        self._email = value.lower()

    @property
    def password(self):
        raise AttributeError("Password is write-only.")

    @password.setter
    def password(self, value):
        if len(value) < 8:
            raise ValueError("Password must be at least 8 characters.")
        import hashlib
        self._password = hashlib.sha256(value.encode()).hexdigest()

    def check_password(self, candidate):
        import hashlib
        return self._password == hashlib.sha256(candidate.encode()).hexdigest()

    @property
    def created(self):
        return self._created.strftime("%d %b %Y %H:%M")

    def __str__(self):
        return f"User: {self.username} <{self.email}> (joined {self.created})"


user = UserProfile("alice_w", "Alice@Example.COM", "securePass1")
print(user)

print(user.check_password("securePass1"))  # True
print(user.check_password("wrongPass"))    # False

user.email = "alice@newdomain.com"
print(user.email)

try:
    user.username = "bob"
except AttributeError as e:
    print(f"Immutable: {e}")
```

```
try:
    print(user.password)
except AttributeError as e:
    print(f"Write-only: {e}")
```

Output:

```
User: alice_w <alice@example.com> (joined 21 Mar 2026 08:15)
True
False
alice@newdomain.com
Immutable: property 'username' of 'UserProfile' object has no setter
Write-only: Password is write-only.
```

A write-only property — a getter that intentionally raises `AttributeError` — is an uncommon but legitimate pattern for sensitive data like passwords, private keys, or tokens that should be stored (hashed) but never readable in plain text. The password can be set and checked, but never retrieved.

4.4 Data Validation as Encapsulation

One of the most direct benefits of encapsulation is the ability to enforce invariants: conditions that must always be true about an object's state. An invariant might be "a bank account balance is never negative", "a student's grade is between 0 and 100", or "a date's month is between 1 and 12".

Without encapsulation, invariants must be enforced at every point in the codebase that modifies the relevant data — which is every line that assigns to the attribute, scattered across files and functions. Miss one, and the invariant breaks silently. With encapsulation, the invariant is enforced in one place: the setter or the constructor. All modifications pass through that single gate.

Well-validated objects are safe to pass around. If `Student(1001, "Alice", 105)` raises a `ValueError` at construction, you never have to worry about a `Student` with an out-of-range grade appearing anywhere else in the system. The class guarantees its own correctness.

What to validate, and how much

Validate everything that has a meaningful constraint: numeric ranges, string formats, type requirements, uniqueness. Do not over-validate: a `name` field probably does not need a regex in a simple system. The question to ask is: "If this value is wrong, where will the program fail?" If the answer is "much later, in a way that is hard to debug", validate it now.

Example 1 — Introduction

An Inventory item with multiple independent invariants enforced across its properties.

```
class InventoryItem:
    VALID_CATEGORIES = {"electronics", "clothing", "food", "tools", "books"}

    def __init__(self, sku, name, category, price, quantity):
```

```
        self.sku      = sku
        self.name     = name
        self.category = category
        self.price    = price
        self.quantity = quantity

    @property
    def sku(self):
        return self._sku

    @sku.setter
    def sku(self, value):
        import re
        if not re.match(r"^[A-Z]{2}[0-9]{4}$", value):
            raise ValueError(f"SKU must be 2 uppercase letters + 4 digits, got
{value!r}.")
        self._sku = value

    @property
    def category(self):
        return self._category

    @category.setter
    def category(self, value):
        if value.lower() not in self.VALID_CATEGORIES:
            raise ValueError(f"Category must be one of
{self.VALID_CATEGORIES}.")
        self._category = value.lower()

    @property
    def price(self):
        return self._price

    @price.setter
    def price(self, value):
        if not isinstance(value, (int, float)) or value <= 0:
            raise ValueError(f"Price must be a positive number.")
        self._price = round(float(value), 2)

    @property
```

```
    def quantity(self):
        return self._quantity

    @quantity.setter
    def quantity(self, value):
        if not isinstance(value, int) or value < 0:
            raise ValueError("Quantity must be a non-negative integer.")
        self._quantity = value

    def __str__(self):
        return (f"[{self.sku}] {self.name} ({self.category}) |
${self.price:.2f} x {self.quantity}")


item = InventoryItem("EL0042", "Wireless Keyboard", "electronics", 89.00, 14)
print(item)

item.quantity = 10      # valid update
item.price    = 79.99   # valid price reduction
print(item)

try:
    InventoryItem("bad-sku", "Widget", "electronics", 10.00, 5)
except ValueError as e:
    print(f"Error: {e}")

try:
    item.price = 0
except ValueError as e:
    print(f"Error: {e}")
```

Output:

```
[EL0042] Wireless Keyboard (electronics) | $89.00 x 14
[EL0042] Wireless Keyboard (electronics) | $79.99 x 10
Error: SKU must be 2 uppercase letters + 4 digits, got 'bad-sku'.
Error: Price must be a positive number.
```

Example 2 — Variation

Cross-field validation: an event booking where start time must always precede end time, enforced in a coordinated setter.

```python
from datetime import datetime, timedelta

class BookingSlot:
    """A time-bounded booking slot. Invariant: start < end always."""

    def __init__(self, room, start: datetime, end: datetime):
        self.room  = room
        self._start = None
        self._end   = None
        self._set_times(start, end)

    def _set_times(self, start, end):
        """Internal setter that validates both times together."""
        if not isinstance(start, datetime) or not isinstance(end, datetime):
            raise TypeError("start and end must be datetime objects.")
        if end <= start:
            raise ValueError("end time must be after start time.")
        duration = end - start
        if duration > timedelta(hours=8):
            raise ValueError("Booking cannot exceed 8 hours.")
        self._start = start
        self._end   = end

    @property
    def start(self):
        return self._start

    @property
    def end(self):
        return self._end

    @property
    def duration_hours(self):
        return (self._end - self._start).seconds / 3600

    def reschedule(self, new_start: datetime, new_end: datetime):
        """Reschedule: validates both new times atomically."""
        self._set_times(new_start, new_end)
```

```
    def __str__(self):
        return (f"Room {self.room}: {self._start:%H:%M} - {self._end:%H:%M}
({self.duration_hours:.1f}h)")


start = datetime(2026, 4, 1, 9, 0)
end   = datetime(2026, 4, 1, 11, 30)
slot  = BookingSlot("B12", start, end)
print(slot)

slot.reschedule(datetime(2026, 4, 1, 14, 0),
                datetime(2026, 4, 1, 15, 30))
print(slot)

try:
    BookingSlot("B12", end, start)   # end before start
except ValueError as e:
    print(f"Error: {e}")
```

Output:

```
Room B12: 09:00 - 11:30 (2.5h)
Room B12: 14:00 - 15:30 (1.5h)
Error: end time must be after start time.
```

> **Note:** Cross-field validation — where the validity of one attribute depends on another — is best handled by a private method like _set_times that validates both atomically, rather than two independent setters. Separate setters create a window where one field has been updated and the other has not, leaving the object temporarily invalid.

Example 3 — Real-world application

A student grade book where every operation maintains the invariant that grades are in range and the stored list is never directly accessible.

```
class GradeBook:
    """Manages a student's grade records with full validation.

    Invariants:
      - Each grade is a float in [0.0, 100.0]
      - The internal list is never exposed directly
      - Subject names are non-empty strings
    """
```

```
    def __init__(self, student_name):
        self.student_name = student_name
        self.__grades     = {}   # subject -> list of grades

    def add_grade(self, subject, grade):
        subject = self._validate_subject(subject)
        grade   = self._validate_grade(grade)
        self.__grades.setdefault(subject, []).append(grade)

    def average(self, subject=None):
        if subject:
            subject = self._validate_subject(subject)
            scores  = self.__grades.get(subject, [])
            if not scores:
                return None
            return sum(scores) / len(scores)
        all_scores = [g for scores in self.__grades.values() for g in scores]
        return sum(all_scores) / len(all_scores) if all_scores else None

    def subjects(self):
        """Return a copy of subject names — not the internal dict."""
        return list(self.__grades.keys())

    def grades_for(self, subject):
        """Return a copy of the grade list — not the internal list."""
        subject = self._validate_subject(subject)
        return list(self.__grades.get(subject, []))

    def report(self):
        print(f"Grade Book: {self.student_name}")
        for subject, scores in self.__grades.items():
            avg = sum(scores) / len(scores)
            print(f"  {subject:20s} {scores}  avg={avg:.1f}")
        overall = self.average()
        if overall:
            print(f"  Overall average: {overall:.1f}")

    @staticmethod
    def _validate_subject(subject):
        if not isinstance(subject, str) or not subject.strip():
```

```
            raise ValueError("Subject must be a non-empty string.")
        return subject.strip().title()

    @staticmethod
    def _validate_grade(grade):
        if not isinstance(grade, (int, float)) or not (0.0 <= grade <= 100.0):
            raise ValueError(f"Grade must be between 0 and 100, got
{grade!r}.")
        return round(float(grade), 1)


gb = GradeBook("Alice Wong")
gb.add_grade("Mathematics", 88)
gb.add_grade("Mathematics", 92)
gb.add_grade("english",     75)  # normalised to "English"
gb.add_grade("science",     83)
gb.report()

print("\nMaths grades:", gb.grades_for("Mathematics"))

try:
    gb.add_grade("History", 105)
except ValueError as e:
    print(f"\nError: {e}")
```

Output:

```
Grade Book: Alice Wong
  Mathematics          [88.0, 92.0]  avg=90.0
  English              [75.0]  avg=75.0
  Science              [83.0]  avg=83.0
  Overall average: 84.5

Maths grades: [88.0, 92.0]

Error: Grade must be between 0 and 100, got 105.
```

4.5 Encapsulating Collections

When a class holds a collection internally — a list of items, a dict of records, a set of IDs — exposing that collection directly gives callers unrestricted access to an object's core state. They can append, delete, clear, or reorder elements without going through any validation logic, bypassing every invariant the class is trying to maintain.

The solution is to never expose the internal collection directly. Instead, provide controlled methods that add, remove, and query elements. When a caller needs to read the contents, return a copy or a view, not the original.

This is one of the most commonly overlooked forms of encapsulation. It is easy to write `self.items = []` as a public attribute and then provide methods around it, but a caller who receives a reference to the list has the same power over it as the class itself. Returning `list(self._items)` from a getter hands the caller a snapshot they can do what they like with — without affecting the internal state.

Example 1 — Introduction

The exposure problem: a class that returns its internal list directly, and why this is dangerous.

```
# --- Dangerous: internal list exposed directly ---
class ShoppingCartBad:
    def __init__(self):
        self.items = []     # public list: caller has full control

    def total(self):
        return sum(price for _, price in self.items)


cart = ShoppingCartBad()
cart.items.append(("Laptop", 999.00))
cart.items.append(("Mouse",   29.00))
print(f"Total: ${cart.total():.2f}")

# Caller can bypass the class entirely
cart.items.clear()          # all items wiped, no notification
cart.items.append(("Laptop", -999.00))  # negative price, no validation
print(f"Total: ${cart.total():.2f}")


# --- Safe: internal list encapsulated ---
class ShoppingCartGood:
    def __init__(self):
        self.__items = []

    def add(self, name, price):
        if price <= 0:
            raise ValueError("Price must be positive.")
        self.__items.append((name, round(float(price), 2)))
```

```
    def remove(self, name):
        self.__items = [(n, p) for n, p in self.__items if n != name]

    def items(self):
        return list(self.__items)  # copy, not the original

    def total(self):
        return sum(p for _, p in self.__items)

    def __len__(self):
        return len(self.__items)


cart2 = ShoppingCartGood()
cart2.add("Laptop", 999.00)
cart2.add("Mouse",   29.00)
print(f"Items: {cart2.items()}")
print(f"Total: ${cart2.total():.2f}")

try:
    cart2.add("Cable", -5.00)
except ValueError as e:
    print(f"Blocked: {e}")
```

Output:

```
Total: $1028.00
Total: $-999.00
[('Laptop', 999.0), ('Mouse', 29.0)]
Total: $1028.00
Blocked: Price must be positive.
```

Example 2 — Variation

A team roster that maintains a set internally, exposing only membership queries and controlled add/remove operations.

```
class TeamRoster:
    def __init__(self, team_name, max_size):
        self.team_name = team_name
        self.max_size  = max_size
```

```
        self.__members = set()

    def add_member(self, name):
        name = name.strip().title()
        if not name:
            raise ValueError("Member name cannot be empty.")
        if len(self.__members) >= self.max_size:
            raise RuntimeError(f"{self.team_name} is at capacity
({self.max_size}).")
        if name in self.__members:
            print(f"{name} is already on the roster.")
            return
        self.__members.add(name)
        print(f"Added: {name}")

    def remove_member(self, name):
        name = name.strip().title()
        if name not in self.__members:
            print(f"{name} is not on the roster.")
            return
        self.__members.discard(name)
        print(f"Removed: {name}")

    def is_member(self, name):
        return name.strip().title() in self.__members

    def members(self):
        """Return a sorted copy — not the internal set."""
        return sorted(self.__members)

    def size(self):
        return len(self.__members)

    def __str__(self):
        return f"{self.team_name} ({self.size()}/{self.max_size}):
{self.members()}"


roster = TeamRoster("Pythons", max_size=4)
roster.add_member("Alice Wong")
```

```
roster.add_member("bob smith")   # normalised to Bob Smith
roster.add_member("Alice Wong")  # duplicate
roster.add_member("Cara Lee")
print(roster)

print(f"Is Alice a member? {roster.is_member('Alice Wong')}")
roster.remove_member("Bob Smith")
print(roster)
```

Output:

```
Added: Alice Wong
Added: Bob Smith
Alice Wong is already on the roster.
Added: Cara Lee
Pythons (3/4): ['Alice Wong', 'Bob Smith', 'Cara Lee']
Is Alice a member? True
Removed: Bob Smith
Pythons (2/4): ['Alice Wong', 'Cara Lee']
```

Example 3 — Real-world application

A student course management system encapsulating a dict of enrolled courses, with all mutations going through validated methods.

```
class CourseEnrolment:
    """Manages a student's course enrolments.

    The internal dict maps course_code -> course_name.
    It is never directly exposed; all reads return copies.
    """

    MAX_COURSES = 6

    def __init__(self, student_id, student_name):
        self.student_id   = student_id
        self.student_name = student_name
        self.__courses    = {}

    def enrol(self, code, name):
        code = code.strip().upper()
        if not code:
            raise ValueError("Course code cannot be empty.")
```

```
        if len(self.__courses) >= self.MAX_COURSES:
            raise RuntimeError(f"Cannot enrol in more than {self.MAX_COURSES}
courses.")
        if code in self.__courses:
            print(f"Already enrolled in {code}.")
            return
        self.__courses[code] = name.strip()
        print(f"Enrolled in {code}: {name.strip()}")

    def withdraw(self, code):
        code = code.strip().upper()
        if code not in self.__courses:
            print(f"Not enrolled in {code}.")
            return
        removed = self.__courses.pop(code)
        print(f"Withdrawn from {code}: {removed}")

    def is_enrolled(self, code):
        return code.strip().upper() in self.__courses

    def courses(self):
        """Return a copy of the enrolment dict."""
        return dict(self.__courses)

    def credit_points(self, points_per_course=6):
        return len(self.__courses) * points_per_course

    def transcript(self):
        print(f"\nStudent: {self.student_name} ({self.student_id})")
        print(f"Enrolled courses ({len(self.__courses)}):")
        for code, name in self.__courses.items():
            print(f"  {code:8s}  {name}")
        print(f"Credit points: {self.credit_points()}")


enrolment = CourseEnrolment("S100001", "Alice Wong")
enrolment.enrol("IFB104", "Building IT Systems")
enrolment.enrol("IFB105", "Introduction to Programming")
enrolment.enrol("IFB103", "IT Systems Design")
enrolment.transcript()
```

```python
enrolment.withdraw("IFB105")
enrolment.enrol("IFB201", "Software Engineering")
enrolment.transcript()

# The returned dict is a copy: modifying it does not affect enrolment
snapshot = enrolment.courses()
snapshot["FAKE001"] = "Fake Course"
print(f"\nInternal course count: {len(enrolment.courses())} (snapshot was modified)")
```

Output:

```
Enrolled in IFB104: Building IT Systems
Enrolled in IFB105: Introduction to Programming
Enrolled in IFB103: IT Systems Design

Student: Alice Wong (S100001)
Enrolled courses (3):
  IFB104    Building IT Systems
  IFB105    Introduction to Programming
  IFB103    IT Systems Design
Credit points: 18
Withdrawn from IFB105: Introduction to Programming
Enrolled in IFB201: Software Engineering

Student: Alice Wong (S100001)
Enrolled courses (3):
  IFB104    Building IT Systems
  IFB103    IT Systems Design
  IFB201    Software Engineering
Credit points: 18

Internal course count: 3 (snapshot was modified)
```

The final lines demonstrate the key protection: `snapshot["FAKE001"] = "Fake Course"` modifies the caller's copy, not the internal dict. The course count inside `CourseEnrolment` remains 3. This would not be true if `courses()` returned `self.__courses` directly.

4.6 Encapsulation in Practice — The Interface Mindset

Encapsulation is not just a set of naming rules. It is a way of thinking about what a class exposes and what it hides. The key question is: "What is this class's contract with the outside world?" Everything that answers that question is part of the public interface. Everything else is an implementation detail.

An implementation detail is something that could change without affecting any external code. The data structure used to store items, the exact algorithm used to compute a result, the names of private helpers — all of these should be free to change. If external code depends on them, refactoring becomes risky.

The interface mindset means designing from the outside in: before writing any implementation, ask "What should callers be able to do with this object? What should they never be able to do?" The answers define the public interface. The implementation is everything inside that interface that makes it work.

Designing the interface first

A useful habit before writing a class: list its public methods and properties as comments. No implementation yet — just the names and what they do. This forces you to think about the caller's perspective before getting absorbed in the internal mechanics.

Example 1 — Introduction

Interface-first design: writing the public API as comments before implementing any of it.

```
# Design session for a Playlist class:
#
# Public interface:
#   add_track(title, artist, duration_seconds)
#   remove_track(title)
#   play_next()  -> returns the next track dict or None
#   shuffle()    -> randomises playback order
#   total_duration -> property: total seconds
#   track_count  -> property: number of tracks
#   tracks()     -> returns a copy of current track list
#
# Internal (not part of public contract):
#   __tracks        (the actual list)
#   __current_index
#   _format_duration(seconds)  (formatting helper)

import random


class Playlist:
    def __init__(self, name):
        self.name            = name
```

```
        self.__tracks      = []
        self.__current_idx = 0

    def add_track(self, title, artist, duration_seconds):
        if duration_seconds <= 0:
            raise ValueError("Duration must be positive.")
        self.__tracks.append({
            "title":    title.strip(),
            "artist":   artist.strip(),
            "duration": int(duration_seconds),
        })

    def remove_track(self, title):
        title = title.strip()
        self.__tracks = [t for t in self.__tracks if t["title"] != title]

    def play_next(self):
        if not self.__tracks:
            return None
        track = self.__tracks[self.__current_idx % len(self.__tracks)]
        self.__current_idx += 1
        return dict(track)

    def shuffle(self):
        random.shuffle(self.__tracks)
        self.__current_idx = 0

    @property
    def total_duration(self):
        return sum(t["duration"] for t in self.__tracks)

    @property
    def track_count(self):
        return len(self.__tracks)

    def tracks(self):
        return [dict(t) for t in self.__tracks]

    def _format_duration(self, seconds):
```

```
        return f"{seconds // 60}:{seconds % 60:02d}"

    def __str__(self):
        dur = self._format_duration(self.total_duration)
        return f"Playlist: {self.name} ({self.track_count} tracks, {dur})"


pl = Playlist("Morning Run")
pl.add_track("Run the World",    "Beyoncé", 235)
pl.add_track("Can't Stop Me",  "David Guetta", 198)
pl.add_track("Eye of the Tiger","Survivor", 245)
print(pl)

next_track = pl.play_next()
print(f"Now playing: {next_track['title']} by {next_track['artist']}")
```

Output:

```
Playlist: Morning Run (3 tracks, 11:18)
Now playing: Run the World by Beyoncé
```

Example 2 — Variation

A library book loan system designed with a clear interface: callers can borrow, return, and query, but never touch the internal loan record directly.

```
from datetime import datetime, timedelta

class Book:
    def __init__(self, isbn, title, author):
        self.isbn   = isbn
        self.title  = title
        self.author = author

    def __str__(self):
        return f'"{self.title}" by {self.author}'


class LoanRecord:
    LOAN_DAYS = 14

    def __init__(self, book, borrower):
```

```
        self.__book     = book
        self.__borrower = borrower
        self.__due      = datetime.now() + timedelta(days=self.LOAN_DAYS)
        self.__returned = False

    def mark_returned(self):
        self.__returned = True

    @property
    def is_active(self):
        return not self.__returned

    @property
    def is_overdue(self):
        return self.is_active and datetime.now() > self.__due

    @property
    def book_title(self):
        return self.__book.title

    @property
    def borrower(self):
        return self.__borrower

    def days_until_due(self):
        if self.__returned:
            return None
        delta = self.__due - datetime.now()
        return max(0, delta.days)

    def __str__(self):
        status = "returned" if self.__returned else \
                 ("OVERDUE" if self.is_overdue else f"{self.days_until_due()}d
remaining")
        return f"{self.__borrower}: {self.__book} [{status}]"


class Library:
    def __init__(self, name):
```

```
        self.name    = name
        self.__books = {}
        self.__loans = []

    def add_book(self, book):
        self.__books[book.isbn] = book

    def lend(self, isbn, borrower):
        book = self.__books.get(isbn)
        if not book:
            raise ValueError(f"Book {isbn!r} not found.")
        active = [l for l in self.__loans if l.book_title == book.title and
l.is_active]
        if active:
            print(f"{book.title} is currently on loan.")
            return None
        record = LoanRecord(book, borrower)
        self.__loans.append(record)
        print(f"Loaned: {record}")
        return record

    def accept_return(self, isbn, borrower):
        book   = self.__books.get(isbn)
        if not book:
            return
        record = next((l for l in self.__loans
                       if l.book_title == book.title
                       and l.borrower == borrower
                       and l.is_active), None)
        if record:
            record.mark_returned()
            print(f"Returned: {book.title} from {borrower}.")

    def active_loans(self):
        return [str(l) for l in self.__loans if l.is_active]


lib = Library("Southside Library")
lib.add_book(Book("978-0001", "Dune",        "Frank Herbert"))
lib.add_book(Book("978-0002", "Neuromancer","William Gibson"))
```

```
lib.lend("978-0001", "Alice")
lib.lend("978-0001", "Bob")    # already on loan
lib.lend("978-0002", "Carol")

print("\nActive loans:")
for loan in lib.active_loans():
    print(" ", loan)

lib.accept_return("978-0001", "Alice")
lib.lend("978-0001", "Bob")    # now available
```

Output:

```
Loaned: Alice: "Dune" by Frank Herbert [14d remaining]
Dune is currently on loan.
Loaned: Carol: "Neuromancer" by William Gibson [14d remaining]

Active loans:
  Alice: "Dune" by Frank Herbert [14d remaining]
  Carol: "Neuromancer" by William Gibson [14d remaining]
Returned: Dune from Alice.
Loaned: Bob: "Dune" by Frank Herbert [14d remaining]
```

Example 3 — Real-world application

A game engine component system: each Entity has a component registry whose internals are hidden, exposing only add, get, has, and remove operations.

```
class Component:
    """Base class for all entity components."""
    pass


class HealthComponent(Component):
    def __init__(self, max_hp):
        self.max_hp     = max_hp
        self.current_hp = max_hp

    def take_damage(self, amount):
        self.current_hp = max(0, self.current_hp - amount)
```

```
    def is_alive(self):
        return self.current_hp > 0

    def __str__(self):
        return f"HP {self.current_hp}/{self.max_hp}"


class PositionComponent(Component):
    def __init__(self, x=0, y=0):
        self.x = x
        self.y = y

    def move(self, dx, dy):
        self.x += dx
        self.y += dy

    def __str__(self):
        return f"Pos ({self.x}, {self.y})"


class Entity:
    """Game entity. Components stored in a private registry.

    Public interface: add_component, get_component,
                      has_component, remove_component
    """

    def __init__(self, name):
        self.name             = name
        self.__components     = {}

    def add_component(self, component):
        key = type(component).__name__
        if key in self.__components:
            raise ValueError(f"Entity already has a {key}.")
        self.__components[key] = component

    def get_component(self, component_type):
        key = component_type.__name__
```

```
        if key not in self.__components:
            raise KeyError(f"Entity has no {key}.")
        return self.__components[key]

    def has_component(self, component_type):
        return component_type.__name__ in self.__components

    def remove_component(self, component_type):
        self.__components.pop(component_type.__name__, None)

    def __str__(self):
        parts = [self.name] + [str(c) for c in self.__components.values()]
        return " | ".join(parts)


hero = Entity("Hero")
hero.add_component(HealthComponent(100))
hero.add_component(PositionComponent(5, 10))
print(hero)

health = hero.get_component(HealthComponent)
health.take_damage(35)

pos = hero.get_component(PositionComponent)
pos.move(3, -2)

print(hero)
print(f"Alive: {health.is_alive()}")

try:
    hero.add_component(HealthComponent(50))  # duplicate
except ValueError as e:
    print(f"Error: {e}")
```

Output:

```
Hero | HP 100/100 | Pos (5, 10)
Hero | HP 65/100 | Pos (8, 8)
Alive: True
Error: Entity already has a HealthComponent.
```

4.7 When to Encapsulate and When Not To

Encapsulation is a tool, not a rule applied uniformly to every attribute. Over-encapsulation produces bloated classes with trivial getters and setters for every field, adding complexity without providing any real protection or value. Under-encapsulation leaves state unguarded and invariants unenforced.

The decision of what to encapsulate comes down to a few practical questions. Answering them honestly produces the right level of protection for each situation.

Questions to ask before encapsulating

- Does this attribute have invariants or constraints? If assigning any value to it could leave the object in an invalid state, protect it with a setter and validator.
- Could this implementation detail change? If the internal representation might change (e.g. swapping a list for a dict, changing a storage format), hide it behind a method so callers are insulated from the change.
- Is this data sensitive? Passwords, keys, PINs, and personal health information should be private and never directly readable.
- Is this a simple data container with no behaviour? A class that simply groups related data (like a named tuple equivalent) may not need any encapsulation at all. Python's dataclasses are designed for exactly this case.
- Will subclasses need access? Use protected (single underscore) rather than private (double underscore) for members that subclasses legitimately need to override or extend.

Example 1 — Introduction

A simple data container (dataclass) where encapsulation would add complexity without value.

```
from dataclasses import dataclass


# When a class is purely a data holder with no behaviour,
# a dataclass with public attributes is the correct choice.
# No getters, no setters, no properties needed.


@dataclass
class Coordinate:
    latitude:  float
    longitude: float
    label:     str = ""



@dataclass
class ColourRGB:
    red:   int
    green: int
```

```
    blue: int

    def to_hex(self):
        return f"#{self.red:02X}{self.green:02X}{self.blue:02X}"


pos = Coordinate(-27.4698, 153.0251, "Brisbane CBD")
print(pos)
print(f"lat={pos.latitude}, lon={pos.longitude}")

red = ColourRGB(255, 0, 0)
print(red)
print(red.to_hex())
```

Output:

```
Coordinate(latitude=-27.4698, longitude=153.0251, label='Brisbane CBD')
lat=-27.4698, lon=153.0251
ColourRGB(red=255, green=0, blue=0)
#FF0000
```

Example 2 — Variation

Calibrating protection: the same class at three levels of encapsulation, illustrating when each is appropriate.

```
# Level 0: no encapsulation
# Appropriate when: simple script, no constraints, throwaway code
class PointMinimal:
    def __init__(self, x, y):
        self.x = x
        self.y = y


# Level 1: protected with convention
# Appropriate when: subclasses need access, library code, soft guideline
class PointProtected:
    def __init__(self, x, y):
        self._x = float(x)
        self._y = float(y)

    @property
```

```
    def x(self): return self._x

    @property
    def y(self): return self._y

    def distance_to(self, other):
        return ((self._x - other._x)**2 + (self._y - other._y)**2) ** 0.5


# Level 2: fully private
# Appropriate when: immutable value object, no subclassing intended,
#                   internal coordinate system may change
class PointPrivate:
    def __init__(self, x, y):
        self.__x = float(x)
        self.__y = float(y)

    @property
    def x(self): return self.__x

    @property
    def y(self): return self.__y

    def distance_to(self, other):
        return ((self.__x - other.x)**2 + (self.__y - other.y)**2) ** 0.5


p1 = PointPrivate(0, 0)
p2 = PointPrivate(3, 4)
print(f"Distance: {p1.distance_to(p2):.2f}")

# Read-only: cannot modify via property
try:
    p1.x = 99
except AttributeError as e:
    print(f"Immutable: {e}")
```

Output:

```
Distance: 5.00
```

```
Immutable: property 'x' of 'PointPrivate' object has no setter
```

Example 3 — Real-world application

A mixed-visibility class: some attributes fully public, some protected for subclass use, some private. Each choice is justified.

```
class Employee:
    """
    Visibility decisions:
      name, role      : public — safe to read/write freely
      _department     : protected — HR subclasses may need direct access
      __salary        : private — sensitive; only payroll methods touch this
      __access_log    : private — internal audit trail; no external access
    """

    def __init__(self, employee_id, name, role, department, salary):
        self.employee_id  = employee_id
        self.name         = name
        self.role         = role
        self._department  = department
        self.__salary     = salary
        self.__access_log = []

    @property
    def salary(self):
        self.__access_log.append("salary read")
        return self.__salary

    @salary.setter
    def salary(self, value):
        if value < 0:
            raise ValueError("Salary cannot be negative.")
        self.__access_log.append(f"salary updated: {self.__salary} -> {value}")
        self.__salary = value

    def give_raise(self, percent):
        increase = self.__salary * (percent / 100)
        self.__salary += increase
        self.__access_log.append(f"raise applied: {percent}%")
        print(f"{self.name} received a {percent}% raise.")
```

```
    def audit_log(self):
        return list(self.__access_log)

    def __str__(self):
        return f"{self.employee_id}: {self.name} | {self.role} |
{self._department}"


emp = Employee("E001", "Alice Wong", "Engineer", "Technology", 95000)
print(emp)

emp.give_raise(8)
print(f"New salary: ${emp.salary:,.2f}")

emp.name = "Alicia Wong"      # public: fine
emp._department = "R&D"       # protected: allowed but flagged by linters

try:
    emp.__salary = 1          # private: does not affect the real attribute
except:
    pass

# Mangling means this created a NEW attribute, not the private one
print(f"Real salary: ${emp.salary:,.2f}")
print("Audit:", emp.audit_log())
```

Output:

```
E001: Alice Wong | Engineer | Technology
Alice Wong received an 8% raise.
New salary: $102,600.00
Real salary: $102,600.00
Audit: ['raise applied: 8%', 'salary read', 'salary read']
```

The final block demonstrates a subtle point: `emp.__salary = 1` outside the class does not overwrite the private attribute. Due to name mangling, it creates a new attribute named `__salary` on the instance (not mangled, because we are outside the class definition), while the real `_Employee__salary` is untouched. This reinforces that private attributes are genuinely protected by mangling, not just convention.

Chapter 4 Summary

- Python signals attribute visibility through naming conventions: plain names are public (part of the contract), a single leading underscore is protected (internal / subclass use), and a double leading underscore is private (strictly this class only, name-mangled by the interpreter).
- Name mangling renames __attr to _ClassName__attr at the class body level. This prevents accidental collision between parent and subclass attributes with the same name, and makes private attributes inaccessible under their original name from outside the class. The mangled name is discoverable via vars() and accessible if you know it — mangling is a guardrail, not a security mechanism.
- Explicit getter and setter methods (get_x, set_x) work but clutter the interface. The @property decorator provides the same protection with attribute-style syntax for callers. Prefer properties in new code; recognise getter/setter patterns when reading older Python.
- A write-only property (getter that raises AttributeError) is a legitimate pattern for sensitive data such as passwords or API keys that must be stored but should never be read back in plain form.
- Encapsulation enforces invariants: conditions that must always be true about an object's state. Validation in setters and constructors ensures an object is always in a valid state after any operation. Cross-field validation (where two attributes constrain each other) should use a private helper method that validates both atomically.
- Collections held as instance attributes should never be exposed directly. Return copies (list(), dict()) from accessor methods so callers cannot bypass validation by modifying the internal structure. Provide controlled add, remove, and query methods instead.
- The interface mindset: design from the outside in. Decide what callers should be able to do, what they should never be able to do, and what is an implementation detail free to change. List the public interface as a comment before writing any implementation.
- Not everything needs encapsulation. Simple data containers (use dataclasses), throwaway scripts, and attributes with no meaningful constraints are better left as plain public attributes. The cost of unnecessary encapsulation is verbosity and complexity without benefit.

Guided Exercises

Complete the following exercises. Each targets a specific concept from this chapter.

1. Create a class called SafeCounter with a private __count attribute. Provide a property count that is read-only (no setter). Add methods increment(amount=1), decrement(amount=1), and reset(). decrement() must not allow the count to fall below zero. Add a property is_zero that returns True when the count is zero. Test all methods and the read-only property.

> ***Hint:*** *Store the value in __count. In the count property, omit the setter so it is read-only. In decrement(), use max(0, self.__count - amount) to prevent negative values.*

2. Write a class called SecurePin that stores a 4-digit PIN as a private hashed value. The pin property should be write-only (the getter raises AttributeError). Add a method check(candidate) that returns True if the candidate matches the stored PIN. Add a change_pin(old_pin, new_pin) method that only succeeds if old_pin is correct and new_pin is exactly 4 digits. Use hashlib.sha256 for hashing.

> ***Hint:*** *Store the hash in __pin_hash. The check() method hashes the candidate and compares. For the write-only pattern, define the getter as: raise AttributeError("PIN is write-only.").*

3. Build a Basket class that encapsulates a private list of (item_name, price) tuples. Provide methods: add(name, price), remove(name), total(), items() returning a copy of the list, and item_count(). Validate that price is positive in add(). Demonstrate that modifying the list returned by items() does not affect the basket.

> ***Hint:*** *Store as self.__items = []. The items() method should return list(self.__items). After calling items(), append something to the returned list and verify basket.item_count() is unchanged.*

4. Design a Rectangle class with a clear interface: width and height are validated properties (must be positive), area and perimeter are read-only computed properties. Add a scale(factor) method that multiplies both dimensions by factor, validating that factor is positive. Add a @classmethod square(cls, side) that creates a square Rectangle. Test all paths including invalid inputs.

> ***Hint:*** *Assign self.width = width and self.height = height in __init__ to route through setters. The scale() method should assign to self.width and self.height using the setters, not directly to _width and _height.*

5. Create a StudentRegistry class that holds student records in a private dict keyed by student ID. Provide methods: register(id, name, grade), update_grade(id, new_grade), deregister(id), find(id), and all_students() returning a copy of the dict. Grade must be 0–100. Demonstrate that modifying the dict returned by all_students() does not affect the registry.

> ***Hint:*** *Store as self.__registry = {}. register() should validate that the ID is not already in use. all_students() should return dict(self.__registry). The copy prevents external code from modifying the internal state.*

Challenge Tasks

Open-ended tasks. No hints provided. Design your solution before writing any code.

1. Design and implement a BankAccount class with the following requirements: balance is a private attribute exposed through a read-only property; deposit(amount) and withdraw(amount) are the only way to change the balance; withdraw() raises an InsufficientFundsError (a custom exception you define) if the amount exceeds the balance; every successful transaction is recorded in a private transaction history list; a statement() method prints all transactions and the current balance; an interest(rate) method applies interest to the balance and records it as a transaction. Write a complete test scenario with at least six transactions including one failed withdrawal.

2. Build an EnhancedGradeBook class that extends the GradeBook from Section 4.4. Add: a highest_grade(subject) method and a lowest_grade(subject) method; a grades_above(threshold) method that returns a dict of subject -> [grades] where at least one grade exceeds the threshold; a to_dict() method that serialises the grade book to a plain dict (without exposing the internal structure); and a @classmethod from_dict(cls, data) that reconstructs a GradeBook from that dict. Ensure that the internal list is never exposed in any of these methods.

3. Design a GameInventory system for a role-playing game. Each Item has a name, type (weapon/armour/consumable), weight, and value. The inventory has a weight capacity and a maximum item count. Items can be added, removed, and queried by type. The inventory exposes: add_item(item), remove_item(name), items_by_type(type), total_weight (computed property), total_value (computed property), and is_full (computed property). All internal storage must be private. Attempting to add an item when the inventory is full or would exceed the weight limit should raise a descriptive exception. Write a test that fills an inventory to capacity, queries by type, removes items, and attempts an invalid addition.

CHAPTER 5 **Inheritance**

Book 01: Object-Oriented Programming in Python

> *Inheritance allows one class to acquire the attributes and methods of another, enabling code reuse and the expression of real-world hierarchies in your program structure. This chapter covers every aspect of Python inheritance: defining subclasses, overriding methods, using super() to extend rather than replace parent behaviour, understanding the Method Resolution Order that governs multiple inheritance, and working with mixin classes. The chapter closes with the most important design question in OOP — when inheritance is the right tool and when composition serves better. Inheritance used well makes programs more expressive and easier to extend; used carelessly, it creates rigid, fragile hierarchies that resist every change.*

5.1 The Inheritance Relationship — is-a vs has-a

Inheritance models an is-a relationship. A `Dog` is an `Animal`. A `SavingsAccount` is a `BankAccount`. A `Manager` is an `Employee`. When this relationship holds genuinely, inheritance is the correct structure: the subclass shares the parent's interface, can be used wherever the parent is expected, and adds or specialises behaviour on top.

The alternative is composition, which models a has-a relationship. A `Car` has an `Engine`. A `Library` has a collection of `Books`. A `Player` has a `Score`. The Car does not inherit from Engine — it contains one. When the relationship is one of containing or using rather than being, composition is the right tool.

Choosing correctly matters because the consequences are different. Inheritance creates a tight coupling: changes to the parent ripple to all children. Composition is looser: a Car can swap its Engine for a different one without changing the Car's interface. Getting the choice wrong produces the most common OOP design problems — deep hierarchies that are brittle, classes forced to inherit behaviour they do not need, and code that is rigid where it should be flexible.

The Liskov Substitution Principle

A reliable test for whether inheritance is appropriate: a subclass instance must be substitutable for a parent class instance wherever the parent is expected, without breaking the program. If a `Square` inheriting from `Rectangle` causes a width-setting method to behave unexpectedly (because a square must keep both dimensions equal), the is-a relationship does not hold in a meaningful way, and inheritance is the wrong model.

Example 1 — Introduction

A genuine is-a hierarchy: Animal → Dog and Cat. Each subclass is a valid Animal everywhere an Animal is expected.

```
class Animal:
    def __init__(self, name, species):
        self.name    = name
        self.species = species
```

```
    def eat(self, food):
        print(f"{self.name} eats {food}.")

    def describe(self):
        print(f"{self.name} is a {self.species}.")


class Dog(Animal):
    def __init__(self, name, breed):
        super().__init__(name, "Canis lupus familiaris")
        self.breed = breed

    def fetch(self, item):
        print(f"{self.name} fetches the {item}!")


class Cat(Animal):
    def __init__(self, name, indoor=True):
        super().__init__(name, "Felis catus")
        self.indoor = indoor

    def purr(self):
        print(f"{self.name} purrs contentedly.")


dog = Dog("Rex", "Labrador")
cat = Cat("Whiskers")

# Both work as Animals — is-a holds
animals = [dog, cat]
for a in animals:
    a.describe()        # Animal method works on both
    a.eat("kibble")     # Animal method works on both

# Subclass-specific behaviour
dog.fetch("ball")
cat.purr()
```

Output:
```
Rex is a Canis lupus familiaris.
Rex eats kibble.
Whiskers is a Felis catus.
Whiskers eats kibble.
Rex fetches the ball!
Whiskers purrs contentedly.
```

Example 2 — Variation

A has-a relationship correctly modelled with composition: a Car has an Engine, not is an Engine.

```
class Engine:
    def __init__(self, cylinders, displacement_cc):
        self.cylinders       = cylinders
        self.displacement_cc = displacement_cc
        self._running        = False

    def start(self):
        self._running = True
        print(f"Engine ({self.cylinders}-cyl, {self.displacement_cc}cc)
started.")

    def stop(self):
        self._running = False
        print("Engine stopped.")

    def is_running(self):
        return self._running


class Car:
    """Car HAS-A Engine — composition, not inheritance."""

    def __init__(self, make, model, engine):
        self.make   = make
        self.model  = model
        self.engine = engine     # composition: Car contains an Engine
        self._speed = 0

    def start(self):
```

```python
        self.engine.start()      # delegates to the Engine
        print(f"{self.make} {self.model} is ready.")

    def accelerate(self, kmh):
        if not self.engine.is_running():
            print("Start the engine first.")
            return
        self._speed += kmh
        print(f"Speed: {self._speed} km/h")


v8     = Engine(8, 5000)
hybrid = Engine(4, 1800)

sports = Car("Ferrari", "Roma",   v8)
family = Car("Toyota",  "Camry",  hybrid)

sports.start()
sports.accelerate(60)
sports.accelerate(40)
```

Output:

```
Engine (8-cyl, 5000cc) started.
Ferrari Roma is ready.
Speed: 60 km/h
Speed: 100 km/h
```

Example 3 — Real-world application

A staff management system: Employee is a genuine base class. Manager is-an Employee. Department has-a list of Employees.

```python
class Employee:
    def __init__(self, emp_id, name, salary):
        self.emp_id = emp_id
        self.name   = name
        self.salary = salary

    def annual_cost(self):
        return self.salary * 12
```

```
    def __str__(self):
        return f"[{self.emp_id}] {self.name}  ${self.salary:,.2f}/mo"


class Manager(Employee):
    """Manager IS-AN Employee with an additional bonus."""

    def __init__(self, emp_id, name, salary, bonus_pct):
        super().__init__(emp_id, name, salary)
        self.bonus_pct = bonus_pct

    def annual_cost(self):
        base  = super().annual_cost()
        bonus = base * (self.bonus_pct / 100)
        return base + bonus

    def __str__(self):
        return super().__str__() + f"  (Mgr, {self.bonus_pct}% bonus)"


class Department:
    """Department HAS-A list of Employees — composition."""

    def __init__(self, name):
        self.name      = name
        self._staff    = []

    def hire(self, employee):
        self._staff.append(employee)

    def headcount(self):
        return len(self._staff)

    def total_annual_cost(self):
        return sum(e.annual_cost() for e in self._staff)

    def roster(self):
        print(f"\n=== {self.name} Department ===")
```

```
        for emp in self._staff:
            print(f"  {emp}")
        print(f"  Annual cost: ${self.total_annual_cost():,.2f}")


dept = Department("Engineering")
dept.hire(Employee("E001", "Alice Wong",  8500))
dept.hire(Employee("E002", "Bob Smith",   7800))
dept.hire(Manager ("E003", "Cara Lee",   12000, 20))
dept.roster()
```

Output:

```
=== Engineering Department ===
  [E001] Alice Wong  $8,500.00/mo
  [E002] Bob Smith  $7,800.00/mo
  [E003] Cara Lee  $12,000.00/mo  (Mgr, 20% bonus)
  Annual cost: $374,400.00
```

5.2 Defining a Subclass

A subclass is defined by placing the parent class name in parentheses after the subclass name: `class Dog(Animal):`. The subclass inherits every attribute and method from the parent. It can use them as-is, override them with a specialised version, or add new ones that only it provides.

A subclass does not automatically call the parent's `__init__`. If the subclass defines its own constructor, it must explicitly call `super().__init__(...)` with any arguments the parent requires. Failing to do so leaves the parent's attributes uninitialised, which causes `AttributeError` errors later when parent methods try to access them.

`super()` returns a proxy object that delegates method calls to the parent class in the MRO (Method Resolution Order). In most single-inheritance situations, `super()` simply means the immediate parent. Its full significance in multiple inheritance is covered in Section 5.5.

Inherited, overridden, and new members

- Inherited: method exists in parent, not redefined in subclass — the parent's version is used.
- Overridden: method is redefined in the subclass with the same name — the subclass version is used.
- New: method exists only in the subclass — not accessible via a parent class reference.

Example 1 — Introduction

A Shape hierarchy: the base class defines interface; subclasses add their own geometry.

```
import math
```

```
class Shape:
    def __init__(self, colour="black"):
        self.colour = colour

    def area(self):
        raise NotImplementedError("Subclasses must implement area().")

    def perimeter(self):
        raise NotImplementedError("Subclasses must implement perimeter().")

    def describe(self):
        print(f"{self.__class__.__name__} ({self.colour}):
area={self.area():.2f}, perimeter={self.perimeter():.2f}")


class Rectangle(Shape):
    def __init__(self, width, height, colour="black"):
        super().__init__(colour)    # must call parent __init__
        self.width  = width
        self.height = height

    def area(self):
        return self.width * self.height

    def perimeter(self):
        return 2 * (self.width + self.height)


class Circle(Shape):
    def __init__(self, radius, colour="black"):
        super().__init__(colour)
        self.radius = radius

    def area(self):
        return math.pi * self.radius ** 2

    def perimeter(self):
        return 2 * math.pi * self.radius
```

```python
shapes = [
    Rectangle(5, 3, "blue"),
    Circle(4, "red"),
    Rectangle(6, 6, "green"),
]

for s in shapes:
    s.describe()
```

Output:

```
Rectangle (blue): area=15.00, perimeter=16.00
Circle (red): area=50.27, perimeter=25.13
Rectangle (green): area=36.00, perimeter=24.00
```

Example 2 — Variation

Inspecting the inheritance chain: isinstance(), issubclass(), and __mro__ at runtime.

```python
class Vehicle:
    pass

class Car(Vehicle):
    pass

class ElectricCar(Car):
    pass

ec = ElectricCar()

# isinstance checks the full hierarchy
print(isinstance(ec, ElectricCar))  # True
print(isinstance(ec, Car))          # True  — inherits from Car
print(isinstance(ec, Vehicle))      # True  — inherits from Vehicle
print(isinstance(ec, list))         # False

# issubclass checks class relationships
print(issubclass(ElectricCar, Car))     # True
print(issubclass(ElectricCar, Vehicle)) # True
print(issubclass(Car, ElectricCar))     # False — not reversed
```

```
# __mro__ shows the lookup order
print(ElectricCar.__mro__)
```

Output:

```
True
True
True
False
True
True
False
(<class '__main__.ElectricCar'>, <class '__main__.Car'>, <class
'__main__.Vehicle'>, <class 'object'>)
```

Example 3 — Real-world application

A financial account hierarchy: Account → SavingsAccount and CheckingAccount, each adding distinct behaviour while sharing base account logic.

```
class Account:
    def __init__(self, account_number, owner, opening_balance=0.0):
        self.account_number = account_number
        self.owner          = owner
        self._balance       = float(opening_balance)
        self._transactions  = []

    def deposit(self, amount):
        if amount <= 0:
            raise ValueError("Deposit must be positive.")
        self._balance += amount
        self._transactions.append(f"Deposit  +${amount:.2f}")

    def get_balance(self):
        return self._balance

    def statement(self):
        print(f"\n{self.__class__.__name__}: {self.account_number}
({self.owner})")
        for t in self._transactions:
            print(f"  {t}")
        print(f"  Balance: ${self._balance:,.2f}")
```

```
class SavingsAccount(Account):
    """Savings: earns interest, no overdraft."""

    def __init__(self, account_number, owner, opening_balance, interest_rate):
        super().__init__(account_number, owner, opening_balance)
        self.interest_rate = interest_rate

    def apply_interest(self):
        interest = self._balance * self.interest_rate
        self._balance += interest
        self._transactions.append(f"Interest +${interest:.2f}
({self.interest_rate*100:.1f}%)")

    def withdraw(self, amount):
        if amount > self._balance:
            raise ValueError("Insufficient funds in savings account.")
        self._balance -= amount
        self._transactions.append(f"Withdraw -${amount:.2f}")


class CheckingAccount(Account):
    """Checking: allows overdraft up to a limit."""

    def __init__(self, account_number, owner, opening_balance,
overdraft_limit):
        super().__init__(account_number, owner, opening_balance)
        self.overdraft_limit = overdraft_limit

    def withdraw(self, amount):
        if amount > self._balance + self.overdraft_limit:
            raise ValueError("Exceeds overdraft limit.")
        self._balance -= amount
        fee = 15.00 if self._balance < 0 else 0
        if fee:
            self._balance -= fee
            self._transactions.append(f"Withdraw -${amount:.2f} (overdraft fee
-${fee:.2f})")
        else:
```

```
            self._transactions.append(f"Withdraw -${amount:.2f}")


savings  = SavingsAccount("SA-001", "Alice Wong",  5000.00, 0.04)
checking = CheckingAccount("CA-001", "Bob Smith",   500.00,  200.00)

savings.deposit(1000)
savings.apply_interest()
savings.withdraw(500)
savings.statement()

checking.deposit(100)
checking.withdraw(750)    # into overdraft
checking.statement()
```

Output:

```
SavingsAccount: SA-001 (Alice Wong)
  Deposit  +$1000.00
  Interest +$240.00 (4.0%)
  Withdraw -$500.00
  Balance: $5,740.00

CheckingAccount: CA-001 (Bob Smith)
  Deposit  +$100.00
  Withdraw -$750.00 (overdraft fee -$15.00)
  Balance: $-165.00
```

5.3 Overriding Methods

Overriding means defining a method in a subclass with the same name as a method in the parent. When the method is called on a subclass instance, Python finds the subclass version first and executes it instead of the parent's version. The parent's version is not gone — it is reachable via `super()` — but it is no longer the default.

Overriding is the primary mechanism for specialisation: the parent defines the general behaviour, and each subclass overrides the parts that differ for its particular case. A well-designed parent class anticipates which methods will be overridden and documents them clearly as extension points.

There are three distinct override patterns: complete replacement (the subclass provides an entirely new implementation with no call to the parent), extension (the subclass calls `super()` to run the parent's version first, then adds to it), and pre-processing (the subclass does something first, then delegates to the parent). Choosing the right pattern keeps code correct and readable.

Override patterns

- Complete replacement: `def speak(self): return "Woof!"` — parent's speak() is entirely replaced.
- Extension (after): `super().method(); # add more` — parent runs first, subclass adds to it.
- Pre-processing (before): `# do something; super().method()` — subclass acts first, then delegates.

Example 1 — Introduction

Complete replacement: each subclass overrides speak() with a wholly different implementation.

```
class Animal:
    def __init__(self, name):
        self.name = name

    def speak(self):
        return f"{self.name} makes a sound."

    def introduce(self):
        print(f"I am {self.name}. {self.speak()}")


class Dog(Animal):
    def speak(self):                    # complete replacement
        return f"{self.name} says: Woof!"


class Cat(Animal):
    def speak(self):                    # complete replacement
        return f"{self.name} says: Meow!"


class Duck(Animal):
    def speak(self):                    # complete replacement
        return f"{self.name} says: Quack!"


animals = [Dog("Rex"), Cat("Whiskers"), Duck("Donald"), Animal("Mystery")]

for a in animals:
    a.introduce()
```

Output:

```
I am Rex. Rex says: Woof!
I am Whiskers. Whiskers says: Meow!
I am Donald. Donald says: Quack!
I am Mystery. Mystery makes a sound.
```

Example 2 — Variation

Extension pattern: subclass calls super() to preserve the parent's behaviour and then adds to it.

```
class Vehicle:
    def __init__(self, make, model):
        self.make  = make
        self.model = model
        self._log  = []

    def start_sequence(self):
        self._log.append("Engine check")
        self._log.append("Safety systems online")
        print(f"{self.make} {self.model}: standard start complete.")

    def show_log(self):
        for entry in self._log:
            print(f"  - {entry}")


class ElectricVehicle(Vehicle):
    def start_sequence(self):
        super().start_sequence()          # run parent checks first
        self._log.append("Battery status: 87%")
        self._log.append("Regenerative braking: active")
        print("EV systems initialised.")


class AutonomousVehicle(ElectricVehicle):
    def start_sequence(self):
        super().start_sequence()          # EV checks, then standard
        self._log.append("LIDAR calibrated")
        self._log.append("Map data loaded")
        print("Autonomous systems ready.")
```

```
av = AutonomousVehicle("Waymo", "One")
av.start_sequence()
print("\nStart log:")
av.show_log()
```

Output:

```
Waymo One: standard start complete.
EV systems initialised.
Autonomous systems ready.

Start log:
  - Engine check
  - Safety systems online
  - Battery status: 87%
  - Regenerative braking: active
  - LIDAR calibrated
  - Map data loaded
```

Example 3 — Real-world application

A notification system: the base Notification class handles delivery logging; subclasses override the send mechanism while still triggering the shared logging behaviour.

```
from datetime import datetime

class Notification:
    def __init__(self, recipient, subject, body):
        self.recipient = recipient
        self.subject   = subject
        self.body      = body
        self._sent_at  = None

    def _pre_send(self):
        """Pre-processing hook: runs before delivery."""
        print(f"[{self.__class__.__name__}] Preparing notification for
{self.recipient}...")

    def _deliver(self):
        """Override this in subclasses to change delivery method."""
        raise NotImplementedError("Subclasses must implement _deliver().")
```

```
    def send(self):
        """Template method: orchestrates the full send lifecycle."""
        self._pre_send()
        self._deliver()
        self._sent_at = datetime.now().strftime("%H:%M:%S")
        print(f"  Delivered at {self._sent_at}.")


class EmailNotification(Notification):
    def __init__(self, recipient, subject, body, cc=None):
        super().__init__(recipient, subject, body)
        self.cc = cc

    def _deliver(self):
        cc_info = f" (CC: {self.cc})" if self.cc else ""
        print(f"  EMAIL → {self.recipient}{cc_info}")
        print(f"  Subject: {self.subject}")


class SMSNotification(Notification):
    def __init__(self, recipient_number, body):
        super().__init__(recipient_number, "SMS", body)

    def _deliver(self):
        preview = self.body[:40] + "..." if len(self.body) > 40 else self.body
        print(f"  SMS → {self.recipient}: {preview!r}")


class PushNotification(Notification):
    def __init__(self, device_token, subject, body):
        super().__init__(device_token, subject, body)

    def _deliver(self):
        print(f"  PUSH → device {self.recipient[:12]}...")
        print(f"  Alert: {self.subject}")


notifications = [
    EmailNotification("alice@example.com", "Order Confirmed",
```

```
                    "Your order #1042 has been confirmed.",
cc="orders@shop.com"),
    SMSNotification("0412000001", "Your verification code is 482916."),
    PushNotification("tok_abc123xyz789", "Flash Sale!", "50% off all items
today!"),
]

for n in notifications:
    n.send()
    print()
```

Output:

```
[EmailNotification] Preparing notification for alice@example.com...
  EMAIL → alice@example.com (CC: orders@shop.com)
  Subject: Order Confirmed
  Delivered at 08:15:32.

[SMSNotification] Preparing notification for 0412000001...
  SMS → 0412000001: 'Your verification code is 482916.'
  Delivered at 08:15:32.

[PushNotification] Preparing notification for tok_abc123xyz789...
  PUSH → device tok_abc123xy...
  Alert: Flash Sale!
  Delivered at 08:15:32.
```

The `send()` method in `Notification` is a template method: it defines the overall algorithm (pre-send → deliver → log) while delegating the variable step (`_deliver`) to subclasses. This pattern keeps the shared lifecycle management in one place while allowing subclasses to plug in their specific delivery logic.

5.4 The super() Function

`super()` returns a proxy object that delegates attribute and method lookups to the next class in the Method Resolution Order (MRO). In straightforward single inheritance, this is always the immediate parent. In multiple inheritance (covered in Section 5.5), the MRO determines which class is "next", and `super()` respects that order.

The most common use of `super()` is calling the parent's `__init__` from a subclass constructor. Without this call, the parent's attributes are never set up, and any parent method that accesses them will raise an `AttributeError`.

`super()` is also used to call a parent's version of a method that the subclass is overriding. This is the extension override pattern: run the parent's logic first (or last), then add the subclass's contribution.

It avoids duplicating the parent's code inside the subclass and means the subclass's behaviour updates automatically if the parent's implementation changes.

super() vs hard-coding the parent name

Always use `super()` rather than `ParentClass.method(self, ...)`. Hard-coding the parent name breaks multiple inheritance — the MRO is bypassed and the cooperative call chain is broken. It also means that if the class is refactored and its parent changes, every hard-coded reference must be updated manually.

Example 1 — Introduction

super().__init__() in a two-level hierarchy: each level adds its own attributes and calls up the chain.

```
class Person:
    def __init__(self, name, email):
        self.name  = name
        self.email = email
        print(f"Person.__init__: {name}")

    def contact(self):
        return f"{self.name} <{self.email}>"


class Employee(Person):
    def __init__(self, name, email, employee_id, department):
        super().__init__(name, email)          # calls Person.__init__
        self.employee_id = employee_id
        self.department  = department
        print(f"Employee.__init__: {employee_id}")

    def badge(self):
        return f"{self.employee_id} | {self.name} | {self.department}"


class Manager(Employee):
    def __init__(self, name, email, employee_id, department, team_size):
        super().__init__(name, email, employee_id, department)  # calls
Employee.__init__
        self.team_size = team_size
        print(f"Manager.__init__: team_size={team_size}")

    def summary(self):
        return f"{self.badge()}  (manages {self.team_size} people)"
```

```
mgr = Manager("Cara Lee", "cara@example.com", "E003", "Technology", 8)
print()
print(mgr.contact())
print(mgr.summary())
```

Output:

```
Person.__init__: Cara Lee
Employee.__init__: E003
Manager.__init__: team_size=8

Cara Lee <cara@example.com>
E003 | Cara Lee | Technology  (manages 8 people)
```

Example 2 — Variation

Using super() to extend a parent method rather than replace it: a logging decorator pattern using inheritance.

```
class DataStore:
    def __init__(self, name):
        self.name   = name
        self._data  = {}

    def save(self, key, value):
        self._data[key] = value

    def load(self, key):
        return self._data.get(key)

    def keys(self):
        return list(self._data.keys())


class AuditedDataStore(DataStore):
    """Extends DataStore with an audit trail on every write."""

    def __init__(self, name):
        super().__init__(name)
        self._audit = []
```

```
    def save(self, key, value):
        super().save(key, value)          # parent handles the actual save
        self._audit.append(f"WRITE  {key!r} = {value!r}")

    def load(self, key):
        result = super().load(key)        # parent handles the actual load
        self._audit.append(f"READ   {key!r} -> {result!r}")
        return result

    def audit_log(self):
        return list(self._audit)


store = AuditedDataStore("ConfigStore")
store.save("host", "localhost")
store.save("port", 5432)
store.save("debug", True)

print(store.load("host"))
print(store.load("missing"))

print("\nAudit log:")
for entry in store.audit_log():
    print(f"  {entry}")
```

Output:

```
localhost
None

Audit log:
  WRITE  'host' = 'localhost'
  WRITE  'port' = 5432
  WRITE  'debug' = True
  READ   'host' -> 'localhost'
  READ   'missing' -> None
```

Example 3 — Real-world application

A game character system where super() chains through three levels to build up a character's full description and stats.

```
class Entity:
    def __init__(self, name, x=0, y=0):
        self.name = name
        self.x    = x
        self.y    = y

    def stats(self):
        return f"Entity: {self.name} at ({self.x},{self.y})"

    def move(self, dx, dy):
        self.x += dx
        self.y += dy


class Character(Entity):
    def __init__(self, name, x=0, y=0, hp=100, mp=50):
        super().__init__(name, x, y)
        self.hp = hp
        self.mp = mp

    def stats(self):
        base = super().stats()             # get Entity stats
        return f"{base} | HP:{self.hp} MP:{self.mp}"

    def take_damage(self, amount):
        self.hp = max(0, self.hp - amount)


class Warrior(Character):
    def __init__(self, name, x=0, y=0, hp=150, mp=20, armour=30):
        super().__init__(name, x, y, hp, mp)
        self.armour = armour

    def stats(self):
        base = super().stats()             # get Character stats
        return f"{base} | Armour:{self.armour}"

    def take_damage(self, amount):
        mitigated = max(0, amount - self.armour)
```

```python
        super().take_damage(mitigated)      # parent handles the HP reduction
        blocked = amount - mitigated
        if blocked:
            print(f"  Armour blocked {blocked} damage.")


w = Warrior("Thorin", x=5, y=5)
print(w.stats())

print("\nTaking 50 damage (blocked by armour):")
w.take_damage(50)
print(w.stats())

print("\nTaking 100 damage:")
w.take_damage(100)
print(w.stats())
```

Output:

```
Entity: Thorin at (5,5) | HP:150 MP:20 | Armour:30

Taking 50 damage (blocked by armour):
  Armour blocked 30 damage.
Entity: Thorin at (5,5) | HP:130 MP:20 | Armour:30

Taking 100 damage:
  Armour blocked 30 damage.
Entity: Thorin at (5,5) | HP:60 MP:20 | Armour:30
```

`super().stats()` at each level calls up the chain: `Warrior.stats()` → `Character.stats()` → `Entity.stats()`. Each level appends its own data. `super().take_damage()` in Warrior delegates the HP reduction to `Character.take_damage()`, which handles the `max(0, ...)` guard. Neither class duplicates the other's logic.

5.5 Multiple Inheritance and the MRO

Python allows a class to inherit from more than one parent: `class C(A, B):`. This is multiple inheritance. When `C` calls a method, Python must decide which parent's version to use if both define it. The answer is the Method Resolution Order (MRO): a linear sequence that determines precisely which class is searched first, second, third, and so on.

Python uses the C3 linearisation algorithm to compute the MRO. The result is always: the class itself, then its parents left-to-right, and the parents of parents, with no class appearing twice and no class appearing before all of its subclasses. The full MRO for any class is accessible via `ClassName.__mro__` or `ClassName.mro()`.

The key to making multiple inheritance work correctly is cooperative `super()` calls. Every class in the hierarchy should call `super().__init__(...)` and pass along all keyword arguments it does not consume, using `**kwargs`. This ensures the full chain of constructors runs, even when the MRO is not linear.

> **Note:** Multiple inheritance is powerful but complex. Python's standard library uses it in several places (collections.abc, io module). In application code, it is most commonly seen in the form of mixin classes (Section 5.6). For general class hierarchies, prefer single inheritance; reach for multiple inheritance only when the use case genuinely requires it.

Example 1 — Introduction

Basic multiple inheritance: a class inheriting from two parents and the MRO determining which method is used.

```
class A:
    def greet(self):
        return "Hello from A"

    def describe(self):
        return "I am A"


class B(A):
    def greet(self):
        return "Hello from B"


class C(A):
    def greet(self):
        return "Hello from C"


class D(B, C):
    """Inherits from B and C, both of which inherit from A."""
    pass


d = D()
```

```
# MRO: D -> B -> C -> A -> object
print(D.__mro__)

# greet() found in B first (B is before C in the MRO)
print(d.greet())

# describe() not in B or C, falls through to A
print(d.describe())
```

Output:

```
(<class '__main__.D'>, <class '__main__.B'>, <class '__main__.C'>, <class
'__main__.A'>, <class 'object'>)
Hello from B
I am A
```

Example 2 — Variation

*Cooperative super() calls: every class passes **kwargs up the chain so all __init__ methods run correctly.*

```
class Base:
    def __init__(self, **kwargs):
        print(f"Base.__init__ called")
        super().__init__(**kwargs)


class LoggingMixin:
    def __init__(self, **kwargs):
        print(f"LoggingMixin.__init__ called")
        super().__init__(**kwargs)
        self._log = []

    def log(self, message):
        self._log.append(message)
        print(f"LOG: {message}")


class TimestampMixin:
    def __init__(self, **kwargs):
        from datetime import datetime
        print(f"TimestampMixin.__init__ called")
        super().__init__(**kwargs)
```

```
        self.created_at = datetime.now().strftime("%Y-%m-%d")


class AuditedService(LoggingMixin, TimestampMixin, Base):
    def __init__(self, service_name, **kwargs):
        self.service_name = service_name
        print(f"AuditedService.__init__ called")
        super().__init__(**kwargs)


print("MRO:", [c.__name__ for c in AuditedService.__mro__])
print()

svc = AuditedService("PaymentService")
print()
svc.log("Transaction #4421 processed.")
print(f"Service: {svc.service_name}")
print(f"Created: {svc.created_at}")
```

Output:

```
MRO: ['AuditedService', 'LoggingMixin', 'TimestampMixin', 'Base', 'object']

AuditedService.__init__ called
LoggingMixin.__init__ called
TimestampMixin.__init__ called
Base.__init__ called

LOG: Transaction #4421 processed.
Service: PaymentService
Created: 2026-03-21
```

Example 3 — Real-world application

A realistic multiple-inheritance scenario: a ReportDocument that inherits from both a Document class and a Printable class.

```
class Document:
    def __init__(self, title, author, **kwargs):
        super().__init__(**kwargs)
        self.title  = title
        self.author = author
```

```
        self._pages = []

    def add_page(self, content):
        self._pages.append(content)

    def page_count(self):
        return len(self._pages)

    def __str__(self):
        return f'"{self.title}" by {self.author} ({self.page_count()} pages)'


class Printable:
    def __init__(self, printer_name="Default Printer", **kwargs):
        super().__init__(**kwargs)
        self.printer_name = printer_name

    def print_document(self):
        print(f"Sending to [{self.printer_name}]...")
        if hasattr(self, "_pages"):
            for i, page in enumerate(self._pages, 1):
                print(f"  Page {i}: {page[:40]}...")
        print("Print job complete.")

    def print_preview(self):
        print(f"Preview: {self}")


class ReportDocument(Document, Printable):
    def __init__(self, title, author, printer_name="Report Printer", **kwargs):
        super().__init__(title=title, author=author,
                         printer_name=printer_name, **kwargs)
        self._report_id = f"RPT-{hash(title) % 10000:04d}"

    def header(self):
        return f"[{self._report_id}] {self.title}"
```

```python
report = ReportDocument("Q1 Financial Summary", "Finance Team")
report.add_page("Executive summary: revenue up 12% year-on-year.")
report.add_page("Detailed figures: see attached spreadsheets.")
report.add_page("Recommendations: expand into three new markets.")

print(report)
print(report.header())
print()
report.print_preview()
print()
report.print_document()
```

Output:

```
"Q1 Financial Summary" by Finance Team (3 pages)
[RPT-XXXX] Q1 Financial Summary

Preview: "Q1 Financial Summary" by Finance Team (3 pages)

Sending to [Report Printer]...
  Page 1: Executive summary: revenue up 12% year...
  Page 2: Detailed figures: see attached spreadshe...
  Page 3: Recommendations: expand into three new m...
Print job complete.
```

5.6 Mixin Classes

A mixin is a class that provides a bundle of related methods intended to be mixed into other classes via multiple inheritance. Mixins are not meant to be instantiated directly and usually have no meaningful `__init__`. They add reusable capabilities — serialisation, logging, validation, comparison operators — to any class that inherits from them, without those capabilities being part of the main inheritance hierarchy.

The key characteristics of a mixin: it should do one thing, it should not hold significant state of its own, it should not depend on the internal attributes of the classes it is mixed into (only on a well-defined interface), and it should always call `super()` so the cooperative chain is not broken.

Mixins are one of the most legitimate and common uses of multiple inheritance in Python. Django uses them extensively: `LoginRequiredMixin`, `PermissionRequiredMixin`, `UserPassesTestMixin` are all mixins that add access-control behaviour to any view class. The standard library's `collections.abc` module defines abstract mixins for sequences, mappings, and iterables.

Example 1 — Introduction

A ReprMixin and a ToDictMixin: each adds one reusable capability that any class can acquire by inheriting from it.

```python
class ReprMixin:
    """Adds a clean __repr__ based on public instance attributes."""

    def __repr__(self):
        attrs = {k: v for k, v in vars(self).items() if not k.startswith("_")}
        attr_str = ", ".join(f"{k}={v!r}" for k, v in attrs.items())
        return f"{self.__class__.__name__}({attr_str})"


class ToDictMixin:
    """Adds a to_dict() method that serialises public attributes."""

    def to_dict(self):
        return {k: v for k, v in vars(self).items() if not k.startswith("_")}


class Product(ReprMixin, ToDictMixin):
    def __init__(self, sku, name, price):
        self.sku   = sku
        self.name  = name
        self.price = price


class Customer(ReprMixin, ToDictMixin):
    def __init__(self, customer_id, name, email):
        self.customer_id = customer_id
        self.name        = name
        self.email       = email


p = Product("P001", "Laptop Stand", 49.00)
c = Customer("C001", "Alice Wong",  "alice@example.com")

print(repr(p))
print(p.to_dict())
print()
print(repr(c))
print(c.to_dict())
```

```
Output:
Product(sku='P001', name='Laptop Stand', price=49.0)
{'sku': 'P001', 'name': 'Laptop Stand', 'price': 49.0}

Customer(customer_id='C001', name='Alice Wong', email='alice@example.com')
{'customer_id': 'C001', 'name': 'Alice Wong', 'email': 'alice@example.com'}
```

Example 2 — Variation

A ComparableMixin that adds all comparison operators from a single defined __lt__ method.

```
class ComparableMixin:
    """Provides <=, >, >= by deriving from __lt__ and __eq__.

    The using class must define __lt__ and __eq__.
    """

    def __le__(self, other):
        return self < other or self == other

    def __gt__(self, other):
        return not (self < other or self == other)

    def __ge__(self, other):
        return not self < other


class Temperature(ComparableMixin):
    def __init__(self, celsius):
        self.celsius = celsius

    def __lt__(self, other):
        return self.celsius < other.celsius

    def __eq__(self, other):
        return self.celsius == other.celsius

    def __repr__(self):
        return f"Temperature({self.celsius}°C)"
```

```python
class Weight(ComparableMixin):
    def __init__(self, kg):
        self.kg = kg

    def __lt__(self, other):
        return self.kg < other.kg

    def __eq__(self, other):
        return self.kg == other.kg

    def __repr__(self):
        return f"Weight({self.kg}kg)"


t1 = Temperature(20)
t2 = Temperature(35)
print(f"{t1} < {t2}:  {t1 < t2}")
print(f"{t1} <= {t2}: {t1 <= t2}")
print(f"{t2} > {t1}:  {t2 > t1}")

temps = [Temperature(38), Temperature(22), Temperature(15), Temperature(29)]
print(f"Sorted: {sorted(temps)}")

w1, w2 = Weight(5.5), Weight(3.2)
print(f"{w1} >= {w2}: {w1 >= w2}")
```

Output:

```
Temperature(20°C) < Temperature(35°C):  True
Temperature(20°C) <= Temperature(35°C): True
Temperature(35°C) > Temperature(20°C):  True
Sorted: [Temperature(15°C), Temperature(22°C), Temperature(29°C),
Temperature(38°C)]
Weight(5.5kg) >= Weight(3.2kg): True
```

Note: Python's functools.total_ordering decorator does exactly this — derives the other comparison operators from __lt__ and __eq__. ComparableMixin above demonstrates the pattern manually. In production code, prefer @functools.total_ordering over a hand-rolled mixin for comparison operators.

Example 3 — Real-world application

A web framework-style mixin system: view classes gain authentication and permission checking by mixing in specialised behaviours.

```
class View:
    """Base view: handles the request/response lifecycle."""

    def dispatch(self, request):
        method = request.get("method", "GET").upper()
        if method == "GET":
            return self.get(request)
        if method == "POST":
            return self.post(request)
        return {"status": 405, "body": "Method Not Allowed"}

    def get(self, request):
        return {"status": 200, "body": "OK"}

    def post(self, request):
        return {"status": 200, "body": "OK"}


class LoginRequiredMixin:
    """Mixin: redirects to login if user is not authenticated."""

    def dispatch(self, request):
        if not request.get("user"):
            return {"status": 401, "body": "Login required."}
        return super().dispatch(request)


class PermissionRequiredMixin:
    """Mixin: blocks access if user lacks required permission."""
    required_permission = "view"

    def dispatch(self, request):
        user_perms = request.get("permissions", [])
        if self.required_permission not in user_perms:
            return {"status": 403, "body": "Permission denied."}
        return super().dispatch(request)
```

```
class DashboardView(LoginRequiredMixin, PermissionRequiredMixin, View):
    required_permission = "admin"

    def get(self, request):
        user = request["user"]
        return {"status": 200, "body": f"Welcome to the dashboard, {user}!"}


view = DashboardView()

anon_request    = {"method": "GET"}
user_request    = {"method": "GET", "user": "alice", "permissions": ["view"]}
admin_request   = {"method": "GET", "user": "alice", "permissions":
["view","admin"]}

print(view.dispatch(anon_request))
print(view.dispatch(user_request))
print(view.dispatch(admin_request))
```

Output:

```
{'status': 401, 'body': 'Login required.'}
{'status': 403, 'body': 'Permission denied.'}
{'status': 200, 'body': 'Welcome to the dashboard, alice!'}
```

The MRO for `DashboardView` is `[DashboardView, LoginRequiredMixin, PermissionRequiredMixin, View, object]`. When `dispatch()` is called, LoginRequiredMixin checks authentication first. If it passes, it calls `super().dispatch()`, which runs PermissionRequiredMixin's check. If that passes, it calls `super().dispatch()` on the base `View`. Each mixin does exactly one thing and cooperates with the chain via `super()`.

5.7 Composition vs Inheritance — Choosing the Right Tool

The choice between inheritance and composition is one of the most consequential design decisions in OOP. Python's flexibility means both are always available, which makes the decision genuinely yours. The conventional guidance — "favour composition over inheritance" — is widely repeated but often misunderstood as "never use inheritance". The accurate version is: use inheritance when the is-a relationship holds and the Liskov Substitution Principle is satisfied; use composition when one object uses or contains another.

Inheritance creates a permanent coupling. A subclass depends on its parent's implementation details — if the parent changes, all children are affected. Deep hierarchies (four or more levels) become very difficult to reason about because any method call may pass through several layers of overrides before doing anything. Composition is more flexible: the Car can hold any Engine object, not just the one it was designed with.

The practical indicators for each choice are straightforward. Prefer inheritance when you want a subclass to be usable wherever the parent is used, when the subclass represents a specialised kind of the parent, or when you want to override specific methods while inheriting the rest. Prefer composition when you want to reuse behaviour from a class that the new class is not a specialisation of, or when you want to swap implementations at runtime.

The "favour composition" heuristic in practice

A useful test: could you replace the parent class with a different one and still have the subclass work correctly? If the subclass is tightly coupled to the parent's internal methods and attributes, the answer is probably no, and composition would have been more flexible.

Example 1 — Introduction

Refactoring from inheritance to composition: an EmailSender that becomes more flexible when the transport mechanism is injected rather than inherited.

```
# --- Inheritance version: tightly coupled to SMTP ---
class SMTPTransport:
    def send_raw(self, to, subject, body):
        print(f"SMTP → {to}: [{subject}] {body[:30]}...")


class EmailSenderInheritance(SMTPTransport):
    """Inherits from SMTPTransport. Cannot easily swap transport."""

    def send_welcome(self, user_email, name):
        self.send_raw(user_email, "Welcome!", f"Hello {name}, welcome aboard.")


# --- Composition version: transport is injected ---
class MockTransport:
    """Test transport: captures messages instead of sending them."""
    def __init__(self):
        self.sent = []

    def send_raw(self, to, subject, body):
        self.sent.append({"to": to, "subject": subject})
        print(f"MOCK captured: {to} / {subject}")


class EmailSenderComposition:
```

```python
    """Uses any transport object — swap without changing this class."""

    def __init__(self, transport):
        self._transport = transport    # has-a transport, not is-a transport

    def send_welcome(self, user_email, name):
        self._transport.send_raw(
            user_email, "Welcome!",
            f"Hello {name}, welcome aboard."
        )


print("--- Inheritance version ---")
sender_v1 = EmailSenderInheritance()
sender_v1.send_welcome("alice@example.com", "Alice")

print("\n--- Composition version with SMTP ---")
smtp      = SMTPTransport()
sender_v2 = EmailSenderComposition(smtp)
sender_v2.send_welcome("alice@example.com", "Alice")

print("\n--- Composition version with Mock (for testing) ---")
mock      = MockTransport()
sender_v3 = EmailSenderComposition(mock)
sender_v3.send_welcome("alice@example.com", "Alice")
print(f"Captured: {mock.sent}")
```

Output:

```
--- Inheritance version ---
SMTP → alice@example.com: [Welcome!] Hello Alice, welcome aboard....

--- Composition version with SMTP ---
SMTP → alice@example.com: [Welcome!] Hello Alice, welcome aboard....

--- Composition version with Mock (for testing) ---
MOCK captured: alice@example.com / Welcome!
[{'to': 'alice@example.com', 'subject': 'Welcome!'}]
```

Example 2 — Variation

When inheritance is clearly correct: a shape hierarchy where every subclass genuinely is-a Shape and must be usable wherever a Shape is expected.

```
import math

class Shape:
    def area(self)      -> float: raise NotImplementedError
    def perimeter(self) -> float: raise NotImplementedError

    def scale(self, factor):
        """Scale all dimensions by factor. Subclasses must implement."""
        raise NotImplementedError

    def describe(self):
        print(f"{self.__class__.__name__:12s} area={self.area():8.2f}
perimeter={self.perimeter():.2f}")


class Rectangle(Shape):
    def __init__(self, w, h): self.w, self.h = w, h
    def area(self):      return self.w * self.h
    def perimeter(self): return 2 * (self.w + self.h)
    def scale(self, f):  self.w *= f; self.h *= f


class Circle(Shape):
    def __init__(self, r): self.r = r
    def area(self):      return math.pi * self.r ** 2
    def perimeter(self): return 2 * math.pi * self.r
    def scale(self, f):  self.r *= f


class Triangle(Shape):
    def __init__(self, a, b, c): self.a, self.b, self.c = a, b, c
    def area(self):
        s = (self.a + self.b + self.c) / 2
        return math.sqrt(s * (s-self.a) * (s-self.b) * (s-self.c))
    def perimeter(self): return self.a + self.b + self.c
    def scale(self, f):  self.a*=f; self.b*=f; self.c*=f
```

```
shapes = [Rectangle(4, 3), Circle(5), Triangle(3, 4, 5)]

print("Before scaling:")
for s in shapes: s.describe()

for s in shapes: s.scale(2)

print("\nAfter scaling by 2:")
for s in shapes: s.describe()

# All shapes usable wherever Shape is expected
total_area = sum(s.area() for s in shapes)
print(f"\nTotal area of all shapes: {total_area:.2f}")
```

Output:

```
Before scaling:
Rectangle     area=   12.00  perimeter=14.00
Circle        area=   78.54  perimeter=31.42
Triangle      area=    6.00  perimeter=12.00

After scaling by 2:
Rectangle     area=   48.00  perimeter=28.00
Circle        area=  314.16  perimeter=62.83
Triangle      area=   24.00  perimeter=24.00

Total area of all shapes: 386.16
```

Example 3 — Real-world application

A game character system refactored to use composition for abilities — more flexible than an inheritance chain of Warrior, Mage, Paladin.

```
class Ability:
    """Composable game ability."""
    def __init__(self, name, damage, cost):
        self.name   = name
        self.damage = damage
        self.cost   = cost

    def __str__(self):
```

```
        return f"{self.name} (dmg:{self.damage}, cost:{self.cost})"


class Character:
    """Character HAS abilities rather than IS a Warrior or Mage.

    Abilities are injected, allowing any combination at runtime.
    """

    def __init__(self, name, hp, mp):
        self.name      = name
        self.hp        = hp
        self.mp        = mp
        self._abilities = {}

    def learn(self, ability):
        self._abilities[ability.name] = ability
        print(f"{self.name} learned: {ability.name}")

    def use(self, ability_name, target):
        ability = self._abilities.get(ability_name)
        if not ability:
            print(f"{self.name} does not know {ability_name!r}.")
            return
        if self.mp < ability.cost:
            print(f"Not enough MP to use {ability.name}.")
            return
        self.mp -= ability.cost
        target.hp = max(0, target.hp - ability.damage)
        print(f"{self.name} uses {ability.name} on {target.name}! (-
{ability.damage} HP, {target.name} HP: {target.hp})")

    def status(self):
        print(f"{self.name}: HP={self.hp} MP={self.mp} | Abilities:
{list(self._abilities.keys())}")


# Define abilities independently
fireball   = Ability("Fireball",     55, 30)
heal       = Ability("Heal",          0, 25)
```

```
sword_slash= Ability("Sword Slash", 35,  5)
shield      = Ability("Shield",        0, 10)

# Create characters and compose their abilities freely
warrior = Character("Thorin", hp=150, mp=40)
warrior.learn(sword_slash)
warrior.learn(shield)

mage = Character("Lyra", hp=80, mp=120)
mage.learn(fireball)
mage.learn(heal)

# A paladin: warrior abilities + healing (no separate class needed)
paladin = Character("Aldric", hp=120, mp=80)
paladin.learn(sword_slash)
paladin.learn(heal)

print()
warrior.status()
mage.status()
paladin.status()
print()
mage.use("Fireball", warrior)
paladin.use("Heal", warrior)
warrior.status()
```

Output:

```
Thorin learned: Sword Slash
Thorin learned: Shield
Lyra learned: Fireball
Lyra learned: Heal
Aldric learned: Sword Slash
Aldric learned: Heal

Thorin: HP=150 MP=40 | Abilities: ['Sword Slash', 'Shield']
Lyra: HP=80 MP=120 | Abilities: ['Fireball', 'Heal']
Aldric: HP=120 MP=80 | Abilities: ['Sword Slash', 'Heal']

Lyra uses Fireball on Thorin! (-55 HP, Thorin HP: 95)
Aldric uses Heal on Thorin! (-0 HP, Thorin HP: 95)
```

```
Thorin: HP=95 MP=40 | Abilities: ['Sword Slash', 'Shield']
```

Adding a new character type (Necromancer, Bard, Ranger) requires creating new `Ability` objects and combining them — no new class, no modification to the hierarchy. This is composition's defining advantage: the behaviour set is open to extension without touching existing code.

Chapter 5 Summary

- Inheritance models an is-a relationship. A subclass is a specialised version of its parent and must be usable wherever the parent is expected (Liskov Substitution Principle). Composition models a has-a relationship and is more flexible when one object uses or contains another.
- A subclass is defined by listing the parent in parentheses: class Dog(Animal):. It inherits all parent attributes and methods. Methods can be used as-is (inherited), redefined (overridden), or added new (subclass-only). isinstance() and issubclass() respect the full inheritance hierarchy.
- Overriding a method in a subclass replaces the parent's version for that class. Three patterns apply: complete replacement (new implementation, no super() call), extension (call super() and add to it), and pre-processing (act first, then call super()). Choose based on whether the parent's logic is still needed.
- super() returns a proxy to the next class in the MRO. Always use super().__init__() in a subclass constructor to ensure parent attributes are initialised. Prefer super() over hard-coding the parent class name, which breaks multiple inheritance and requires manual updates on refactoring.
- Python's MRO (computed by C3 linearisation) defines the order in which classes are searched for methods in multiple inheritance. The MRO is accessible via ClassName.__mro__. Cooperative super() calls using **kwargs ensure all __init__ methods in the MRO run correctly.
- Mixins are lightweight classes designed to be mixed in via multiple inheritance. They add a single reusable capability (logging, serialisation, comparison operators, access control) to any class. A well-designed mixin does one thing, holds minimal state, and always calls super() to keep the cooperative chain intact.
- Favour composition over inheritance when an object uses another rather than being a specialised version of it. Composition allows runtime flexibility (swapping implementations), avoids tight parent-child coupling, and keeps hierarchies shallow and easy to reason about.
- Deep inheritance hierarchies (four or more levels) are a warning sign. Each level adds cognitive overhead and increases the risk that a parent change breaks all descendants. Mixins, composition, and protocol-based design (covered in Chapter 6) are alternatives that achieve code reuse with less coupling.

Guided Exercises

Complete the following exercises. Each targets a specific concept from this chapter.

1. Create a three-level inheritance hierarchy: Vehicle → Car → ElectricCar. Vehicle stores make, model, and year. Car adds num_doors and a fuel_type attribute. ElectricCar adds range_km and a charge() method. Each __init__ must call super().__init__() with the appropriate arguments. Add a describe() method at each level that calls super().describe() and appends its own details. Create one instance of each class and call describe() on each.

Hint: In Vehicle.describe(), print the basic details. In Car.describe(), call super().describe() then print the car-specific info. In ElectricCar.describe(), call super().describe() then print the EV-specific info.

2. Write a Shape base class with abstract-style methods area() and perimeter() that raise NotImplementedError. Create three subclasses: Rectangle, Circle, and Triangle. Each must implement both methods. Add a compare(other) method to Shape that prints which of the two shapes has the larger area. Test by creating pairs of shapes and calling compare().

Hint: *In compare(), use self.area() and other.area() directly — Python dispatches to the correct subclass implementation automatically via polymorphism.*

3. Create an Employee base class and two subclasses: SalariedEmployee (fixed monthly salary) and HourlyEmployee (hourly rate and hours worked). Both must inherit common attributes (employee_id, name) from Employee via super(). Add a pay() method to each subclass that returns the calculated pay for the month. Add a pay_summary(employees) module-level function that takes a list of mixed Employee objects and prints a formatted payroll report.

Hint: *The pay_summary() function should call e.pay() on each employee in the list without knowing which subclass it is — this is polymorphism. Employee itself does not need a pay() method.*

4. Define a JSONMixin that adds a to_json() method returning a JSON string of all public instance attributes, and a @classmethod from_json(cls, json_string) that reconstructs an instance from that JSON string. Apply this mixin to both a Product class and a Customer class. Demonstrate round-tripping: create an instance, serialise to JSON, reconstruct from JSON, and verify the attributes match.

Hint: *import json. In to_json(), use json.dumps(vars(self) filtered for public keys). In from_json(), parse the string with json.loads(), then use cls(**data) to reconstruct.*

5. Build a simple mixin called ValidatedMixin that provides a validate() method. The method should iterate over a class-level dict called VALIDATORS, where each key is an attribute name and each value is a callable (e.g. a lambda or function) that returns True if the value is valid. validate() should check all attributes listed in VALIDATORS and raise a ValueError listing all invalid fields. Apply it to a form-style UserRegistration class that validates username, email, and age.

Hint: *Define VALIDATORS = {"username": lambda v: len(v) >= 3, "email": lambda v: "@" in v, "age": lambda v: 18 <= v <= 120} in the class body. In validate(), use getattr(self, field) to fetch each value.*

Challenge Tasks

Open-ended tasks. No hints provided. Design your solution before writing any code.

1. Design a library media system with the following hierarchy: MediaItem (base) → Book, AudioBook, and DVD (subclasses). MediaItem stores title, creator, year, and loan status. Each subclass adds its own specific attributes (e.g. Book has page_count and isbn; DVD has runtime_minutes and rating; AudioBook has narrator and duration_hours). All constructors must chain correctly via super(). Add a checkout(borrower) method to the base class that records who borrowed it and when (use datetime).

Add a return_item() method. A subclass-specific display() method should show all relevant details. Create a mixed catalogue and demonstrate checkout, return, and display for items of all three types.

2. Implement a plugin system using mixins. Define a base Logger mixin that stores log messages in a private list and provides a log(message) method and a get_log() method. Define a Cacheable mixin that stores method results in a private dict keyed by method name + arguments and returns cached results on repeated calls (implement via a cache(method_name, key, compute_fn) helper). Define a Retryable mixin that provides a retry(fn, attempts=3) method that retries a failing callable up to the specified number of times. Create a DataFetcher class that inherits from all three mixins and uses all three capabilities: log each fetch attempt, cache successful results, and retry failed ones. Write a complete demonstration.

3. Refactor the following scenario from inheritance to composition and justify your design. You have: Vehicle (make, model, speed) → FuelVehicle (fuel_level, refuel()) → HybridVehicle (battery_level, charge(), switch_mode()). The problem is that HybridVehicle needs both fuel and battery behaviour, but the inheritance chain is awkward and HybridVehicle is tightly coupled to FuelVehicle internals. Redesign using composition: create separate FuelSystem and ElectricSystem components. HybridVehicle should contain both. Demonstrate that the refactored design makes it straightforward to create a fully electric vehicle, a fully fuel vehicle, and a hybrid — all from the same Vehicle base and component classes, with no duplicated code.

CHAPTER 6 **Polymorphism**

Book 01: Object-Oriented Programming in Python

> *Polymorphism — from the Greek for "many forms" — is the ability of different objects to respond to the same method call in ways appropriate to their own type. It is what allows a loop to call speak() on a list of Animals without caring whether each is a Dog, Cat, or Duck. This chapter examines every form polymorphism takes in Python: method overriding through inheritance, duck typing and the power of informal interfaces, operator overloading through dunder methods, and polymorphism across collections of mixed objects. The chapter closes with the role of isinstance() — when it genuinely helps, and when reaching for it signals that polymorphism has been bypassed rather than embraced.*

6.1 What Polymorphism Means in Python

Polymorphism is the third pillar of OOP and arguably the one that delivers the most immediate practical benefit. It allows a single piece of code to work correctly with many different types of object, as long as those objects implement the required interface. The calling code does not need to know the exact type of object it is working with; it only needs to know what methods it can call.

In Python, polymorphism takes two distinct forms. The first is subtype polymorphism: different subclasses of a common parent each override a shared method, and calling that method on any instance dispatches to the correct subclass version. The second is duck typing: Python does not require a formal class relationship for polymorphism to work. Any object that has the right methods can be used wherever those methods are called, regardless of its class hierarchy.

Python's built-in functions are a constant, quiet demonstration of polymorphism. `len()` works on strings, lists, tuples, dicts, sets, and any object with a `__len__` method. `str()` works on any object with `__str__`. `sorted()` works on any iterable of objects that support comparison. The function does not inspect the type — it calls the method, and the object responds appropriately.

Dispatch: how Python finds the right method

When you call `animal.speak()`, Python first looks for `speak` in the instance's own namespace, then in its class, then in its parent classes following the MRO. This lookup — called attribute dispatch — happens at runtime, not at compile time. It is what makes polymorphism possible: the method that runs is determined by the actual type of the object at the moment of the call, not by the type of the variable holding it.

Example 1 — Introduction

The simplest polymorphism: a loop calling the same method on objects of different types.

```
class Dog:
    def __init__(self, name): self.name = name
    def speak(self): return f"{self.name} says: Woof!"
    def __str__(self): return f"Dog({self.name})"
```

```
class Cat:
    def __init__(self, name): self.name = name
    def speak(self): return f"{self.name} says: Meow!"
    def __str__(self): return f"Cat({self.name})"

class Duck:
    def __init__(self, name): self.name = name
    def speak(self): return f"{self.name} says: Quack!"
    def __str__(self): return f"Duck({self.name})"


# No common base class — pure duck typing
animals = [Dog("Rex"), Cat("Whiskers"), Duck("Donald"), Dog("Buddy")]

for animal in animals:
    print(animal.speak())    # correct method called for each type
```

Output:

```
Rex says: Woof!
Whiskers says: Meow!
Donald says: Quack!
Buddy says: Woof!
```

Example 2 — Variation

Python's built-in functions demonstrate polymorphism: len(), str(), and sorted() work on any object that implements the required protocol.

```
class WordCollection:
    def __init__(self, words):
        self._words = list(words)

    def __len__(self):
        return len(self._words)

    def __str__(self):
        return f"WordCollection({self._words})"

    def __iter__(self):
        return iter(self._words)
```

```
class NumberRange:
    def __init__(self, start, stop):
        self._start = start
        self._stop  = stop

    def __len__(self):
        return max(0, self._stop - self._start)

    def __str__(self):
        return f"NumberRange({self._start}..{self._stop})"

    def __iter__(self):
        return iter(range(self._start, self._stop))


wc = WordCollection(["python", "java", "rust", "go"])
nr = NumberRange(5, 10)

# len() works on any object with __len__
print(len(wc))
print(len(nr))

# str() works on any object with __str__
print(str(wc))
print(str(nr))

# for-loop and list() work on any object with __iter__
print(list(wc))
print(list(nr))
```

Output:

```
4
5
WordCollection(['python', 'java', 'rust', 'go'])
NumberRange(5..10)
['python', 'java', 'rust', 'go']
[5, 6, 7, 8, 9]
```

Example 3 — Real-world application

A rendering pipeline that draws different shapes without knowing their types: polymorphism enabling a uniform processing loop.

```
import math

class Shape:
    colour = "black"

    def area(self) -> float:
        raise NotImplementedError

    def draw(self):
        raise NotImplementedError


class Circle(Shape):
    def __init__(self, cx, cy, radius, colour="blue"):
        self.cx, self.cy = cx, cy
        self.radius     = radius
        self.colour     = colour

    def area(self):
        return math.pi * self.radius ** 2

    def draw(self):
        print(f"  Drawing Circle at ({self.cx},{self.cy}) r={self.radius}
[{self.colour}] area={self.area():.2f}")


class Rectangle(Shape):
    def __init__(self, x, y, w, h, colour="red"):
        self.x, self.y = x, y
        self.w, self.h = w, h
        self.colour    = colour

    def area(self):
        return self.w * self.h

    def draw(self):
```

```
        print(f"  Drawing Rect at ({self.x},{self.y}) {self.w}x{self.h}
[{self.colour}] area={self.area():.2f}")


class Triangle(Shape):
    def __init__(self, base, height, colour="green"):
        self.base   = base
        self.height = height
        self.colour = colour

    def area(self):
        return 0.5 * self.base * self.height

    def draw(self):
        print(f"  Drawing Triangle base={self.base} h={self.height}
[{self.colour}] area={self.area():.2f}")


def render_scene(shapes):
    """Renders any collection of shapes polymorphically."""
    print("=== Rendering scene ===")
    for shape in shapes:
        shape.draw()    # correct draw() called for each type
    total_area = sum(s.area() for s in shapes)
    print(f"  Total area: {total_area:.2f}")


scene = [
    Circle(10, 10, 5, "blue"),
    Rectangle(0, 0, 8, 4, "red"),
    Triangle(6, 9, "green"),
    Circle(20, 15, 3, "purple"),
]

render_scene(scene)
```

Output:

```
=== Rendering scene ===
  Drawing Circle at (10,10) r=5 [blue] area=78.54
  Drawing Rect at (0,0) 8x4 [red] area=32.00
```

```
Drawing Triangle base=6 h=9 [green] area=27.00
Drawing Circle at (20,15) r=3 [purple] area=28.27
Total area: 165.81
```

`render_scene` is completely decoupled from the specific shape types. Adding a new shape (Hexagon, Ellipse, Star) requires writing that shape's class — not modifying `render_scene`. This is the open/closed principle expressed through polymorphism: the function is open to new shape types without being modified.

6.2 Duck Typing

Duck typing is Python's most distinctive approach to polymorphism. The name comes from the phrase: "If it walks like a duck and quacks like a duck, then it is a duck." In practical terms: Python does not check an object's type before calling a method. If the object has the method, the call succeeds. If it does not, Python raises an `AttributeError` at runtime.

This is fundamentally different from statically-typed languages like Java, where you must declare that an object implements an interface before it can be used as one. In Python, any object that has the right methods is automatically compatible, regardless of its class hierarchy. There is no need to inherit from a common base class or declare an interface explicitly.

Duck typing produces highly flexible, loosely coupled code. A function that calls `.read()` on its argument works equally well with a file object, a `StringIO` object, a network socket, or any custom class that provides a `read()` method. The function does not know or care about the type — it only cares about the behaviour.

The trade-off

Duck typing requires discipline. Because Python does not enforce interfaces, a caller may pass an object that is missing the expected method, and the failure happens at runtime rather than at design time. This is mitigated by clear documentation, type hints (Section 6.7), and abstract base classes (Chapter 7), but it remains a genuine consideration for library and API design.

Example 1 — Introduction

Duck typing in action: a function that works with any object providing a write() method, regardless of its type.

```
import io

class CSVWriter:
    """Writes rows to any file-like object with a write() method."""

    def __init__(self, destination):
        self._dest = destination    # duck typed: anything with write()

    def write_header(self, fields):
        self._dest.write(",".join(fields) + "\n")
```

```python
    def write_row(self, values):
        self._dest.write(",".join(str(v) for v in values) + "\n")


# Works with a real file
with open("/tmp/test_output.csv", "w") as f:
    writer = CSVWriter(f)
    writer.write_header(["id", "name", "grade"])
    writer.write_row([1001, "Alice Wong", 91.5])
    writer.write_row([1002, "Bob Smith",  72.0])

# Works with an in-memory StringIO — no change to CSVWriter
buffer = io.StringIO()
writer = CSVWriter(buffer)
writer.write_header(["product", "price", "qty"])
writer.write_row(["Laptop Stand", 49.00, 15])
writer.write_row(["USB-C Hub",    39.00, 22])

print(buffer.getvalue())

# Works with a custom logger — still no change to CSVWriter
class LogWriter:
    def write(self, text):
        print(f"[LOG] {text.strip()}")

log_writer = CSVWriter(LogWriter())
log_writer.write_header(["event", "timestamp"])
log_writer.write_row(["login", "2026-03-21 08:15"])
```

Output:

```
product,price,qty
Laptop Stand,49.0,15
USB-C Hub,39.0,22

[LOG] event,timestamp
[LOG] login,2026-03-21 08:15
```

Example 2 — Variation

A sort key demonstrating duck typing: sorted() works on any objects that implement __lt__, regardless of their class.

```
class Student:
    def __init__(self, name, gpa):
        self.name = name
        self.gpa  = gpa

    def __lt__(self, other):
        return self.gpa < other.gpa     # compare by GPA

    def __repr__(self):
        return f"Student({self.name}, {self.gpa})"


class Product:
    def __init__(self, name, price):
        self.name  = name
        self.price = price

    def __lt__(self, other):
        return self.price < other.price  # compare by price

    def __repr__(self):
        return f"Product({self.name}, ${self.price:.2f})"


students = [
    Student("Alice", 3.8), Student("Bob", 3.2),
    Student("Cara",  3.9), Student("Dan", 3.5),
]

products = [
    Product("Laptop Stand", 49.00), Product("Webcam",  69.00),
    Product("USB-C Hub",    39.00), Product("Keyboard",89.00),
]

# sorted() uses __lt__ — works for both types without modification
print(sorted(students))
```

```
print(sorted(products))


# min() and max() also use __lt__
print(f"Top student:   {max(students)}")
print(f"Cheapest item: {min(products)}")
```

Output:

```
[Student(Bob, 3.2), Student(Dan, 3.5), Student(Alice, 3.8), Student(Cara, 3.9)]
[Product(USB-C Hub, $39.00), Product(Laptop Stand, $49.00), Product(Webcam,
$69.00), Product(Keyboard, $89.00)]
Top student:   Student(Cara, 3.9)
Cheapest item: Product(USB-C Hub, $39.00)
```

Example 3 — Real-world application

A data pipeline that processes any data source providing read() and close() — file, network stream, or in-memory buffer all work without modification.

```
import io

class DataPipeline:
    """Processes records from any source with read() and close() methods.

    The source can be a file, a network stream, an in-memory buffer,
    or any custom object that provides the same interface.
    """

    def __init__(self, source, transformer=None):
        self._source      = source
        self._transformer = transformer or (lambda x: x)
        self._records     = []

    def process(self):
        try:
            raw = self._source.read()
            for line in raw.strip().splitlines():
                if line.strip():
                    self._records.append(self._transformer(line.strip()))
        finally:
            self._source.close()
        return self
```

```
    def filter(self, predicate):
        self._records = [r for r in self._records if predicate(r)]
        return self

    def results(self):
        return list(self._records)


# Source 1: in-memory StringIO (no file system needed)
csv_data = io.StringIO(
    "Alice Wong,91.5\n"
    "Bob Smith,42.0\n"
    "Cara Lee,78.5\n"
    "Dan Park,55.0\n"
)

def parse_student(line):
    name, grade = line.split(",")
    return {"name": name.strip(), "grade": float(grade)}

results = (
    DataPipeline(csv_data, parse_student)
    .process()
    .filter(lambda r: r["grade"] >= 50)
    .results()
)

print("Passing students:")
for r in results:
    print(f"  {r['name']:15s}  {r['grade']}")



# Source 2: a custom "network" source with the same interface
class MockNetworkSource:
    """Simulates a network stream — has read() and close()."""
    def __init__(self, data):
        self._data   = data
        self._closed = False
```

```
    def read(self):
        if self._closed:
            raise IOError("Stream already closed.")
        return self._data

    def close(self):
        self._closed = True
        print("  Network stream closed.")


network = MockNetworkSource("WARN: disk space low\nERROR: DB timeout\nINFO:
backup done")

errors = (
    DataPipeline(network)
    .process()
    .filter(lambda line: line.startswith("ERROR"))
    .results()
)

print("\nErrors from network stream:")
for e in errors:
    print(f"  {e}")
```

Output:

```
Passing students:
  Alice Wong       91.5
  Cara Lee         78.5
  Dan Park         55.0

  Network stream closed.

Errors from network stream:
  ERROR: DB timeout
```

`DataPipeline` never uses `isinstance()` or checks the type of its source. It calls `read()` and `close()` and trusts that the source provides them. This is the duck typing contract: the pipeline's documentation states "source must have read() and close()" and any object that satisfies that description is accepted.

6.3 Method Overriding as Polymorphism

Method overriding, covered mechanically in Chapter 5, is also the most explicit form of polymorphism. When a hierarchy of classes shares a common interface (a set of method signatures inherited from a base class), any code that works with the base class automatically works with every subclass. The behaviour varies per subclass, but the calling code is unaffected.

This is subtype polymorphism: a `SavingsAccount` can be used wherever a `BankAccount` is expected. A `Manager` can be used wherever an `Employee` is expected. Code that processes a list of `BankAccount` objects correctly processes a mixed list of `SavingsAccount` and `CheckingAccount` objects without any modification.

The power is in the abstraction: you write the processing logic once, targeting the base class interface. Every subclass added later is automatically supported. This is the open/closed principle again, expressed through a class hierarchy.

The template method pattern

A common polymorphism pattern is the template method: the base class defines the overall algorithm as a method, delegates variable steps to protected methods, and subclasses override only those variable steps. The base class's template method never changes; the subclasses provide the specific behaviour.

Example 1 — Introduction

A tax calculation system: the base TaxCalculator defines the calculation structure; subclasses supply jurisdiction-specific rates and rules.

```
class TaxCalculator:
    """Template method pattern for tax calculation.

    Subclasses implement _income_tax_rate(), _gst_rate(),
    and optionally _levy(). calculate() orchestrates the full
    calculation using those subclass-supplied values.
    """

    def _income_tax_rate(self, income): raise NotImplementedError
    def _gst_rate(self): raise NotImplementedError
    def _levy(self, income): return 0.0    # optional, default zero

    def calculate(self, gross_income, expenditure):
        income_tax = gross_income * self._income_tax_rate(gross_income)
        gst        = expenditure  * self._gst_rate()
        levy       = self._levy(gross_income)
        total_tax  = income_tax + gst + levy
        return {
            "gross_income":  gross_income,
            "income_tax":    round(income_tax, 2),
```

```
            "gst":          round(gst, 2),
            "levy":         round(levy, 2),
            "total_tax":    round(total_tax, 2),
            "net_income":   round(gross_income - income_tax - levy, 2),
        }


class AustralianTax(TaxCalculator):
    """Australian simplified tax rates (illustrative)."""

    def _income_tax_rate(self, income):
        if income <= 18_200:  return 0.0
        if income <= 45_000:  return 0.19
        if income <= 120_000: return 0.325
        return 0.37

    def _gst_rate(self): return 0.10

    def _levy(self, income):
        return income * 0.02 if income > 22_000 else 0.0


class UKTax(TaxCalculator):
    """UK simplified tax rates (illustrative)."""

    def _income_tax_rate(self, income):
        if income <= 12_570: return 0.0
        if income <= 50_270: return 0.20
        return 0.40

    def _gst_rate(self): return 0.20    # VAT


def print_summary(calculator, label, income, expenditure):
    result = calculator.calculate(income, expenditure)
    print(f"\n{label} (income=${income:,}, expenditure=${expenditure:,})")
    for key, val in result.items():
        print(f"  {key:15s}: ${val:,.2f}")
```

```
au = AustralianTax()
uk = UKTax()

print_summary(au, "Australia", 80_000, 25_000)
print_summary(uk, "UK",        80_000, 25_000)
```

Output:

```
Australia (income=$80,000, expenditure=$25,000)
  gross_income    : $80,000.00
  income_tax      : $26,000.00
  gst             : $2,500.00
  levy            : $1,600.00
  total_tax       : $30,100.00
  net_income      : $52,400.00

UK (income=$80,000, expenditure=$25,000)
  gross_income    : $80,000.00
  income_tax      : $15,452.00
  gst             : $5,000.00
  levy            : $0.00
  total_tax       : $20,452.00
  net_income      : $64,548.00
```

Example 2 — Variation

A report generator: the base class defines how a report is formatted; subclasses control the output format (text, CSV, HTML).

```
class ReportGenerator:
    def __init__(self, title, rows):
        self.title = title
        self.rows  = rows    # list of dicts

    def _format_header(self, fields):
        raise NotImplementedError

    def _format_row(self, row, fields):
        raise NotImplementedError
```

```
    def _format_footer(self, row_count):
        return ""

    def generate(self):
        if not self.rows: return ""
        fields = list(self.rows[0].keys())
        lines  = [self._format_header(fields)]
        for row in self.rows:
            lines.append(self._format_row(row, fields))
        footer = self._format_footer(len(self.rows))
        if footer: lines.append(footer)
        return "\n".join(lines)


class TextReport(ReportGenerator):
    def _format_header(self, fields):
        header = "  ".join(f"{f:15s}" for f in fields)
        return f"{self.title}\n{"-" * len(header)}\n{header}"

    def _format_row(self, row, fields):
        return "  ".join(f"{str(row[f]):15s}" for f in fields)

    def _format_footer(self, count):
        return f"({count} records)"


class CSVReport(ReportGenerator):
    def _format_header(self, fields):
        return ",".join(fields)

    def _format_row(self, row, fields):
        return ",".join(str(row[f]) for f in fields)


class HTMLReport(ReportGenerator):
    def _format_header(self, fields):
        cells = "".join(f"<th>{f}</th>" for f in fields)
        return f"<table>\n<tr>{cells}</tr>"
```

```
    def _format_row(self, row, fields):
        cells = "".join(f"<td>{row[f]}</td>" for f in fields)
        return f"<tr>{cells}</tr>"

    def _format_footer(self, count):
        return "</table>"


data = [
    {"name": "Alice Wong",  "grade": 91.5, "status": "Pass"},
    {"name": "Bob Smith",   "grade": 42.0, "status": "Fail"},
    {"name": "Cara Lee",    "grade": 78.5, "status": "Pass"},
]

for generator in [TextReport("Results", data),
                  CSVReport("Results", data)]:
    print(generator.generate())
    print()
```

Output:

```
Results
------------------------------------------------
name             grade            status
Alice Wong       91.5             Pass
Bob Smith        42.0             Fail
Cara Lee         78.5             Pass
(3 records)

name,grade,status
Alice Wong,91.5,Pass
Bob Smith,42.0,Fail
Cara Lee,78.5,Pass
```

Example 3 — Real-world application

A game enemy system using overriding for polymorphic behaviour: the game loop processes all enemy types uniformly.

```
import random


class Enemy:
```

```
    def __init__(self, name, hp, speed):
        self.name  = name
        self.hp    = hp
        self.speed = speed

    def take_damage(self, amount):
        self.hp = max(0, self.hp - amount)

    def is_alive(self): return self.hp > 0

    def attack(self, player_hp):
        raise NotImplementedError

    def update(self):
        raise NotImplementedError

    def status(self):
        bar = "\u2588" * (self.hp // 10) + "\u2591" * (10 - self.hp // 10)
        return f"{self.name:12s} [{bar}] {self.hp} HP"


class Goblin(Enemy):
    def __init__(self, name):
        super().__init__(name, hp=60, speed=3)
        self.swarm_bonus = 2

    def attack(self, player_hp):
        dmg = random.randint(5, 12)
        print(f"  {self.name} scratches! -{dmg} HP")
        return player_hp - dmg

    def update(self):
        self.swarm_bonus = min(5, self.swarm_bonus + 1)


class Troll(Enemy):
    def __init__(self, name):
        super().__init__(name, hp=200, speed=1)
        self.rage = False
```

```
    def take_damage(self, amount):
        super().take_damage(amount)
        if self.hp < 100:
            self.rage = True

    def attack(self, player_hp):
        dmg = random.randint(25, 45) * (2 if self.rage else 1)
        mode = "RAGES and smashes" if self.rage else "smashes"
        print(f"  {self.name} {mode}! -{dmg} HP")
        return player_hp - dmg

    def update(self):
        if self.is_alive() and self.hp < 200:
            regen = 5
            self.hp = min(200, self.hp + regen)


class Archer(Enemy):
    def __init__(self, name):
        super().__init__(name, hp=80, speed=4)
        self._arrows = 3

    def attack(self, player_hp):
        if self._arrows > 0:
            self._arrows -= 1
            dmg = random.randint(15, 25)
            print(f"  {self.name} fires an arrow! -{dmg} HP ({self._arrows}
left)")
            return player_hp - dmg
        dmg = random.randint(3, 8)
        print(f"  {self.name} uses dagger! -{dmg} HP")
        return player_hp - dmg

    def update(self): pass


# Game loop — processes all enemy types polymorphically
enemies = [Goblin("Grak"), Troll("Grum"), Archer("Sylva")]
```

```
player_hp = 200

print("--- Round 1 ---")
for enemy in enemies:
    if enemy.is_alive():
        player_hp = enemy.attack(player_hp)
        enemy.take_damage(random.randint(20, 40))
        enemy.update()

print(f"\nPlayer HP: {player_hp}")
print("Enemy status:")
for e in enemies:
    print(f"  {e.status()}")
```

Output:

```
--- Round 1 ---
  Grak scratches! -9 HP
  Grum smashes! -33 HP
  Sylva fires an arrow! -19 HP (2 left)

Player HP: 139
Enemy status:
  Grak         [████░░░░░░] 40 HP
  Grum         [███████░░░] 170 HP
  Sylva        [██████░░░░] 60 HP
```

6.4 Operator Overloading

Operator overloading is a form of polymorphism that allows objects to respond to Python's built-in operators: `+`, `-`, `*`, `/`, `==`, `<`, `>`, `len()`, `str()`, and many more. Each operator corresponds to a dunder method. When Python encounters `a + b`, it calls `a.__add__(b)`. When it encounters `len(x)`, it calls `x.__len__()`. When it calls `str(x)`, it calls `x.__str__()`.

Overloading these operators makes custom objects behave naturally with Python's syntax. A `Vector` that supports `+` can be added with `v1 + v2` rather than `v1.add(v2)`. A `Money` object that supports `*` can be multiplied by a scalar. A `Duration` that supports `>` can be compared in a sorted() call. This is not just cosmetic convenience — it means custom objects integrate seamlessly with Python's built-in functions and standard library.

Key dunder methods for operators

- Arithmetic: `__add__`, `__sub__`, `__mul__`, `__truediv__`, `__floordiv__`, `__mod__`, `__pow__`
- Comparison: `__eq__`, `__ne__`, `__lt__`, `__le__`, `__gt__`, `__ge__`

- Unary: `__neg__`, `__pos__`, `__abs__`
- Representation: `__str__`, `__repr__`, `__format__`
- Container: `__len__`, `__getitem__`, `__setitem__`, `__contains__`, `__iter__`
- Reflected arithmetic: `__radd__`, `__rsub__`, etc. — called when the left operand does not support the operation

Example 1 — Introduction

A Vector2D class with arithmetic and comparison operators, making it behave naturally with Python's built-in syntax.

```
import math

class Vector2D:
    def __init__(self, x, y):
        self.x = x
        self.y = y

    def __add__(self, other):
        return Vector2D(self.x + other.x, self.y + other.y)

    def __sub__(self, other):
        return Vector2D(self.x - other.x, self.y - other.y)

    def __mul__(self, scalar):
        return Vector2D(self.x * scalar, self.y * scalar)

    def __rmul__(self, scalar):
        return self.__mul__(scalar)    # handles: 3 * v

    def __neg__(self):
        return Vector2D(-self.x, -self.y)

    def __abs__(self):
        return math.sqrt(self.x**2 + self.y**2)

    def __eq__(self, other):
        return self.x == other.x and self.y == other.y

    def __repr__(self):
        return f"Vector2D({self.x}, {self.y})"
```

```
    def dot(self, other):
        return self.x * other.x + self.y * other.y


v1 = Vector2D(3, 4)
v2 = Vector2D(1, 2)

print(v1 + v2)          # __add__
print(v1 - v2)          # __sub__
print(v1 * 3)           # __mul__
print(2 * v1)           # __rmul__
print(-v1)              # __neg__
print(abs(v1))          # __abs__  (magnitude)
print(v1 == Vector2D(3, 4))  # __eq__
print(v1.dot(v2))
```

Output:

```
Vector2D(4, 6)
Vector2D(2, 2)
Vector2D(9, 12)
Vector2D(6, 8)
Vector2D(-3, -4)
5.0
True
11
```

Example 2 — Variation

A Money class with currency-aware arithmetic and comparison, raising TypeError for incompatible currencies.

```
from decimal import Decimal

class Money:
    def __init__(self, amount, currency="AUD"):
        self.amount   = Decimal(str(amount)).quantize(Decimal("0.01"))
        self.currency = currency.upper()

    def _check_currency(self, other):
        if self.currency != other.currency:
```

```
            raise TypeError(
                f"Cannot operate on {self.currency} and {other.currency}."
            )

    def __add__(self, other):
        self._check_currency(other)
        return Money(self.amount + other.amount, self.currency)

    def __sub__(self, other):
        self._check_currency(other)
        return Money(self.amount - other.amount, self.currency)

    def __mul__(self, factor):
        return Money(self.amount * Decimal(str(factor)), self.currency)

    def __rmul__(self, factor):
        return self.__mul__(factor)

    def __eq__(self, other):
        return self.currency == other.currency and self.amount == other.amount

    def __lt__(self, other):
        self._check_currency(other)
        return self.amount < other.amount

    def __repr__(self):
        return f"{self.currency} {self.amount}"


price    = Money(49.95, "AUD")
shipping = Money(9.50,  "AUD")
discount = Money(5.00,  "AUD")

total = price + shipping - discount
print(f"Total:     {total}")
print(f"GST (10%): {total * 0.10}")

prices = [Money(89, "AUD"), Money(39, "AUD"), Money(69, "AUD")]
print(f"Cheapest: {min(prices)}")
```

```python
print(f"Most expensive: {max(prices)}")

try:
    Money(10, "AUD") + Money(10, "USD")
except TypeError as e:
    print(f"Error: {e}")
```

Output:

```
Total:    AUD 54.45
GST (10%): AUD 5.45
Cheapest: AUD 39.00
Most expensive: AUD 89.00
Error: Cannot operate on AUD and USD.
```

Example 3 — Real-world application

A Matrix class with arithmetic operators and indexing, making it work naturally with Python's operator syntax.

```python
class Matrix:
    """Simple 2D matrix with operator support."""

    def __init__(self, data):
        self._data = [list(row) for row in data]
        self.rows  = len(self._data)
        self.cols  = len(self._data[0]) if self._data else 0

    def __getitem__(self, index):
        row, col = index
        return self._data[row][col]

    def __setitem__(self, index, value):
        row, col = index
        self._data[row][col] = value

    def __add__(self, other):
        if self.rows != other.rows or self.cols != other.cols:
            raise ValueError("Matrix dimensions must match for addition.")
        return Matrix([
            [self._data[r][c] + other._data[r][c]
             for c in range(self.cols)]
            for r in range(self.rows)
```

```
        ])

    def __mul__(self, other):
        if isinstance(other, (int, float)):
            return Matrix([[v * other for v in row] for row in self._data])
        if self.cols != other.rows:
            raise ValueError("Incompatible dimensions for multiplication.")
        result = [[0] * other.cols for _ in range(self.rows)]
        for r in range(self.rows):
            for c in range(other.cols):
                result[r][c] = sum(
                    self._data[r][k] * other._data[k][c]
                    for k in range(self.cols)
                )
        return Matrix(result)

    def __eq__(self, other):
        return self._data == other._data

    def __repr__(self):
        rows = ["  [" + "  ".join(f"{v:5.1f}" for v in row) + "]"
                for row in self._data]
        return "Matrix(\n" + "\n".join(rows) + "\n)"


a = Matrix([[1, 2], [3, 4]])
b = Matrix([[5, 6], [7, 8]])

print("A + B =")
print(a + b)

print("A * 2 =")
print(a * 2)

print("A * B =")
print(a * b)

print(f"a[0,1] = {a[0,1]}")
a[1,0] = 99
```

```
print(f"After a[1,0]=99: a[1,0] = {a[1,0]}")
```

Output:

```
A + B =
Matrix(
  [  6.0    8.0]
  [ 10.0   12.0]
)
A * 2 =
Matrix(
  [  2.0    4.0]
  [  6.0    8.0]
)
A * B =
Matrix(
  [ 19.0   22.0]
  [ 43.0   50.0]
)
a[0,1] = 2
After a[1,0]=99: a[1,0] = 99
```

6.5 Polymorphism with Collections of Mixed Objects

One of the most practical applications of polymorphism is processing a mixed collection of related objects through a uniform interface. A list containing `SavingsAccount`, `CheckingAccount`, and `TermDeposit` objects can all have their `balance` queried and their `statement()` called without the processing code knowing or caring which type each element is.

This pattern appears throughout real software: a drawing application processes a list of mixed Shape objects; a web framework dispatches requests to a list of mixed view handlers; a game engine updates a list of mixed entity types. In every case, the code operating on the collection targets the shared interface, not the specific types.

Python's polymorphism here is particularly clean because even unrelated types can participate, as long as they share the method names being called. A list containing a Django model, a dataclass, and a custom class can all be serialised by the same function, provided each has a `to_dict()` method.

Example 1 — Introduction

A payroll system processing a mixed list of Employee subclasses through the uniform pay() interface.

```
class Employee:
    def __init__(self, emp_id, name):
        self.emp_id = emp_id
        self.name   = name
```

```
    def pay(self): raise NotImplementedError

    def pay_slip(self):
        amount = self.pay()
        print(f"  {self.emp_id:6s}  {self.name:20s}  ${amount:9,.2f}
[{self.__class__.__name__}]")


class SalariedEmployee(Employee):
    def __init__(self, emp_id, name, monthly_salary):
        super().__init__(emp_id, name)
        self.monthly_salary = monthly_salary

    def pay(self): return self.monthly_salary


class HourlyEmployee(Employee):
    def __init__(self, emp_id, name, hourly_rate, hours_worked):
        super().__init__(emp_id, name)
        self.hourly_rate  = hourly_rate
        self.hours_worked = hours_worked

    def pay(self):
        regular  = min(self.hours_worked, 40) * self.hourly_rate
        overtime = max(0, self.hours_worked - 40) * self.hourly_rate * 1.5
        return regular + overtime


class Contractor(Employee):
    def __init__(self, emp_id, name, day_rate, days_worked):
        super().__init__(emp_id, name)
        self.day_rate    = day_rate
        self.days_worked = days_worked

    def pay(self): return self.day_rate * self.days_worked


def run_payroll(staff):
```

```
    print(f"{"ID":6s}  {"Name":20s}  {"Amount":>12s}  Type")
    print("-" * 55)
    for employee in staff:
        employee.pay_slip()    # polymorphic call
    total = sum(e.pay() for e in staff)
    print("-" * 55)
    print(f"  {"Total payroll":26s}  ${total:9,.2f}")


payroll = [
    SalariedEmployee("E001", "Alice Wong",        9500.00),
    HourlyEmployee  ("E002", "Bob Smith",  55.00, 45),
    SalariedEmployee("E003", "Cara Lee",          12000.00),
    Contractor      ("E004", "Dan Park",   800.00, 12),
    HourlyEmployee  ("E005", "Eva Chen",   48.00, 38),
]

run_payroll(payroll)
```

Output:

```
ID      Name                    Amount  Type
-------------------------------------------------------
  E001    Alice Wong              $9,500.00  [SalariedEmployee]
  E002    Bob Smith               $2,612.50  [HourlyEmployee]
  E003    Cara Lee               $12,000.00  [SalariedEmployee]
  E004    Dan Park                $9,600.00  [Contractor]
  E005    Eva Chen                $1,824.00  [HourlyEmployee]
-------------------------------------------------------
    Total payroll              $35,536.50
```

Example 2 — Variation

An event system that dispatches events to a heterogeneous list of handlers, each responding according to its own logic.

```
class Event:
    def __init__(self, event_type, data):
        self.event_type = event_type
        self.data       = data

    def __repr__(self):
        return f"Event({self.event_type!r}, {self.data})"
```

```
class EmailHandler:
    def handle(self, event):
        if event.event_type in ("purchase", "registration"):
            print(f"  [Email] Sending confirmation to {event.data.get('email',
'N/A')}")


class LogHandler:
    def handle(self, event):
        print(f"  [Log]   {event.event_type}: {event.data}")


class AnalyticsHandler:
    def __init__(self):
        self._counts = {}

    def handle(self, event):
        self._counts[event.event_type] = \
            self._counts.get(event.event_type, 0) + 1

    def report(self):
        print("  [Analytics] Event counts:", dict(self._counts))


class FraudDetector:
    def handle(self, event):
        if event.event_type == "purchase":
            amount = event.data.get("amount", 0)
            if amount > 5000:
                print(f"  [Fraud] HIGH-VALUE ALERT: ${amount} purchase!")


def dispatch(events, handlers):
    for event in events:
        print(f"\nDispatching: {event}")
        for handler in handlers:
            handler.handle(event)   # polymorphic call
```

```
analytics = AnalyticsHandler()
handlers  = [LogHandler(), EmailHandler(), analytics, FraudDetector()]

events = [
    Event("registration", {"email": "alice@example.com", "name": "Alice"}),
    Event("purchase",     {"email": "alice@example.com", "amount": 149.00}),
    Event("purchase",     {"email": "bob@example.com",  "amount": 8500.00}),
    Event("page_view",    {"page": "/products"}),
]

dispatch(events, handlers)
print()
analytics.report()
```

Output:

```
Dispatching: Event('registration', {'email': 'alice@example.com', 'name':
'Alice'})
  [Log]   registration: {'email': 'alice@example.com', 'name': 'Alice'}
  [Email] Sending confirmation to alice@example.com

Dispatching: Event('purchase', {'email': 'alice@example.com', 'amount': 149.0})
  [Log]   purchase: {'email': 'alice@example.com', 'amount': 149.0}
  [Email] Sending confirmation to alice@example.com

Dispatching: Event('purchase', {'email': 'bob@example.com', 'amount': 8500.0})
  [Log]   purchase: {'email': 'bob@example.com', 'amount': 8500.0}
  [Email] Sending confirmation to bob@example.com
  [Fraud] HIGH-VALUE ALERT: $8500.0 purchase!

Dispatching: Event('page_view', {'page': '/products'})
  [Log]   page_view: {'page': '/products'}

  [Analytics] Event counts: {'registration': 1, 'purchase': 2, 'page_view': 1}
```

Example 3 — Real-world application

A data export system that serialises a heterogeneous list of domain objects to multiple output formats.

```
import json
```

```
class Exportable:
    """Mixin: any class with to_dict() can be exported."""
    def to_dict(self): raise NotImplementedError


class Customer(Exportable):
    def __init__(self, customer_id, name, email, tier):
        self.customer_id = customer_id
        self.name        = name
        self.email       = email
        self.tier        = tier

    def to_dict(self):
        return {"type": "customer", "id": self.customer_id,
                "name": self.name, "email": self.email, "tier": self.tier}


class Order(Exportable):
    def __init__(self, order_id, customer_id, total, status):
        self.order_id    = order_id
        self.customer_id = customer_id
        self.total       = total
        self.status      = status

    def to_dict(self):
        return {"type": "order", "id": self.order_id,
                "customer": self.customer_id,
                "total": self.total, "status": self.status}



class Exporter:
    def __init__(self, objects):
        self._objects = objects

    def to_json(self):
        return json.dumps([o.to_dict() for o in self._objects], indent=2)

    def to_csv(self):
```

```
        if not self._objects: return ""
        dicts  = [o.to_dict() for o in self._objects]
        fields = list(dicts[0].keys())
        rows   = [",".join(fields)]
        for d in dicts:
            rows.append(",".join(str(d.get(f, "")) for f in fields))
        return "\n".join(rows)

    def summary(self):
        from collections import Counter
        types = Counter(o.to_dict()["type"] for o in self._objects)
        print("Export summary:", dict(types))


records = [
    Customer("C001", "Alice Wong",  "alice@example.com", "gold"),
    Order   ("O001", "C001",        249.00, "shipped"),
    Customer("C002", "Bob Smith",   "bob@example.com",   "silver"),
    Order   ("O002", "C002",        89.50,  "pending"),
    Order   ("O003", "C001",        1299.00,"processing"),
]

exporter = Exporter(records)
exporter.summary()

print("\nCSV:")
print(exporter.to_csv()[:300])
```

Output:

```
Export summary: {'customer': 2, 'order': 3}

CSV:
type,id,name,email,tier,customer,total,status
customer,C001,Alice Wong,alice@example.com,gold,,,
order,O001,,,,,249.0,shipped
customer,C002,Bob Smith,bob@example.com,silver,,,
order,O002,,,,,89.5,pending
order,O003,,,,,1299.0,processing
```

6.6 The isinstance() Check — When It Helps and When It Hinders

`isinstance()` is a powerful tool but also a temptation. The temptation is to use it as a substitute for polymorphism: instead of calling a method on an object and trusting it to respond correctly, you check the type first and branch on it. This approach re-centralises the type-specific logic in the calling code, which is exactly what polymorphism is designed to avoid.

A function that checks `isinstance(obj, Dog)` and then `isinstance(obj, Cat)` to decide what to do is a signal that the type hierarchy is not being used polymorphically. Every time a new subclass is added, this function must be updated. Every check that should not be necessary becomes a maintenance burden.

There are genuine, legitimate uses for `isinstance()`: validating function arguments before processing them, implementing operators that need to know whether the other operand is a compatible type, dispatching to completely different code paths based on type in places where the class hierarchy cannot be modified, and safety checks in library APIs. The key distinction is intent: using `isinstance()` to guard against wrong input is different from using it to replicate behaviour that belongs in the class.

The anti-pattern to avoid

The clearest signal of misuse is isinstance() inside a loop or in a function that processes a collection of objects. If you find yourself writing `if isinstance(obj, TypeA): ... elif isinstance(obj, TypeB): ...`, ask whether that logic belongs as a method on TypeA and TypeB instead.

Example 1 — Introduction

Anti-pattern vs correct pattern: isinstance() used to replicate polymorphism, then refactored to use it properly.

```
# Anti-pattern: isinstance() used as a substitute for polymorphism
class Cat:
    def __init__(self, name): self.name = name

class Dog:
    def __init__(self, name): self.name = name

class Bird:
    def __init__(self, name): self.name = name



def make_sound_bad(animal):
    """Every new animal type requires modifying this function."""
    if isinstance(animal, Dog):
        return f"{animal.name} says: Woof!"
    elif isinstance(animal, Cat):
        return f"{animal.name} says: Meow!"
    elif isinstance(animal, Bird):
        return f"{animal.name} says: Tweet!"
```

```python
    else:
        return f"{animal.name} makes a sound."


# Correct pattern: behaviour belongs in the class
class CatP:
    def __init__(self, name): self.name = name
    def speak(self): return f"{self.name} says: Meow!"

class DogP:
    def __init__(self, name): self.name = name
    def speak(self): return f"{self.name} says: Woof!"

class BirdP:
    def __init__(self, name): self.name = name
    def speak(self): return f"{self.name} says: Tweet!"

class SnakeP:
    def __init__(self, name): self.name = name
    def speak(self): return f"{self.name} says: Hiss!"


def make_sound_good(animal):
    """Adding Snake required no change to this function."""
    return animal.speak()


bad_animals = [Dog("Rex"), Cat("Whiskers"), Bird("Tweety")]
for a in bad_animals:
    print(make_sound_bad(a))

print()

good_animals = [DogP("Rex"), CatP("Whiskers"), BirdP("Tweety"), SnakeP("Sly")]
for a in good_animals:
    print(make_sound_good(a))
```

Output:

```
Rex says: Woof!
```

```
Whiskers says: Meow!
Tweety says: Tweet!

Rex says: Woof!
Whiskers says: Meow!
Tweety says: Tweet!
Sly says: Hiss!
```

Example 2 — Variation

Legitimate uses of isinstance(): argument validation, operator safety, and type-specific formatting.

```
class Vector2D:
    def __init__(self, x, y):
        self.x = x
        self.y = y

    def __add__(self, other):
        # Legitimate: guard before operating on other
        if not isinstance(other, Vector2D):
            return NotImplemented    # signal: not handled here
        return Vector2D(self.x + other.x, self.y + other.y)

    def __mul__(self, scalar):
        # Legitimate: different behaviour for scalar vs vector
        if isinstance(scalar, (int, float)):
            return Vector2D(self.x * scalar, self.y * scalar)
        if isinstance(scalar, Vector2D):
            return self.x * scalar.x + self.y * scalar.y  # dot product
        return NotImplemented

    def __repr__(self):
        return f"Vector2D({self.x}, {self.y})"


def format_value(value):
    """Legitimate: format different types appropriately."""
    if isinstance(value, float):
        return f"{value:.4f}"
    if isinstance(value, int):
        return f"{value:,}"
```

```
    if isinstance(value, (list, tuple)):
        return f"[{len(value)} items]"
    return str(value)


v1 = Vector2D(3, 4)
v2 = Vector2D(1, 2)


print(v1 + v2)          # Vector + Vector
print(v1 * 2)           # Vector * scalar
print(v1 * v2)          # Vector * Vector (dot product)

result = v1 + "hello"   # returns NotImplemented, Python handles gracefully
print(result)


print(format_value(3.14159))
print(format_value(1_000_000))
print(format_value([1, 2, 3, 4, 5]))
print(format_value("hello"))
```

Output:

```
Vector2D(4, 6)
Vector2D(6, 8)
11
NotImplemented
3.1416
1,000,000
[5 items]
hello
```

> **Note:** Returning NotImplemented (not raising NotImplementedError) from an arithmetic dunder method tells Python to try the reflected operation on the other operand. This is the correct way to signal "I don't know how to handle this combination" without raising an error immediately.

Example 3 — Real-world application

A document processing library that uses isinstance() for legitimate input validation, while still processing the document polymorphically.

```
class Document:
    def __init__(self, content):
        self.content = content
```

```
    def word_count(self):
        return len(self.content.split())

    def summary(self, max_words=20):
        words = self.content.split()[:max_words]
        return " ".join(words) + ("..." if len(self.content.split()) >
max_words else "")


class EmailDocument(Document):
    def __init__(self, content, sender, recipient):
        super().__init__(content)
        self.sender    = sender
        self.recipient = recipient

    def summary(self, max_words=20):
        base = super().summary(max_words)
        return f"From {self.sender} to {self.recipient}: {base}"


class ReportDocument(Document):
    def __init__(self, content, report_id, department):
        super().__init__(content)
        self.report_id  = report_id
        self.department = department

    def summary(self, max_words=20):
        base = super().summary(max_words)
        return f"[{self.report_id}] ({self.department}): {base}"


def process_documents(documents, max_words=15):
    """Validates input type, then processes polymorphically.

    isinstance() used only for input validation — not for
    type-specific branching inside the loop.
    """
    if not isinstance(documents, (list, tuple)):
```

```python
        raise TypeError("documents must be a list or tuple.")
    if not all(isinstance(d, Document) for d in documents):
        raise TypeError("All items must be Document instances.")

    print(f"Processing {len(documents)} document(s):\n")
    for doc in documents:
        print(f"  Words: {doc.word_count():4d}  |  {doc.summary(max_words)}")


docs = [
    EmailDocument("Please find attached the quarterly review. All figures are
as discussed.",
                  "ceo@company.com", "board@company.com"),
    ReportDocument("Revenue increased by 12 percent across all segments.
Operating costs were reduced.",
                   "RPT-2026-Q1", "Finance"),
    Document("Python 3.12 introduces several performance improvements and new
syntax features."),
]

process_documents(docs)

try:
    process_documents("not a list")
except TypeError as e:
    print(f"\nValidation error: {e}")
```

Output:

```
Processing 3 document(s):


  Words:   12  |  From ceo@company.com to board@company.com: Please find
attached the quarterly review. All figures...
  Words:   14  |  [RPT-2026-Q1] (Finance): Revenue increased by 12 percent
across all segments. Operating...
  Words:   13  |  Python 3.12 introduces several performance improvements and
new syntax...


Validation error: documents must be a list or tuple.
```

6.7 Protocols and Structural Subtyping

Duck typing works at runtime: Python calls the method and raises `AttributeError` if it does not exist. But Python's type hint system provides a way to express duck typing formally at the design level, without requiring a class hierarchy: the `Protocol` class from the `typing` module.

A `Protocol` defines a set of methods and attributes that an object must have. Any class that implements those methods satisfies the protocol — without inheriting from it, registering with it, or declaring conformance in any way. Static analysis tools (mypy, Pyright) and IDEs use protocols to catch type mismatches at development time, before code runs.

This is called structural subtyping: compatibility is determined by structure (what methods exist) rather than by nominal type (what the class hierarchy says). It is the formal, tooling-supported expression of duck typing. Python's `typing.Protocol` was introduced in Python 3.8 and is now the standard way to define informal interfaces that tools can check.

Runtime checkable protocols

Adding `@runtime_checkable` to a Protocol allows `isinstance()` to check whether an object conforms to the protocol at runtime. This is the bridge between structural typing and the `isinstance()` checks sometimes needed for argument validation.

Example 1 — Introduction

Defining a Protocol: any class with the required methods satisfies it, with no inheritance required.

```
from typing import Protocol


class Drawable(Protocol):
    """Protocol: anything with draw() and area() is Drawable."""
    def draw(self) -> None: ...
    def area(self) -> float: ...



import math


class Circle:
    """Satisfies Drawable — has draw() and area(). No inheritance needed."""
    def __init__(self, radius): self.radius = radius
    def draw(self): print(f"  Drawing circle r={self.radius}")
    def area(self): return math.pi * self.radius ** 2



class Rectangle:
    """Also satisfies Drawable."""
    def __init__(self, w, h): self.w, self.h = w, h
    def draw(self): print(f"  Drawing rect {self.w}x{self.h}")
```

```
    def area(self): return self.w * self.h


class TextLabel:
    """Also satisfies Drawable — a completely different type."""
    def __init__(self, text): self.text = text
    def draw(self): print(f"  Drawing label: {self.text!r}")
    def area(self): return 0.0


def render_all(shapes: list) -> None:
    """Accepts any list of Drawable objects."""
    total = 0.0
    for shape in shapes:
        shape.draw()          # duck typing: works for any Drawable
        total += shape.area()
    print(f"  Total area: {total:.2f}")


items = [Circle(5), Rectangle(4, 3), TextLabel("Hello"), Circle(2)]
render_all(items)
```

Output:

```
  Drawing circle r=5
  Drawing rect 4x3
  Drawing label: 'Hello'
  Drawing circle r=2
  Total area: 103.27
```

Example 2 — Variation

A runtime-checkable protocol combined with isinstance() for input validation, without requiring inheritance.

```
from typing import Protocol, runtime_checkable

@runtime_checkable
class Serialisable(Protocol):
    """Protocol: any object with to_dict() and from_dict() is Serialisable.

    @runtime_checkable means isinstance() can check conformance.
```

```
    """
    def to_dict(self) -> dict: ...

    @classmethod
    def from_dict(cls, data: dict): ...


class User:
    def __init__(self, user_id, name):
        self.user_id = user_id
        self.name    = name

    def to_dict(self):
        return {"user_id": self.user_id, "name": self.name}

    @classmethod
    def from_dict(cls, data):
        return cls(data["user_id"], data["name"])


class Product:
    def __init__(self, sku, price):
        self.sku   = sku
        self.price = price

    def to_dict(self):
        return {"sku": self.sku, "price": self.price}

    @classmethod
    def from_dict(cls, data):
        return cls(data["sku"], data["price"])


def save_objects(objects, filename):
    """Validates and saves any list of Serialisable objects."""
    import json
    if not all(isinstance(o, Serialisable) for o in objects):
        raise TypeError("All objects must be Serialisable.")
    data = [o.to_dict() for o in objects]
```

```python
    print(f"Saving {len(data)} objects to {filename!r}:")
    for record in data:
        print(f"  {record}")


objects = [
    User("U001", "Alice Wong"),
    Product("P001", 49.95),
    User("U002", "Bob Smith"),
]

save_objects(objects, "data.json")

print()
print(f"User is Serialisable:    {isinstance(User('x','y'), Serialisable)}")
print(f"Product is Serialisable: {isinstance(Product('x', 1), Serialisable)}")
print(f"int is Serialisable:     {isinstance(42, Serialisable)}")
```

Output:

```
Saving 3 objects to 'data.json':
  {'user_id': 'U001', 'name': 'Alice Wong'}
  {'sku': 'P001', 'price': 49.95}
  {'user_id': 'U002', 'name': 'Bob Smith'}

User is Serialisable:    True
Product is Serialisable: True
int is Serialisable:     False
```

Example 3 — Real-world application

A plugin architecture using Protocol to define the interface any plugin must satisfy, regardless of how it is implemented.

```python
from typing import Protocol, runtime_checkable
from datetime import datetime

@runtime_checkable
class DataPlugin(Protocol):
    """Any class with these methods is a valid DataPlugin.

    No inheritance from DataPlugin is required.
```

```
    """
    name: str

    def fetch(self, query: str) -> list: ...
    def transform(self, records: list) -> list: ...


class SQLPlugin:
    """Satisfies DataPlugin: has name, fetch(), and transform()."""
    name = "SQLPlugin"

    def fetch(self, query):
        print(f"  [SQL] Executing: {query}")
        return [{"id": 1, "value": 100}, {"id": 2, "value": 200}]

    def transform(self, records):
        return [{"id": r["id"], "value_doubled": r["value"] * 2}
                for r in records]


class APIPlugin:
    """Satisfies DataPlugin: different implementation, same interface."""
    name = "APIPlugin"

    def fetch(self, query):
        print(f"  [API] GET /data?q={query}")
        return [{"item": "alpha", "score": 0.95},
                {"item": "beta",  "score": 0.72}]

    def transform(self, records):
        return [r for r in records if r["score"] > 0.8]


class Pipeline:
    def __init__(self, plugin):
        if not isinstance(plugin, DataPlugin):
            raise TypeError(f"{plugin!r} does not satisfy DataPlugin
protocol.")
        self._plugin = plugin
```

```
    def run(self, query):
        print(f"\nRunning pipeline via {self._plugin.name}:")
        raw       = self._plugin.fetch(query)
        processed = self._plugin.transform(raw)
        print(f"  Fetched: {len(raw)}, After transform: {len(processed)}")
        for record in processed:
            print(f"    {record}")


for plugin in [SQLPlugin(), APIPlugin()]:
    Pipeline(plugin).run("active_users")

try:
    Pipeline("not a plugin")
except TypeError as e:
    print(f"\nError: {e}")
```

Output:

```
Running pipeline via SQLPlugin:
  [SQL] Executing: active_users
  Fetched: 2, After transform: 2
    {'id': 1, 'value_doubled': 200}
    {'id': 2, 'value_doubled': 400}


Running pipeline via APIPlugin:
  [API] GET /data?q=active_users
  Fetched: 2, After transform: 1
    {'item': 'alpha', 'score': 0.95}

Error: 'not a plugin' does not satisfy DataPlugin protocol.
```

Protocols provide the best of both worlds: the flexibility of duck typing (no inheritance required), with the tooling support of explicit interfaces (IDEs and mypy can check conformance at edit time). They are the modern, idiomatic way to express "this function accepts any object that provides these methods".

Chapter 6 Summary

- Polymorphism allows different objects to respond to the same method call in ways appropriate to their own type. Python achieves this through runtime attribute dispatch: the method that executes is determined by the actual type of the object at call time, not by the variable holding it.
- Duck typing is Python's informal approach to polymorphism: any object with the required methods is compatible, regardless of its class hierarchy. A function that calls .write() works with files, StringIO objects, network sockets, and custom classes, as long as they all provide write().
- Method overriding (Chapter 5) is the explicit form of polymorphism: subclasses override a shared method, and a loop over mixed objects calls the correct subclass version automatically. The template method pattern uses this to define a fixed algorithm with variable steps supplied by subclasses.
- Operator overloading via dunder methods makes custom objects behave naturally with Python's built-in operators. __add__, __mul__, __lt__, __len__, __getitem__, and others allow custom types to integrate with sorted(), min(), max(), len(), and the for-loop without any special cases in the caller.
- Polymorphism with collections of mixed objects is one of the most common and powerful patterns: a list of mixed Employee subclasses all processed through pay(), a list of mixed handlers all called through handle(), a list of mixed shapes all drawn through draw(). The processing function never branches on type.
- isinstance() is legitimate for argument validation, operator safety checks (returning NotImplemented for incompatible types), and input guards in library APIs. It is an anti-pattern when used inside a loop to replicate behaviour that should be in the class itself. If you write if isinstance(obj, TypeA): ... elif isinstance(obj, TypeB): ..., ask whether those branches belong as methods on TypeA and TypeB.
- typing.Protocol defines a structural interface: any class with the required methods satisfies the protocol, without inheriting from it. This is the formal, tooling-supported version of duck typing. @runtime_checkable makes isinstance() work with protocols at runtime.
- The open/closed principle is the practical payoff of polymorphism: code that processes objects through a shared interface is open to new types (add a new subclass or a new class that satisfies the protocol) without any modification to the processing code.

Guided Exercises

Complete the following exercises. Each targets a specific concept from this chapter.

1. Create an abstract-style base class called Instrument with a play(note) method that raises NotImplementedError. Create three subclasses: Guitar, Piano, and Drums. Each must override play() to print a unique description of how the instrument plays the given note. Create a Band class that holds a list of instruments and has a perform(notes) method that calls play() on each instrument for each note in the list. Test with a mixed band.

__Hint:__ The Band.perform() method should loop over self._instruments and call instrument.play(note). This is the polymorphic call — no isinstance() checks needed.

2. Implement a Duration class representing a length of time in total seconds. Overload +, -, *, ==, <, >, and str() so that Duration objects behave naturally. Addition and subtraction should return a new

Duration. Multiplication should accept a numeric scalar. Comparison operators should compare total seconds. __str__ should return a formatted string like "2h 15m 30s". Test by adding, subtracting, and sorting a list of Duration objects.

> ***Hint:*** *Store everything as total_seconds internally. Implement __add__(self, other): return Duration(self.total_seconds + other.total_seconds). For __str__, divide and use modulo to extract hours, minutes, seconds.*

3. Write a function process_payments(payments) that accepts a list of payment objects and prints a summary. Create three classes: CashPayment (amount), CardPayment (amount, card_last_four), and CryptoPayment (amount, coin, wallet_address). Each must have a process() method that prints its own processing message and a receipt() method that returns a formatted receipt string. process_payments() must call both methods on each object without any isinstance() checks.

> ***Hint:*** *Define process() and receipt() on all three classes with the same signatures. process_payments() loops over the list and calls p.process() and p.receipt() on each — polymorphism handles the rest.*

4. Define a Protocol called Resizable with two methods: resize(factor: float) -> None and dimensions() -> tuple. Implement it on three unrelated classes: Photo (width, height), VideoClip (width, height, duration_seconds), and Canvas (width, height). Make it @runtime_checkable. Write a function scale_all(items, factor) that validates all items conform to Resizable, then calls resize() on each and prints their new dimensions.

> ***Hint:*** *from typing import Protocol, runtime_checkable. Use isinstance(item, Resizable) in scale_all() to validate input. Then loop and call item.resize(factor) followed by item.dimensions().*

5. Build a simple expression evaluator using polymorphism. Create a base class Expr with an evaluate() method. Create subclasses: Number (holds a numeric value), Add (holds two Expr objects, returns their sum), Multiply (holds two Expr objects, returns their product), and Negate (holds one Expr, returns its negation). evaluate() should recursively call evaluate() on child expressions. Demonstrate by building and evaluating: (3 + 4) * -2, and -(5 + (2 * 3)).

> ***Hint:*** *Number.evaluate() returns self.value. Add.evaluate() returns self.left.evaluate() + self.right.evaluate(). Negate.evaluate() returns -self.expr.evaluate(). Build the expression tree by nesting objects in the constructor.*

Challenge Tasks

Open-ended tasks. No hints provided. Design your solution before writing any code.

1. Design and implement a polymorphic discount system for a retail application. Define a base Discount class and at least four subclass types: PercentageDiscount (e.g. 15% off), FixedAmountDiscount (e.g. $10 off), BuyXGetYDiscount (e.g. buy 2 get 1 free), and LoyaltyDiscount (percentage that scales with a customer's purchase history). Each must implement apply(original_price, quantity=1) returning the discounted total and describe() returning a human-readable description. Write a checkout(items, discounts) function that processes a list of (item_name, price, quantity) tuples with a list of discounts applied in order. No isinstance() checks in checkout(). Demonstrate with a realistic shopping scenario.

2. Implement a polymorphic serialisation framework. Define a Serialiser Protocol with methods serialise(obj) -> str and deserialise(data: str) -> object. Implement JSONSerialiser, CSVSerialiser, and XMLSerialiser (simplified, string-based XML is fine). Write a DataStore class that accepts any Serialiser and uses it to save and load a list of objects. Demonstrate round-tripping (save then load) with the same data through all three serialisers. Add a @runtime_checkable decorator so the DataStore can validate its serialiser on construction. Note the interface is identical for all three — the DataStore code never checks which serialiser it holds.

3. Build an overloaded Fraction class representing a rational number (numerator / denominator). It must support: construction from two integers (auto-reducing via GCD), all six comparison operators (__eq__, __lt__, __le__, __gt__, __ge__, __ne__), all four arithmetic operators (__add__, __sub__, __mul__, __truediv__) returning a new Fraction, __neg__ and __abs__, __float__ and __int__ for conversion, and a clean __str__ and __repr__. Ensure that all arithmetic operations return a fully reduced Fraction (no 2/4, only 1/2). Include __radd__, __rsub__, __rmul__, and __rtruediv__ so that expressions like 1 + Fraction(1,2) work correctly. Test every operator with at least two cases each.

CHAPTER 7 **Abstraction and Interfaces**

Book 01: Object-Oriented Programming in Python

> *Abstraction is the fourth pillar of OOP and the one most concerned with design rather than mechanics. Where encapsulation hides data, abstraction hides complexity — it presents a simplified interface to the outside world while concealing the implementation details behind it. This chapter examines how Python formalises abstraction through abstract base classes and abstract methods: classes that cannot be instantiated directly but define the contract every concrete subclass must honour. You will learn to use the abc module to enforce interfaces at class-definition time, define abstract properties, use ABCs for robust type checking, and apply these tools to design clean, stable public interfaces that separate what a class does from how it does it.*

7.1 The Purpose of Abstraction

Abstraction is the practice of exposing only what is necessary and hiding everything else. You have been using abstraction throughout this book every time you called a method without knowing or caring how it was implemented. When you call `sorted(items)`, you do not need to understand timsort. When you call `acc.deposit(100)`, you do not need to know how the balance is stored or validated. The method presents a simple interface; the complexity is hidden behind it.

In OOP, abstraction operates at two levels. The first is the class level: a well-designed class hides its internal state and exposes only a clean public interface. This is encapsulation serving abstraction. The second level is the hierarchy level: an abstract class defines a contract — a set of methods that every concrete subclass must implement — without providing any implementation itself. The abstract class answers "what can you do?" while the concrete subclasses answer "how do you do it?"

Without formal abstraction mechanisms, a class hierarchy relies entirely on convention. A base class might define methods that raise `NotImplementedError`, signalling that subclasses should override them. This works in practice but is enforced only at runtime: you discover a missing implementation when you call the method, not when you define the class. Python's `abc` module formalises this: attempting to instantiate a class that has not implemented all required abstract methods raises a `TypeError` immediately, at object creation time.

Abstraction vs encapsulation

The two concepts are related but distinct. Encapsulation is about protecting data and controlling access. Abstraction is about reducing complexity by defining clear interfaces. A class can be well-encapsulated without being abstract (most of the classes in earlier chapters). Abstract classes add the additional constraint that subclasses must implement a specified contract, making the hierarchy more formally defined and its requirements explicit.

Example 1 — Introduction

The problem abstraction solves: a hierarchy that relies on NotImplementedError by convention, with no enforcement at definition time.

```python
# Without abstraction: convention-based, errors found at runtime
class Shape:
    def area(self):
        raise NotImplementedError("Subclasses must implement area().")

    def perimeter(self):
        raise NotImplementedError("Subclasses must implement perimeter().")


class BrokenCircle(Shape):
    """Forgot to implement perimeter — Python does not catch this."""
    def __init__(self, radius):
        self.radius = radius

    def area(self):
        import math
        return math.pi * self.radius ** 2

    # perimeter() missing — not noticed until called


c = BrokenCircle(5)        # no error here
print(c.area())            # works fine

try:
    print(c.perimeter()) # error only discovered when called
except NotImplementedError as e:
    print(f"Runtime error: {e}")

print("BrokenCircle was instantiated successfully — the error was hidden.")
```

Output:

```
78.53981633974483
Runtime error: Subclasses must implement perimeter().
BrokenCircle was instantiated successfully — the error was hidden.
```

Example 2 — Variation

With abstraction enforced by ABC: the missing method is caught at class instantiation time, not at method call time.

```
from abc import ABC, abstractmethod
import math

class Shape(ABC):
    @abstractmethod
    def area(self) -> float:
        """Return the area of the shape."""

    @abstractmethod
    def perimeter(self) -> float:
        """Return the perimeter of the shape."""

    def describe(self):
        """Concrete method: available to all subclasses."""
        print(f"{self.__class__.__name__}: area={self.area():.2f}, 
perimeter={self.perimeter():.2f}")


class Circle(Shape):
    def __init__(self, radius):
        self.radius = radius

    def area(self):
        return math.pi * self.radius ** 2

    def perimeter(self):
        return 2 * math.pi * self.radius


class IncompleteSquare(Shape):
    """Missing perimeter — ABC catches this immediately."""
    def __init__(self, side):
        self.side = side

    def area(self):
        return self.side ** 2
    # perimeter() not implemented
```

```python
# Attempting to instantiate Shape directly fails
try:
    s = Shape()
except TypeError as e:
    print(f"Cannot instantiate abstract class: {e}")

# Circle works perfectly
c = Circle(5)
c.describe()

# IncompleteSquare fails at instantiation, not at method call
try:
    sq = IncompleteSquare(4)
except TypeError as e:
    print(f"Incomplete subclass blocked: {e}")
```

Output:

```
Cannot instantiate abstract class: Can't instantiate abstract class Shape without an implementation for abstract methods 'area', 'perimeter'
Circle: area=78.54, perimeter=31.42
Incomplete subclass blocked: Can't instantiate abstract class IncompleteSquare without an implementation for abstract method 'perimeter'
```

Example 3 — Real-world application

A real-world motivation for abstraction: a payment processing system where different payment providers must all honour the same interface.

```python
from abc import ABC, abstractmethod

class PaymentProcessor(ABC):
    """Abstract contract for all payment processors.

    Any concrete payment processor — Stripe, PayPal, bank transfer,
    cryptocurrency — must implement these three methods. The billing
    system depends only on this interface, not on any specific provider.
    """

    @abstractmethod
    def authorise(self, amount: float, card_token: str) -> bool:
        """Authorise the payment. Return True if approved."""
```

```
    @abstractmethod
    def capture(self, transaction_id: str) -> bool:
        """Capture a previously authorised payment."""

    @abstractmethod
    def refund(self, transaction_id: str, amount: float) -> bool:
        """Issue a full or partial refund."""


class BillingSystem:
    """Processes orders using any PaymentProcessor implementation.

    This class depends only on the abstract interface — it works
    with any concrete processor without modification.
    """

    def __init__(self, processor: PaymentProcessor):
        if not isinstance(processor, PaymentProcessor):
            raise TypeError("processor must be a PaymentProcessor.")
        self._processor = processor

    def checkout(self, amount, card_token):
        print(f"\nProcessing ${amount:.2f}...")
        if self._processor.authorise(amount, card_token):
            txn_id = f"TXN-{hash(card_token) % 100000:05d}"
            if self._processor.capture(txn_id):
                print(f"  Payment complete. Transaction: {txn_id}")
                return txn_id
        print("  Payment declined.")
        return None


class MockProcessor(PaymentProcessor):
    """Test implementation — approves all transactions."""

    def authorise(self, amount, card_token):
        print(f"  [Mock] Authorising ${amount:.2f} for token
{card_token[:8]}...")
        return True
```

```
    def capture(self, transaction_id):
        print(f"  [Mock] Capturing {transaction_id}")
        return True

    def refund(self, transaction_id, amount):
        print(f"  [Mock] Refunding ${amount:.2f} for {transaction_id}")
        return True


billing = BillingSystem(MockProcessor())
txn = billing.checkout(149.00, "tok_visa_4242424242")
if txn:
    billing._processor.refund(txn, 149.00)
```

Output:

```
Processing $149.00...
  [Mock] Authorising $149.00 for token tok_visa...
  [Mock] Capturing TXN-XXXXX
  Payment complete. Transaction: TXN-XXXXX
  [Mock] Refunding $149.00 for TXN-XXXXX
```

`BillingSystem` is written entirely against `PaymentProcessor` — it never mentions `MockProcessor`, Stripe, or PayPal. Swapping the payment provider means passing a different object to the constructor. The billing code never changes. This is the central value of abstraction: stable, provider-independent code that works with any conforming implementation.

7.2 Abstract Base Classes — the abc Module

Python's `abc` module (Abstract Base Classes) provides the machinery for formal abstraction. To create an abstract class, inherit from `ABC` (or use `ABCMeta` as a metaclass). To declare a method that subclasses must implement, decorate it with `@abstractmethod`. A class that inherits from an abstract class but does not implement all abstract methods becomes abstract itself and cannot be instantiated.

The `ABC` class (from `abc import ABC`) is simply a convenience class that uses `ABCMeta` as its metaclass. Both approaches achieve the same result. `ABC` is cleaner for most cases. `ABCMeta` is needed when a class must also inherit from a metaclass of its own.

An abstract class can have concrete methods alongside abstract ones. These concrete methods are inherited by all subclasses and often contain shared logic that builds on the abstract methods. This is the template method pattern from Chapter 6 made formal: the abstract methods define the extension points, the concrete methods define the overall algorithm.

Abstract method bodies

Abstract methods can have a body. If they do, a subclass can call `super().method()` to access it. This is rarely used but occasionally useful when the abstract method provides a default implementation that subclasses extend rather than replace entirely.

Example 1 — Introduction

The basic ABC structure: abstract and concrete methods in the same class, with the concrete method building on the abstract ones.

```
from abc import ABC, abstractmethod


class DataSource(ABC):
    """Abstract base for all data source types.


    Concrete methods: connect(), close(), fetch_all()
    Abstract methods: _open_connection(), _read_records(), _close_connection()


    Subclasses implement the three private abstract methods;
    callers use the three public concrete methods.
    """


    @abstractmethod
    def _open_connection(self) -> None:
        """Open the underlying connection to the data source."""

    @abstractmethod
    def _read_records(self) -> list:
        """Read and return all records as a list of dicts."""

    @abstractmethod
    def _close_connection(self) -> None:
        """Close the underlying connection."""

    # --- Concrete methods: same for all subclasses ---


    def connect(self):
        print(f"[{self.__class__.__name__}] Connecting...")
        self._open_connection()
        print(f"[{self.__class__.__name__}] Connected.")


    def fetch_all(self) -> list:
```

```
        records = self._read_records()
        print(f"[{self.__class__.__name__}] Fetched {len(records)} record(s).")
        return records

    def close(self):
        self._close_connection()
        print(f"[{self.__class__.__name__}] Connection closed.")


class CSVDataSource(DataSource):
    def __init__(self, filepath):
        self._filepath = filepath
        self._data = []

    def _open_connection(self):
        # Simulate reading a CSV file
        self._data = [
            {"id": 1, "name": "Alice", "score": 91.5},
            {"id": 2, "name": "Bob",   "score": 72.0},
            {"id": 3, "name": "Cara",  "score": 88.0},
        ]
        print(f"  Opened CSV: {self._filepath}")

    def _read_records(self):
        return list(self._data)

    def _close_connection(self):
        self._data.clear()


class InMemoryDataSource(DataSource):
    def __init__(self, records):
        self._records = records

    def _open_connection(self):
        print(f"  In-memory source ready ({len(self._records)} records).")

    def _read_records(self):
        return list(self._records)
```

```
    def _close_connection(self):
        pass


for source in [CSVDataSource("students.csv"),
               InMemoryDataSource([{"x": 1}, {"x": 2}])]:
    source.connect()
    records = source.fetch_all()
    source.close()
    print()
```

Output:

```
[CSVDataSource] Connecting...
  Opened CSV: students.csv
[CSVDataSource] Connected.
[CSVDataSource] Fetched 3 record(s).
[CSVDataSource] Connection closed.

[InMemoryDataSource] Connecting...
  In-memory source ready (2 records).
[InMemoryDataSource] Connected.
[InMemoryDataSource] Fetched 2 record(s).
[InMemoryDataSource] Connection closed.
```

Example 2 — Variation

Multiple levels of inheritance with ABC: an abstract subclass adds its own abstract requirements on top of the parent's.

```
from abc import ABC, abstractmethod

class Animal(ABC):
    def __init__(self, name):
        self.name = name

    @abstractmethod
    def speak(self) -> str:
        """Return the sound this animal makes."""

    @abstractmethod
```

```
    def move(self) -> str:
        """Return a description of how this animal moves."""

    def introduce(self):
        """Concrete: same for all animals."""
        print(f"{self.name}: {self.speak()} ({self.move()})")


class Pet(Animal):
    """Still abstract: adds owner requirement but does not implement
speak/move."""

    def __init__(self, name, owner):
        super().__init__(name)
        self.owner = owner

    @abstractmethod
    def trick(self) -> str:
        """Return a trick this pet can perform."""

    def show_trick(self):
        print(f"{self.name} (owned by {self.owner}) performs: {self.trick()}")


class Dog(Pet):
    """Fully concrete: implements all abstract methods from Animal and Pet."""

    def speak(self): return "Woof!"
    def move(self):  return "runs on four legs"
    def trick(self): return "sits on command"


class Cat(Pet):
    def speak(self): return "Meow!"
    def move(self):  return "prowls silently"
    def trick(self): return "high-fives for treats"


class Parrot(Animal):
```

```python
    """Not a pet: implements Animal only."""
    def speak(self): return "Polly wants a cracker!"
    def move(self):  return "flies and perches"


# Pet is still abstract — cannot instantiate directly
try:
    p = Pet("Generic", "Nobody")
except TypeError as e:
    print(f"Abstract: {e}")


animals = [Dog("Rex", "Alice"), Cat("Whiskers", "Bob"), Parrot("Captain")]
for a in animals:
    a.introduce()

print()
for a in animals:
    if isinstance(a, Pet):
        a.show_trick()
```

Output:

```
Abstract: Can't instantiate abstract class Pet without an implementation for
abstract method 'trick'
Rex: Woof! (runs on four legs)
Whiskers: Meow! (prowls silently)
Captain: Polly wants a cracker! (flies and perches)

Rex (owned by Alice) performs: sits on command
Whiskers (owned by Bob) performs: high-fives for treats
```

Example 3 — Real-world application

A storage backend abstraction: the application layer targets the abstract interface; concrete classes implement it for different storage systems.

```python
from abc import ABC, abstractmethod
import json

class StorageBackend(ABC):
    """Abstract interface for all storage backends.
```

```
    The application layer calls save(), load(), delete(), and list_keys().
    The concrete subclass determines where and how data is persisted.
    """

    @abstractmethod
    def save(self, key: str, value: dict) -> None:
        """Persist value under key."""

    @abstractmethod
    def load(self, key: str) -> dict | None:
        """Return the value for key, or None if not found."""

    @abstractmethod
    def delete(self, key: str) -> bool:
        """Delete key. Return True if it existed."""

    @abstractmethod
    def list_keys(self) -> list:
        """Return all stored keys."""

    # Concrete convenience method built on the abstract interface
    def exists(self, key: str) -> bool:
        return self.load(key) is not None

    def save_many(self, items: dict) -> None:
        for key, value in items.items():
            self.save(key, value)


class InMemoryBackend(StorageBackend):
    """Stores data in a dict. Fast, non-persistent. Ideal for testing."""

    def __init__(self):
        self._store = {}

    def save(self, key, value):
        self._store[key] = value
```

```
    def load(self, key):
        return self._store.get(key)

    def delete(self, key):
        if key in self._store:
            del self._store[key]
            return True
        return False

    def list_keys(self):
        return list(self._store.keys())


class JSONFileBackend(StorageBackend):
    """Persists data to a JSON file. Loads entire file on each operation."""

    def __init__(self, filepath):
        self._filepath = filepath
        self._ensure_file()

    def _ensure_file(self):
        try:
            with open(self._filepath, "r") as f:
                json.load(f)
        except (FileNotFoundError, json.JSONDecodeError):
            with open(self._filepath, "w") as f:
                json.dump({}, f)

    def _read(self):
        with open(self._filepath, "r") as f:
            return json.load(f)

    def _write(self, data):
        with open(self._filepath, "w") as f:
            json.dump(data, f, indent=2)

    def save(self, key, value):
        data = self._read()
```

```
        data[key] = value
        self._write(data)

    def load(self, key):
        return self._read().get(key)

    def delete(self, key):
        data = self._read()
        if key in data:
            del data[key]
            self._write(data)
            return True
        return False

    def list_keys(self):
        return list(self._read().keys())


def demo_backend(backend: StorageBackend, label: str):
    print(f"\n=== {label} ===")
    backend.save_many({
        "user:001": {"name": "Alice Wong",  "role": "admin"},
        "user:002": {"name": "Bob Smith",   "role": "user"},
        "user:003": {"name": "Cara Lee",    "role": "user"},
    })
    print(f"Keys: {backend.list_keys()}")
    print(f"Load user:001: {backend.load('user:001')}")
    print(f"Exists user:002: {backend.exists('user:002')}")
    backend.delete("user:002")
    print(f"After delete, exists user:002: {backend.exists('user:002')}")
    print(f"Keys: {backend.list_keys()}")


demo_backend(InMemoryBackend(), "In-Memory Backend")
demo_backend(JSONFileBackend("/tmp/store.json"), "JSON File Backend")
```

Output:

```
=== In-Memory Backend ===
Keys: ['user:001', 'user:002', 'user:003']
Load user:001: {'name': 'Alice Wong', 'role': 'admin'}
```

```
Exists user:002: True
After delete, exists user:002: False
Keys: ['user:001', 'user:003']

=== JSON File Backend ===
Keys: ['user:001', 'user:002', 'user:003']
Load user:001: {'name': 'Alice Wong', 'role': 'admin'}
Exists user:002: True
After delete, exists user:002: False
Keys: ['user:001', 'user:003']
```

7.3 Defining Abstract Methods

An abstract method is defined by decorating a method with `@abstractmethod` inside an `ABC` subclass. The method body is conventionally `...` (Ellipsis) or a docstring only, signalling that no implementation is provided. A subclass that inherits from the ABC must provide a concrete implementation of every abstract method, or it too becomes abstract and cannot be instantiated.

Abstract methods serve as a formal contract enforced at class-definition time. The error message Python raises for a missing implementation is explicit: it names the class and the specific method(s) that were not implemented. This makes debugging much faster than discovering a missing method at runtime, potentially deep inside a call chain.

Python's enforcement of abstract methods is strict but not overly prescriptive. A concrete implementation can have a completely different body from the abstract declaration. The only requirement is that the name matches. Python does not enforce matching signatures — though good practice and type-checking tools like mypy will flag mismatches.

Combining @abstractmethod with other decorators

`@abstractmethod` can be combined with `@classmethod`, `@staticmethod`, and `@property`. The order matters: `@abstractmethod` must be the innermost (closest to the method definition) decorator. Incorrect order produces unexpected behaviour.

- Abstract class method: `@classmethod` then `@abstractmethod` (outer to inner)
- Abstract static method: `@staticmethod` then `@abstractmethod`
- Abstract property: `@property` then `@abstractmethod` — covered in Section 7.5

Example 1 — Introduction

Standard abstract method definitions: the correct syntax, body conventions, and enforcement behaviour.

```
from abc import ABC, abstractmethod


class Validator(ABC):
    """Abstract validator: subclasses define specific validation rules.
```

```
    validate() must be implemented. is_valid() builds on it.
    """

    @abstractmethod
    def validate(self, value) -> tuple:
        """Validate value. Return (True, None) or (False, error_message)."""
        ...   # body is conventionally ... or a docstring

    def is_valid(self, value) -> bool:
        """Concrete convenience: returns just the boolean result."""
        result, _ = self.validate(value)
        return result

    def validate_or_raise(self, value):
        """Concrete: validates and raises ValueError if invalid."""
        ok, msg = self.validate(value)
        if not ok:
            raise ValueError(msg)


class EmailValidator(Validator):
    def validate(self, value):
        import re
        if re.match(r"^[\w.+-]+@[\w-]+\.[\w.]+$", value):
            return (True, None)
        return (False, f"{value!r} is not a valid email address.")


class AgeValidator(Validator):
    def __init__(self, min_age=0, max_age=150):
        self.min_age = min_age
        self.max_age = max_age

    def validate(self, value):
        if not isinstance(value, int):
            return (False, f"Age must be an integer, got
{type(value).__name__}.")
        if not (self.min_age <= value <= self.max_age):
```

```
            return (False, f"Age {value} is outside range [{self.min_age},
{self.max_age}].")
        return (True, None)


class PostcodeValidator(Validator):
    def validate(self, value):
        s = str(value)
        if s.isdigit() and len(s) == 4:
            return (True, None)
        return (False, f"{value!r} is not a valid Australian postcode.")


validators = [
    (EmailValidator(),          ["alice@example.com", "not-an-email"]),
    (AgeValidator(18, 120),     [25, 200, "old"]),
    (PostcodeValidator(),       ["3000", "123", 4000]),
]

for validator, values in validators:
    cls = validator.__class__.__name__
    for v in values:
        ok, msg = validator.validate(v)
        mark = "✓" if ok else "✗"
        info = f"  {msg}" if msg else ""
        print(f"  [{cls}] {mark} {v!r}{info}")
    print()
```

Output:

```
  [EmailValidator] ✓ 'alice@example.com'
  [EmailValidator] ✗ 'not-an-email'  'not-an-email' is not a valid email
address.

  [AgeValidator] ✓ 25
  [AgeValidator] ✗ 200  Age 200 is outside range [18, 120].
  [AgeValidator] ✗ 'old'  Age must be an integer, got str.

  [PostcodeValidator] ✓ '3000'
  [PostcodeValidator] ✗ '123'  '123' is not a valid Australian postcode.
  [PostcodeValidator] ✓ 4000
```

Example 2 — Variation

Combining @abstractmethod with @classmethod and @staticmethod: the correct decorator order.

```
from abc import ABC, abstractmethod

class Codec(ABC):
    """Abstract codec: encode and decode data.

    encode() and decode() are abstract instance methods.
    from_config() is an abstract class method — factory pattern.
    supported_formats() is an abstract static method — class-level metadata.
    """

    @abstractmethod
    def encode(self, data: str) -> bytes:
        """Encode a string to bytes."""

    @abstractmethod
    def decode(self, data: bytes) -> str:
        """Decode bytes to a string."""

    @classmethod
    @abstractmethod
    def from_config(cls, config: dict):
        """Factory: create an instance from a configuration dict."""

    @staticmethod
    @abstractmethod
    def supported_formats() -> list:
        """Return a list of supported format names."""

    # Concrete convenience method
    def roundtrip(self, text: str) -> bool:
        return self.decode(self.encode(text)) == text


class UTF8Codec(Codec):
```

```
    def __init__(self, errors="strict"):
        self.errors = errors

    def encode(self, data):
        return data.encode("utf-8", errors=self.errors)

    def decode(self, data):
        return data.decode("utf-8", errors=self.errors)

    @classmethod
    def from_config(cls, config):
        return cls(errors=config.get("errors", "strict"))

    @staticmethod
    def supported_formats():
        return ["utf-8", "utf-8-bom"]


class ASCIICodec(Codec):
    def encode(self, data):
        return data.encode("ascii", errors="replace")

    def decode(self, data):
        return data.decode("ascii", errors="replace")

    @classmethod
    def from_config(cls, config):
        return cls()

    @staticmethod
    def supported_formats():
        return ["ascii", "us-ascii"]


for CodecClass in [UTF8Codec, ASCIICodec]:
    codec = CodecClass.from_config({})
    text  = "Hello, 世界!" if CodecClass is UTF8Codec else "Hello, World!"
    encoded = codec.encode(text)
    decoded = codec.decode(encoded)
```

```
    print(f"{CodecClass.__name__}:")
    print(f"  Formats:   {codec.supported_formats()}")
    print(f"  Encoded:   {encoded[:20]}...")
    print(f"  Roundtrip: {codec.roundtrip(text)}")
    print()
```

Output:

```
UTF8Codec:
  Formats:   ['utf-8', 'utf-8-bom']
  Encoded:   b'Hello, \xe4\xb8\x96\xe7\x95\x8c!'...
  Roundtrip: True

ASCIICodec:
  Formats:   ['ascii', 'us-ascii']
  Encoded:   b'Hello, World!'...
  Roundtrip: True
```

Example 3 — Real-world application

A report generation framework with abstract methods for content and formatting, and concrete methods for orchestration.

```
from abc import ABC, abstractmethod
from datetime import datetime


class ReportGenerator(ABC):
    """Abstract report generator.

    Subclasses implement _gather_data(), _format_record(record),
    and _output_format(). The concrete generate() method orchestrates
    them into a complete report.
    """

    def __init__(self, title: str):
        self.title     = title
        self.generated = datetime.now().strftime("%Y-%m-%d %H:%M")

    @abstractmethod
    def _gather_data(self) -> list:
        """Return the raw list of records to be reported."""
```

```
    @abstractmethod
    def _format_record(self, record: dict) -> str:
        """Format a single record into a report line."""

    @abstractmethod
    def _output_format(self) -> str:
        """Return the format label (e.g. "TEXT", "CSV", "HTML")."""

    # Concrete orchestration — same for all subclasses
    def generate(self) -> str:
        data    = self._gather_data()
        header  = (f"REPORT: {self.title} | Format: {self._output_format()} | "
                   f"Generated: {self.generated} | Records: {len(data)}")
        divider = "-" * len(header)
        lines   = [header, divider]
        for record in data:
            lines.append(self._format_record(record))
        lines.append(divider)
        return "\n".join(lines)


class StudentReport(ReportGenerator):
    def __init__(self, students):
        super().__init__("Student Results")
        self._students = students

    def _gather_data(self):
        return sorted(self._students, key=lambda s: s["grade"], reverse=True)

    def _format_record(self, record):
        status = "PASS" if record["grade"] >= 50 else "FAIL"
        return f"  {record['name']:20s} {record['grade']:5.1f}  [{status}]"

    def _output_format(self):
        return "TEXT"


class SalesReport(ReportGenerator):
    def __init__(self, transactions):
```

```
        super().__init__("Daily Sales")
        self._transactions = transactions

    def _gather_data(self):
        return self._transactions

    def _format_record(self, record):
        return f"  {record['item']:20s} x{record['qty']}
${record['total']:.2f}"

    def _output_format(self):
        return "TEXT"


students = [
    {"name": "Alice Wong",  "grade": 91.5},
    {"name": "Bob Smith",   "grade": 42.0},
    {"name": "Cara Lee",    "grade": 78.5},
    {"name": "Dan Park",    "grade": 55.0},
]

transactions = [
    {"item": "Laptop Stand",  "qty": 3,  "total": 147.00},
    {"item": "USB-C Hub",     "qty": 5,  "total": 195.00},
    {"item": "Keyboard",      "qty": 2,  "total": 178.00},
]

print(StudentReport(students).generate())
print()
print(SalesReport(transactions).generate())
```

Output:

```
REPORT: Student Results | Format: TEXT | Generated: 2026-03-21 08:15 | Records:
4
--------------------------------------------------------------------
  Alice Wong            91.5  [PASS]
  Cara Lee              78.5  [PASS]
  Dan Park              55.0  [PASS]
  Bob Smith             42.0  [FAIL]
--------------------------------------------------------------------
```

```
REPORT: Daily Sales | Format: TEXT | Generated: 2026-03-21 08:15 | Records: 3
----------------------------------------------------------------------
  Laptop Stand          x3  $147.00
  USB-C Hub             x5  $195.00
  Keyboard              x2  $178.00
----------------------------------------------------------------------
```

7.4 Concrete Implementations of Abstract Classes

A concrete class is one that implements all abstract methods declared in its abstract parent(s). Once all abstract requirements are satisfied, the class can be instantiated normally. The concrete class gains everything the abstract class provides — concrete methods, class attributes, the `isinstance()` relationship — plus its own implementation of the abstract methods.

A single abstract class can have many concrete implementations, each representing a different way to fulfil the same contract. This is the key design benefit: the abstract class defines what must be true; the concrete classes define how. Code targeting the abstract interface works correctly with any of the concrete implementations, present or future.

A useful practice when building a hierarchy is to write the abstract class first, including docstrings that precisely specify what each abstract method must do, and then implement concrete classes one at a time. Writing tests against the abstract interface (using a concrete implementation) ensures the contract is correctly specified before the hierarchy grows.

Example 1 — Introduction

Three concrete implementations of the same abstract Sorter interface, demonstrating that the calling code is entirely independent of the implementation.

```
from abc import ABC, abstractmethod

class Sorter(ABC):
    """Abstract sorting algorithm.

    Concrete classes implement sort(items) and name().
    The abstract class provides a benchmark() convenience method.
    """

    @abstractmethod
    def sort(self, items: list) -> list:
        """Return a new sorted list. Must not modify the input."""

    @abstractmethod
    def name(self) -> str:
        """Return the algorithm name."""
```

```python
    def benchmark(self, items: list):
        import time
        data  = list(items)    # copy to avoid mutation
        start = time.perf_counter()
        result = self.sort(data)
        elapsed = (time.perf_counter() - start) * 1000
        print(f"  {self.name():20s} {len(items):6,} items  {elapsed:.3f}ms")
        return result


class BubbleSorter(Sorter):
    def name(self): return "Bubble Sort"

    def sort(self, items):
        lst = list(items)
        n   = len(lst)
        for i in range(n):
            for j in range(n - i - 1):
                if lst[j] > lst[j + 1]:
                    lst[j], lst[j + 1] = lst[j + 1], lst[j]
        return lst


class InsertionSorter(Sorter):
    def name(self): return "Insertion Sort"

    def sort(self, items):
        lst = list(items)
        for i in range(1, len(lst)):
            key = lst[i]
            j   = i - 1
            while j >= 0 and lst[j] > key:
                lst[j + 1] = lst[j]
                j -= 1
            lst[j + 1] = key
        return lst
```

```
class PythonBuiltinSorter(Sorter):
    """Wraps Python's built-in sort for comparison."""
    def name(self): return "Python Built-in"
    def sort(self, items): return sorted(items)


import random
data = [random.randint(1, 10000) for _ in range(500)]

print("Sorting 500 random integers:")
sorters = [BubbleSorter(), InsertionSorter(), PythonBuiltinSorter()]
for sorter in sorters:
    result = sorter.benchmark(data)
    assert result == sorted(data), f"{sorter.name()} produced incorrect
output!"

print("All sorters produced correct output.")
```

Output:

```
Sorting 500 random integers:
  Bubble Sort           500 items   X.XXXms
  Insertion Sort        500 items   X.XXXms
  Python Built-in       500 items   X.XXXms
All sorters produced correct output.
```

Example 2 — Variation

Concrete implementations of an abstract Logger: console, file, and in-memory loggers all sharing the same interface.

```
from abc import ABC, abstractmethod
from datetime import datetime


class Logger(ABC):
    """Abstract logger. Concrete classes handle the destination.

    All share the same log(), info(), warning(), error() interface.
    """

    LEVELS = {"DEBUG": 0, "INFO": 1, "WARNING": 2, "ERROR": 3}
```

```
    def __init__(self, min_level: str = "INFO"):
        self.min_level = min_level

    @abstractmethod
    def _write(self, entry: str) -> None:
        """Write a formatted log entry to the destination."""

    def _format(self, level: str, message: str) -> str:
        ts = datetime.now().strftime("%H:%M:%S")
        return f"[{ts}] [{level:7s}] {message}"

    def log(self, level: str, message: str) -> None:
        if self.LEVELS.get(level, 0) >= self.LEVELS.get(self.min_level, 0):
            self._write(self._format(level, message))

    def info(self, msg):    self.log("INFO", msg)
    def warning(self, msg): self.log("WARNING", msg)
    def error(self, msg):   self.log("ERROR", msg)
    def debug(self, msg):   self.log("DEBUG", msg)


class ConsoleLogger(Logger):
    def _write(self, entry):
        print(entry)


class MemoryLogger(Logger):
    def __init__(self, min_level="INFO"):
        super().__init__(min_level)
        self._entries = []

    def _write(self, entry):
        self._entries.append(entry)

    def entries(self):
        return list(self._entries)

    def entries_at_level(self, level):
        return [e for e in self._entries if f"[{level}" in e]
```

```python
class MultiLogger(Logger):
    """Fan-out: writes to multiple loggers simultaneously."""

    def __init__(self, *loggers):
        super().__init__("DEBUG")    # MultiLogger itself has no filter
        self._loggers = loggers

    def _write(self, entry):
        for logger in self._loggers:
            logger._write(entry)


console = ConsoleLogger(min_level="INFO")
memory  = MemoryLogger(min_level="WARNING")
multi   = MultiLogger(console, memory)

multi.info("Application started.")
multi.debug("Debug detail — filtered by both loggers.")
multi.warning("Disk usage above 80%.")
multi.error("Failed to connect to database.")

print(f"\nWarnings/Errors captured in memory:")
for entry in memory.entries():
    print(f"  {entry}")
```

Output:

```
[08:15:01] [INFO    ] Application started.
[08:15:01] [WARNING] Disk usage above 80%.
[08:15:01] [ERROR   ] Failed to connect to database.

Warnings/Errors captured in memory:
[08:15:01] [WARNING] Disk usage above 80%.
[08:15:01] [ERROR   ] Failed to connect to database.
```

Example 3 — Real-world application

A caching framework: the abstract Cache defines the interface; concrete backends implement it for in-memory, simple file, and TTL-aware caching.

```
from abc import ABC, abstractmethod
import time

class Cache(ABC):
    """Abstract cache interface.

    All concrete caches must implement get(), set(), delete(),
    and clear(). The abstract class provides exists() and get_or_set().
    """

    @abstractmethod
    def get(self, key: str):
        """Return cached value or None if not present/expired."""

    @abstractmethod
    def set(self, key: str, value, ttl: int = None) -> None:
        """Store value. ttl=seconds until expiry; None=never expires."""

    @abstractmethod
    def delete(self, key: str) -> bool:
        """Remove key. Return True if it existed."""

    @abstractmethod
    def clear(self) -> None:
        """Remove all entries."""

    def exists(self, key: str) -> bool:
        return self.get(key) is not None

    def get_or_set(self, key: str, default_fn, ttl: int = None):
        """Return cached value; if missing, compute, store, and return it."""
        value = self.get(key)
        if value is None:
            value = default_fn()
            self.set(key, value, ttl)
        return value


class SimpleCache(Cache):
```

```
    """In-memory cache with optional TTL."""

    def __init__(self):
        self._store = {}    # key -> (value, expiry_timestamp or None)

    def _is_expired(self, key):
        _, expiry = self._store.get(key, (None, None))
        return expiry is not None and time.time() > expiry

    def get(self, key):
        if key not in self._store or self._is_expired(key):
            if key in self._store:
                del self._store[key]
            return None
        return self._store[key][0]

    def set(self, key, value, ttl=None):
        expiry = time.time() + ttl if ttl is not None else None
        self._store[key] = (value, expiry)

    def delete(self, key):
        if key in self._store:
            del self._store[key]
            return True
        return False

    def clear(self):
        self._store.clear()

    def size(self):
        return len(self._store)


cache = SimpleCache()

# Basic set and get
cache.set("user:001", {"name": "Alice", "role": "admin"})
cache.set("config",   {"debug": False, "version": "2.1"})
```

```python
print(cache.get("user:001"))
print(cache.exists("config"))

# get_or_set: compute only if not cached
call_count = 0
def expensive_lookup():
    global call_count
    call_count += 1
    return {"data": "computed", "calls": call_count}

r1 = cache.get_or_set("result", expensive_lookup)
r2 = cache.get_or_set("result", expensive_lookup)  # cached, no re-computation
print(f"r1={r1}, r2={r2}, calls={call_count}")

# TTL test: short expiry
cache.set("temp", "expires soon", ttl=1)
print(f"Before expiry: {cache.get('temp')}")
time.sleep(1.1)
print(f"After expiry:  {cache.get('temp')}")
```

Output:

```
{'name': 'Alice', 'role': 'admin'}
True
r1={'data': 'computed', 'calls': 1}, r2={'data': 'computed', 'calls': 1},
calls=1
Before expiry: expires soon
After expiry:  None
```

7.5 Abstract Properties

Properties can be made abstract by combining `@property` with `@abstractmethod`. An abstract property declares that every concrete subclass must expose a particular attribute through the property interface — it does not specify whether the value is stored directly, computed, or retrieved from an external source. The concrete class is free to implement the property however it chooses, as long as the property name exists.

Abstract properties are used when the interface requires a value to be accessible as an attribute (not a method call) but the implementation may vary. A `Shape` ABC might declare `area` and `perimeter` as abstract properties rather than abstract methods, ensuring that concrete shapes expose them as attributes (`circle.area`) rather than calls (`circle.area()`).

Abstract read-only properties, writable properties, and properties with deleters can all be made abstract. The concrete subclass must implement at least the getter; if the abstract class declares a setter, the subclass must also implement a setter.

> **Note:** The decorator order for an abstract property is: @property on the outside, then @abstractmethod on the inside — in other words, @abstractmethod is closest to the def. Python 3.3+ deprecated the older @abstractproperty in favour of combining @property and @abstractmethod directly.

Example 1 — Introduction

Abstract properties declared in a base class, implemented differently by two concrete subclasses.

```
from abc import ABC, abstractmethod


class Vehicle(ABC):
    """Abstract vehicle with required property interface.

    All vehicles must expose: make, model, fuel_type, and range_km.
    They may implement these however is appropriate to their type.
    """

    @property
    @abstractmethod
    def make(self) -> str: ...

    @property
    @abstractmethod
    def model(self) -> str: ...

    @property
    @abstractmethod
    def fuel_type(self) -> str: ...

    @property
    @abstractmethod
    def range_km(self) -> float: ...

    def summary(self):
        print(f"{self.make} {self.model} | {self.fuel_type} |
{self.range_km:.0f}km range")


class PetrolCar(Vehicle):
    """Simple implementation: all properties backed by __init__ args."""
```

```
    def __init__(self, make, model, tank_litres, consumption_per_100km):
        self._make    = make
        self._model   = model
        self._tank    = tank_litres
        self._consumption = consumption_per_100km

    @property
    def make(self):  return self._make

    @property
    def model(self): return self._model

    @property
    def fuel_type(self): return "Petrol"

    @property
    def range_km(self):
        return (self._tank / self._consumption) * 100


class ElectricCar(Vehicle):
    """EV: range_km computed from battery and efficiency."""

    def __init__(self, make, model, battery_kwh, kwh_per_100km):
        self._make       = make
        self._model      = model
        self._battery    = battery_kwh
        self._efficiency = kwh_per_100km

    @property
    def make(self):  return self._make

    @property
    def model(self): return self._model

    @property
    def fuel_type(self): return "Electric"

    @property
```

```
    def range_km(self):
        return (self._battery / self._efficiency) * 100


vehicles = [
    PetrolCar("Toyota", "Camry",      55, 8.5),
    PetrolCar("Honda",  "Civic",      47, 6.8),
    ElectricCar("Tesla",  "Model 3",  82, 14.5),
    ElectricCar("BYD",    "Atto 3",   60, 16.8),
]

for v in vehicles:
    v.summary()

# All vehicles comparable through uniform properties
best_range = max(vehicles, key=lambda v: v.range_km)
print(f"\nLongest range: {best_range.make} {best_range.model}
({best_range.range_km:.0f}km)")
```

Output:

```
Toyota Camry | Petrol | 647km range
Honda Civic | Petrol | 691km range
Tesla Model 3 | Electric | 566km range
BYD Atto 3 | Electric | 357km range

Longest range: Honda Civic (691km)
```

Example 2 — Variation

Abstract writable properties: the abstract class declares both getter and setter as abstract; subclasses must implement both.

```
from abc import ABC, abstractmethod

class ConfigStore(ABC):
    """Abstract configuration store with read/write properties.

    Subclasses may persist config in memory, a file, a database, etc.
    The interface is always: store.host, store.host = "value".
    """
```

```
    @property
    @abstractmethod
    def host(self) -> str: ...

    @host.setter
    @abstractmethod
    def host(self, value: str) -> None: ...

    @property
    @abstractmethod
    def port(self) -> int: ...

    @port.setter
    @abstractmethod
    def port(self, value: int) -> None: ...

    @property
    @abstractmethod
    def debug(self) -> bool: ...

    @debug.setter
    @abstractmethod
    def debug(self, value: bool) -> None: ...

    def connection_string(self):
        mode = "debug" if self.debug else "production"
        return f"{self.host}:{self.port} [{mode}]"


class MemoryConfigStore(ConfigStore):
    def __init__(self):
        self._host  = "localhost"
        self._port  = 5432
        self._debug = False

    @property
    def host(self): return self._host
    @host.setter
    def host(self, v): self._host = str(v)
```

```
    @property
    def port(self): return self._port
    @port.setter
    def port(self, v):
        if not (1 <= int(v) <= 65535):
            raise ValueError("Port must be 1-65535.")
        self._port = int(v)

    @property
    def debug(self): return self._debug
    @debug.setter
    def debug(self, v): self._debug = bool(v)


cfg = MemoryConfigStore()
print(cfg.connection_string())

cfg.host  = "db.production.example.com"
cfg.port  = 3306
cfg.debug = False
print(cfg.connection_string())

try:
    cfg.port = 99999
except ValueError as e:
    print(f"Error: {e}")
```

Output:

```
localhost:5432 [production]
db.production.example.com:3306 [production]
Error: Port must be 1-65535.
```

Example 3 — Real-world application

A content management system with abstract properties defining the document interface; concrete subclasses implement them for different content types.

```
from abc import ABC, abstractmethod
from datetime import datetime
```

```
class CMSDocument(ABC):
    """Abstract CMS document. All documents expose a consistent interface.

    Required properties: title, author, created, word_count, content_type
    Required method:     render() -> str
    Concrete method:     metadata() (uses the properties)
    """

    @property
    @abstractmethod
    def title(self) -> str: ...

    @property
    @abstractmethod
    def author(self) -> str: ...

    @property
    @abstractmethod
    def created(self) -> datetime: ...

    @property
    @abstractmethod
    def word_count(self) -> int: ...

    @property
    @abstractmethod
    def content_type(self) -> str: ...

    @abstractmethod
    def render(self) -> str:
        """Return the document as a formatted string."""


    def metadata(self) -> dict:
        """Concrete: build metadata from the abstract properties."""
        return {
            "title":        self.title,
            "author":       self.author,
            "created":      self.created.strftime("%d %b %Y"),
            "words":        self.word_count,
```

```
            "content_type": self.content_type,
        }


class BlogPost(CMSDocument):
    def __init__(self, title, author, body, tags=None):
        self._title   = title
        self._author  = author
        self._body    = body
        self._tags    = tags or []
        self._created = datetime.now()

    @property
    def title(self):        return self._title
    @property
    def author(self):       return self._author
    @property
    def created(self):      return self._created
    @property
    def word_count(self):   return len(self._body.split())
    @property
    def content_type(self): return "Blog Post"

    def render(self):
        tags = " ".join(f"#{t}" for t in self._tags)
        return f"# {self._title}\nBy {self._author}\n\n{self._body}\n\n{tags}"


class ProductDescription(CMSDocument):
    def __init__(self, product_name, author, description, price):
        self._product     = product_name
        self._author      = author
        self._description = description
        self._price       = price
        self._created     = datetime.now()

    @property
    def title(self):        return self._product
    @property
```

```
    def author(self):       return self._author
    @property
    def created(self):      return self._created
    @property
    def word_count(self):   return len(self._description.split())
    @property
    def content_type(self): return "Product Description"

    def render(self):
        return f"PRODUCT: {self._product}\nPrice: 
${self._price:.2f}\n\n{self._description}"


docs = [
    BlogPost("Getting Started with Python",
             "M. North",
             "Python is a versatile language used in data science, web 
development, and automation.",
             tags=["python", "tutorial", "beginner"]),
    ProductDescription("Laptop Stand", "Product Team",
                       "Aluminium alloy construction. Adjustable height. 
Reduces neck strain. Compatible with all laptops.",
                       49.95),
]


for doc in docs:
    print(doc.metadata())
    print(doc.render())
    print()
```

Output:

```
{'title': 'Getting Started with Python', 'author': 'M. North', 'created': '21 
Mar 2026', 'words': 17, 'content_type': 'Blog Post'}
# Getting Started with Python
By M. North


Python is a versatile language used in data science, web development, and 
automation.


#python #tutorial #beginner
```

```
{'title': 'Laptop Stand', 'author': 'Product Team', 'created': '21 Mar 2026',
'words': 14, 'content_type': 'Product Description'}
PRODUCT: Laptop Stand
Price: $49.95

Aluminium alloy construction. Adjustable height. Reduces neck strain.
Compatible with all laptops.
```

7.6 Using ABCs for Type Checking

Python's standard library provides a rich set of pre-built abstract base classes in `collections.abc` and `numbers`. These ABCs define the interfaces for all of Python's built-in protocols: `Iterable`, `Sequence`, `Mapping`, `Callable`, `Hashable`, `Number`, `Integral`, and many more. Any class that implements the required methods automatically satisfies the corresponding ABC.

These standard ABCs are the canonical way to write functions that accept "any sequence-like object" or "any mapping" without restricting the caller to a specific type like `list` or `dict`. A function that type-checks `isinstance(x, Sequence)` accepts lists, tuples, strings, and any custom class with `__len__` and `__getitem__` — without the caller needing to inherit from `Sequence` explicitly.

The mechanism behind this is virtual subclassing: Python's ABCs inspect whether a class provides the required dunder methods, and if it does, `isinstance()` returns True automatically. You can also manually register a class as a virtual subclass using `ABC.register(cls)`, which adds it to the ABC's hierarchy without modifying the class itself.

Virtual subclassing

Virtual subclasses satisfy `isinstance()` checks but do not inherit any methods from the ABC. They are used to retrofit existing classes (including third-party ones) into an abstract hierarchy. The class retains its original implementation; it simply becomes recognised as a member of the abstract family.

Example 1 — Introduction

Using standard ABCs from collections.abc for robust type checking: Iterable, Sequence, and Mapping.

```
from collections.abc import Iterable, Sequence, Mapping, Callable


def process_items(items):
    """Accept any Iterable — list, tuple, generator, custom class."""
    if not isinstance(items, Iterable):
        raise TypeError(f"Expected an Iterable, got {type(items).__name__}")
    return list(items)


def first_item(seq):
    """Accept any Sequence (supports indexing and len)."""
```

```python
    if not isinstance(seq, Sequence):
        raise TypeError(f"Expected a Sequence, got {type(seq).__name__}")
    if not seq:
        return None
    return seq[0]


def lookup(mapping, key, default=None):
    """Accept any Mapping (dict-like)."""
    if not isinstance(mapping, Mapping):
        raise TypeError(f"Expected a Mapping, got {type(mapping).__name__}")
    return mapping.get(key, default)


# Standard types satisfy the ABCs automatically
print(isinstance([1, 2, 3],        Iterable))    # True: list
print(isinstance((1, 2, 3),        Sequence))    # True: tuple
print(isinstance("hello",          Sequence))    # True: string
print(isinstance({"a": 1},         Mapping))     # True: dict
print(isinstance(range(10),        Sequence))    # True: range
print(isinstance(x for x in []), Iterable))    # True: generator
print(isinstance(42,               Iterable))    # False: int


# Using in practice
print(process_items([1, 2, 3]))
print(process_items((x**2 for x in range(4))))
print(first_item("hello"))
print(lookup({"x": 10, "y": 20}, "x"))
```

Output:

```
True
True
True
True
True
True
False
[1, 2, 3]
[0, 1, 4, 9]
h
```

```
10
```

Example 2 — Variation

Virtual subclassing: registering an existing class with an ABC without modifying it.

```
from abc import ABC, abstractmethod

class Printable(ABC):
    @abstractmethod
    def display(self) -> str:
        """Return a display string for this object."""


# Existing class — we cannot (or do not want to) modify it
class LegacyRecord:
    def __init__(self, record_id, data):
        self.record_id = record_id
        self.data      = data

    def display(self):
        return f"Record[{self.record_id}]: {self.data}"


# Register LegacyRecord as a virtual subclass of Printable
# (no inheritance, no modification to LegacyRecord)
Printable.register(LegacyRecord)


class ModernRecord(Printable):
    def __init__(self, uid, payload):
        self.uid     = uid
        self.payload = payload

    def display(self):
        return f"ModernRecord({self.uid}): {self.payload}"
```

```
def print_all(items):
    for item in items:
        if not isinstance(item, Printable):
            print(f"  Skipping: {item!r} is not Printable.")
            continue
        print(f"  {item.display()}")


records = [
    LegacyRecord("L001", {"status": "active"}),
    ModernRecord("M001", {"score": 98.5}),
    "not printable",
    LegacyRecord("L002", {"status": "inactive"}),
]

print_all(records)

print(f"\nLegacyRecord is Printable: {issubclass(LegacyRecord, Printable)}")
print(f"LegacyRecord inherits from Printable: {Printable in
LegacyRecord.__bases__}")
```

Output:

```
  Record[L001]: {'status': 'active'}
  ModernRecord(M001): {'score': 98.5}
  Skipping: 'not printable' is not Printable.
  Record[L002]: {'status': 'inactive'}

LegacyRecord is Printable: True
LegacyRecord inherits from Printable: False
```

Example 3 — Real-world application

A plugin registry using ABCs for type checking: plugins are validated against the abstract interface when they are registered.

```
from abc import ABC, abstractmethod
from typing import Type

class AnalyticsPlugin(ABC):
    """Abstract interface all analytics plugins must implement.
```

```
    Plugins are registered with the PluginRegistry at startup.
    The registry validates conformance before accepting registration.
    """

    @property
    @abstractmethod
    def plugin_name(self) -> str: ...

    @property
    @abstractmethod
    def version(self) -> str: ...

    @abstractmethod
    def initialise(self, config: dict) -> None: ...

    @abstractmethod
    def process_event(self, event: dict) -> dict: ...


class PluginRegistry:
    def __init__(self):
        self._plugins = {}

    def register(self, plugin_instance) -> None:
        if not isinstance(plugin_instance, AnalyticsPlugin):
            raise TypeError(
                f"{type(plugin_instance).__name__} does not implement
AnalyticsPlugin."
            )
        self._plugins[plugin_instance.plugin_name] = plugin_instance
        print(f"  Registered: {plugin_instance.plugin_name}
v{plugin_instance.version}")

    def dispatch(self, event: dict) -> list:
        results = []
        for plugin in self._plugins.values():
            result = plugin.process_event(event)
            if result:
                results.append((plugin.plugin_name, result))
        return results
```

```
class SessionTracker(AnalyticsPlugin):
    @property
    def plugin_name(self): return "SessionTracker"
    @property
    def version(self): return "1.2.0"

    def initialise(self, config):
        self._timeout = config.get("timeout_minutes", 30)

    def process_event(self, event):
        if event.get("type") == "page_view":
            return {"session_update": event.get("user_id"), "page":
event.get("page")}
        return None


class ErrorMonitor(AnalyticsPlugin):
    @property
    def plugin_name(self): return "ErrorMonitor"
    @property
    def version(self): return "2.0.1"

    def initialise(self, config):
        self._threshold = config.get("error_threshold", 5)

    def process_event(self, event):
        if event.get("type") == "error":
            return {"alert": True, "code": event.get("code"), "msg":
event.get("msg")}
        return None



registry = PluginRegistry()


tracker = SessionTracker()
tracker.initialise({"timeout_minutes": 20})
monitor = ErrorMonitor()
```

```
monitor.initialise({})

registry.register(tracker)
registry.register(monitor)

try:
    registry.register("not a plugin")
except TypeError as e:
    print(f"  Rejected: {e}")

events = [
    {"type": "page_view", "user_id": "U001", "page": "/home"},
    {"type": "error",     "code": 500, "msg": "DB timeout"},
    {"type": "page_view", "user_id": "U002", "page": "/products"},
]

print("\nEvent dispatch:")
for event in events:
    results = registry.dispatch(event)
    for name, result in results:
        print(f"  [{name}] {result}")
```

Output:

```
  Registered: SessionTracker v1.2.0
  Registered: ErrorMonitor v2.0.1
  Rejected: str does not implement AnalyticsPlugin.

Event dispatch:
  [SessionTracker] {'session_update': 'U001', 'page': '/home'}
  [ErrorMonitor] {'alert': True, 'code': 500, 'msg': 'DB timeout'}
  [SessionTracker] {'session_update': 'U002', 'page': '/products'}
```

7.7 Designing a Clean Public Interface

The purpose of abstraction is ultimately to create interfaces that are stable, minimal, and easy to use correctly. A well-designed abstract class expresses a clear contract: it tells implementors exactly what they must provide, and it tells callers exactly what they can depend on. A poorly designed one leaks implementation details, requires too many abstract methods, or exposes an interface that is difficult to implement correctly.

Several principles guide interface design. Keep the interface minimal: every abstract method is a requirement imposed on every concrete subclass. The more abstract methods an interface has, the harder it is to add a new implementation. If some methods are genuinely optional, provide default implementations in the ABC rather than making them abstract.

Separate concerns: an abstract class should represent one coherent concept. An ABC that mixes data access, formatting, and notification is probably three separate interfaces that have been conflated. Smaller, focused ABCs are easier to implement and more composable.

Name methods at the right level of abstraction. `_deliver()`, `_read_records()`, and `_close_connection()` are implementation details; `send()`, `fetch_all()`, and `close()` are the caller-facing interface. Abstract methods that begin with underscores signal extension points; those without underscores signal the public contract.

Interface segregation

Large interfaces that force implementors to provide methods they do not need are a design smell. If some concrete classes only implement half the methods meaningfully, the interface should be split. Python makes this straightforward: multiple small ABCs can be combined via multiple inheritance in the concrete class.

Example 1 — Introduction

Designing a minimal, focused interface: a Reader/Writer split that lets concrete classes implement only what they support.

```
from abc import ABC, abstractmethod

# Two small, focused ABCs instead of one large one
class Readable(ABC):
    @abstractmethod
    def read(self, key: str): ...

    @abstractmethod
    def exists(self, key: str) -> bool: ...

    @abstractmethod
    def keys(self) -> list: ...


class Writable(ABC):
    @abstractmethod
    def write(self, key: str, value) -> None: ...

    @abstractmethod
    def delete(self, key: str) -> bool: ...


class ReadWriteStore(Readable, Writable):
```

```
    """Full read/write store: inherits both interfaces."""
    pass


class MemoryStore(ReadWriteStore):
    """Concrete full read/write store."""

    def __init__(self):
        self._data = {}

    def read(self, key):   return self._data.get(key)
    def exists(self, key): return key in self._data
    def keys(self):        return list(self._data.keys())
    def write(self, key, value): self._data[key] = value
    def delete(self, key):
        if key in self._data:
            del self._data[key]
            return True
        return False


class ReadOnlySnapshot(Readable):
    """Read-only view: implements only Readable, not Writable.

    A function that accepts a Readable will work with this class.
    Passing it to a function expecting Writable will fail isinstance().
    """

    def __init__(self, data: dict):
        self._data = dict(data)

    def read(self, key):   return self._data.get(key)
    def exists(self, key): return key in self._data
    def keys(self):        return list(self._data.keys())


def display_all(store: Readable):
    """Only requires Readable — works with any Readable implementation."""
    for key in store.keys():
```

```python
        print(f"  {key}: {store.read(key)}")


mem = MemoryStore()
mem.write("name", "Alice")
mem.write("role", "admin")

snapshot = ReadOnlySnapshot({"name": "Bob", "role": "user", "dept":
"Engineering"})

print("MemoryStore contents:")
display_all(mem)

print("\nSnapshot contents:")
display_all(snapshot)

print(f"\nMemoryStore is Writable: {isinstance(mem, Writable)}")
print(f"Snapshot is Writable:    {isinstance(snapshot, Writable)}")
print(f"Snapshot is Readable:    {isinstance(snapshot, Readable)}")
```

Output:

```
MemoryStore contents:
  name: Alice
  role: admin

Snapshot contents:
  name: Bob
  role: user
  dept: Engineering

MemoryStore is Writable: True
Snapshot is Writable:    False
Snapshot is Readable:    True
```

Example 2 — Variation

Documenting the contract precisely: an ABC whose abstract methods have full docstrings specifying pre-conditions, post-conditions, and error behaviour.

```python
from abc import ABC, abstractmethod
```

```
class MessageQueue(ABC):
    """Abstract message queue.

    Implementors must satisfy these contracts exactly:

      publish(message) -> None
        Pre:  message is a non-empty string.
        Post: message is enqueued; subsequent consume() calls will return it.
        Error: raises ValueError if message is empty.

      consume() -> str | None
        Post: returns and removes the oldest message, or None if queue empty.
        Side-effect: queue shrinks by one.

      peek() -> str | None
        Post: returns the oldest message without removing it, or None if empty.

      size() -> int
        Post: returns the number of unconsumed messages (>= 0).
    """

    @abstractmethod
    def publish(self, message: str) -> None:
        """Enqueue a message. Raises ValueError if message is empty."""

    @abstractmethod
    def consume(self) -> str | None:
        """Remove and return the oldest message, or None if empty."""

    @abstractmethod
    def peek(self) -> str | None:
        """Return the oldest message without removing it, or None if empty."""

    @abstractmethod
    def size(self) -> int:
        """Return the number of unconsumed messages."""

    def is_empty(self) -> bool:
        return self.size() == 0
```

```
    def consume_all(self) -> list:
        messages = []
        while not self.is_empty():
            messages.append(self.consume())
        return messages


class FIFOQueue(MessageQueue):
    """Standard first-in, first-out queue."""
    def __init__(self): self._q = []

    def publish(self, message):
        if not message:
            raise ValueError("Message cannot be empty.")
        self._q.append(message)

    def consume(self): return self._q.pop(0) if self._q else None
    def peek(self):    return self._q[0] if self._q else None
    def size(self):    return len(self._q)


class PriorityQueue(MessageQueue):
    """Messages prefixed with [HIGH] are processed before others."""

    def __init__(self):
        self._high = []
        self._normal = []

    def publish(self, message):
        if not message:
            raise ValueError("Message cannot be empty.")
        if message.startswith("[HIGH]"):
            self._high.append(message)
        else:
            self._normal.append(message)

    def consume(self):
        if self._high:   return self._high.pop(0)
```

```
        if self._normal: return self._normal.pop(0)
        return None

    def peek(self):
        if self._high:   return self._high[0]
        if self._normal: return self._normal[0]
        return None

    def size(self): return len(self._high) + len(self._normal)


def run_queue_demo(queue: MessageQueue, label: str):
    print(f"\n=== {label} ===")
    for msg in ["task-001", "[HIGH] URGENT-002", "task-003", "[HIGH] CRITICAL-
004"]:
        queue.publish(msg)
    print(f"Size: {queue.size()}, Peek: {queue.peek()!r}")
    all_messages = queue.consume_all()
    for m in all_messages:
        print(f"  Consumed: {m}")


run_queue_demo(FIFOQueue(),     "FIFO Queue")
run_queue_demo(PriorityQueue(),"Priority Queue")
```

Output:

```
=== FIFO Queue ===
Size: 4, Peek: 'task-001'
  Consumed: task-001
  Consumed: [HIGH] URGENT-002
  Consumed: task-003
  Consumed: [HIGH] CRITICAL-004

=== Priority Queue ===
Size: 4, Peek: '[HIGH] URGENT-002'
  Consumed: [HIGH] URGENT-002
  Consumed: [HIGH] CRITICAL-004
  Consumed: task-001
  Consumed: task-003
```

Example 3 — Real-world application

A complete, production-style abstract class combining all patterns: abstract methods, abstract properties, concrete methods, documented contract, and type checking.

```
from abc import ABC, abstractmethod
from datetime import datetime

class NotificationService(ABC):
    """Abstract notification service.

    Contract:
      - service_name (property): human-readable name of this service.
      - max_message_length (property): character limit for this channel.
      - send(recipient, subject, body): deliver one notification.
        Raises ValueError if body exceeds max_message_length.
        Raises RuntimeError if delivery fails.
      - send_bulk(recipients, subject, body): deliver to all recipients.
        Concrete implementation uses send() for each.

    All subclasses inherit: send_bulk(), _validate(), _log_sent().
    """

    def __init__(self):
        self._sent_log = []

    @property
    @abstractmethod
    def service_name(self) -> str: ...

    @property
    @abstractmethod
    def max_message_length(self) -> int: ...

    @abstractmethod
    def send(self, recipient: str, subject: str, body: str) -> None: ...

    # --- Concrete methods ---

    def _validate(self, body: str) -> None:
        if len(body) > self.max_message_length:
```

```
            raise ValueError(
                f"Message exceeds {self.service_name} limit
({len(body)}/{self.max_message_length} chars)."
            )

    def _log_sent(self, recipient: str, subject: str) -> None:
        self._sent_log.append({
            "service":   self.service_name,
            "recipient": recipient,
            "subject":   subject,
            "sent_at":   datetime.now().strftime("%H:%M:%S"),
        })

    def send_bulk(self, recipients: list, subject: str, body: str) -> None:
        print(f"[{self.service_name}] Sending to {len(recipients)}
recipients...")
        for recipient in recipients:
            self.send(recipient, subject, body)

    def delivery_report(self) -> None:
        print(f"[{self.service_name}] {len(self._sent_log)} message(s) sent:")
        for entry in self._sent_log[-3:]:
            print(f"  {entry['sent_at']}  {entry['recipient']}
{entry['subject']!r}")


class EmailService(NotificationService):
    @property
    def service_name(self): return "Email"
    @property
    def max_message_length(self): return 100_000

    def send(self, recipient, subject, body):
        self._validate(body)
        print(f"  [Email] → {recipient}: {subject!r}")
        self._log_sent(recipient, subject)


class SMSService(NotificationService):
    @property
```

```python
    def service_name(self): return "SMS"
    @property
    def max_message_length(self): return 160

    def send(self, recipient, subject, body):
        self._validate(body)
        print(f"  [SMS] → {recipient}: {body[:40]!r}...")
        self._log_sent(recipient, subject)


recipients = ["alice@example.com", "bob@example.com", "cara@example.com"]
numbers    = ["0412000001", "0412000002"]

email = EmailService()
email.send_bulk(recipients, "System Alert", "Scheduled maintenance tonight at 22:00 AEST.")
email.delivery_report()

print()
sms = SMSService()
sms.send_bulk(numbers, "Alert", "Maintenance tonight 22:00.")

try:
    sms.send("0412000003", "Long message", "x" * 200)
except ValueError as e:
    print(f"  Error: {e}")
```

Output:

```
[Email] Sending to 3 recipients...
  [Email] → alice@example.com: 'System Alert'
  [Email] → bob@example.com: 'System Alert'
  [Email] → cara@example.com: 'System Alert'
[Email] 3 message(s) sent:
  08:15:01  alice@example.com  'System Alert'
  08:15:01  bob@example.com  'System Alert'
  08:15:01  cara@example.com  'System Alert'

[SMS] Sending to 2 recipients...
  [SMS] → 0412000001: 'Maintenance tonight 22:00.'...
  [SMS] → 0412000002: 'Maintenance tonight 22:00.'...
```

```
Error: Message exceeds SMS limit (200/160 chars).
```

Chapter 7 Summary

- Abstraction presents a simplified interface while hiding complexity. Abstract classes define what must be done (the contract); concrete subclasses define how it is done (the implementation). This separation is what allows calling code to be stable and implementation-independent.
- Python enforces abstraction through the abc module. Inheriting from ABC and decorating methods with @abstractmethod makes those methods required. Attempting to instantiate a class with unimplemented abstract methods raises TypeError immediately at object creation, not at method call time.
- An abstract class can contain both abstract methods (extension points for subclasses) and concrete methods (shared logic built on those extension points). The template method pattern places the orchestration algorithm in a concrete method and the variable steps in abstract methods.
- @abstractmethod can be combined with @classmethod and @staticmethod. The correct order is: @classmethod or @staticmethod on the outside, @abstractmethod on the inside (closest to the def). Abstract class methods are commonly used for factory patterns that should work polymorphically in subclasses.
- Abstract properties are defined by stacking @property and @abstractmethod. They enforce that all concrete subclasses expose a named attribute through the property interface, while leaving the implementation free (stored value, computed value, database lookup, etc.).
- Python's collections.abc and numbers modules provide standard ABCs for built-in protocols (Iterable, Sequence, Mapping, Callable, etc.). Any class that implements the required dunder methods satisfies these ABCs automatically (structural conformance). Virtual subclassing with ABC.register() adds a class to an ABC family without modifying it.
- Interface design principles: keep interfaces minimal (every abstract method is a burden on every implementor), separate concerns (one coherent concept per ABC), name methods at the right level of abstraction (callers see simple verbs; implementors see private extension points), and document the contract precisely in the ABC docstring.
- Interface segregation: large ABCs that force implementors to provide methods they do not need should be split into smaller, focused ABCs. Python makes this natural: concrete classes can inherit from multiple small ABCs simultaneously, satisfying all required interfaces without a monolithic contract.

Guided Exercises

Complete the following exercises. Each targets a specific concept from this chapter.

1. Define an abstract class called Shape with abstract methods area() and perimeter(), and a concrete method describe() that prints the class name, area, and perimeter. Create three concrete subclasses: Rectangle, Circle, and Triangle. Verify that attempting to instantiate Shape directly raises TypeError. Create a list of all three shapes and call describe() on each.

Hint: *from abc import ABC, abstractmethod. In Shape.__init__, accept a colour argument. The describe() method should call self.area() and self.perimeter(), which dispatch to the correct subclass via polymorphism.*

2. Create an abstract class called Exporter with abstract methods export(data: list) -> str and file_extension() -> str, plus a concrete method save(data, filename) that calls export() to get the content and writes it to filename + file_extension(). Implement CSVExporter and JSONExporter as concrete subclasses. Test by exporting the same list of dicts through both exporters.

Hint: *In CSVExporter.export(), build a CSV string from the list of dicts. In JSONExporter.export(), use json.dumps(data, indent=2). The save() method is identical for both — that is the point of the abstract class.*

---

3. Build an abstract class called Authenticator with abstract methods authenticate(username, password) -> bool and get_user(username) -> dict | None, plus a concrete method login(username, password) that calls both and returns a session token on success. Implement MemoryAuthenticator (stores user records in a dict) and a simple HashAuthenticator (stores hashed passwords using hashlib.sha256). Test login() with both implementations using the same calling code.

Hint: *Store users as {"username": ..., "password_hash": ...} in MemoryAuthenticator. The login() concrete method should call authenticate(), and if successful, return a token like f"token_{username}_{int(time.time())}".*

---

4. Define an abstract class called Sensor with abstract properties sensor_id and unit (both read-only), and an abstract method read() -> float. Add a concrete method log_reading() that prints a formatted reading using the properties and read(). Implement TemperatureSensor (simulates readings with random.uniform) and HumiditySensor. Create a list of sensors and call log_reading() on each in a loop.

Hint: *Use @property combined with @abstractmethod for sensor_id and unit. In each concrete class, implement the properties returning fixed strings and implement read() returning a simulated float value.*

5. Use the collections.abc module to write a function called summarise(collection) that: (a) checks whether the argument is a Sequence, Mapping, or other Iterable, and (b) prints an appropriate summary for each case — first and last item for sequences, keys for mappings, and item count for other iterables. Test with a list, a tuple, a string, a dict, a set, and a range.

Hint: *from collections.abc import Sequence, Mapping, Iterable. Check in order: Mapping first (dict is also a Sequence in some ABCs), then Sequence, then Iterable. Use len() where available.*

Challenge Tasks

Open-ended tasks. No hints provided. Design your solution before writing any code.

1. Design and implement a complete abstract data pipeline framework. Define three abstract classes: DataReader (with abstract methods read() -> list and source_description() -> str), DataTransformer (with abstract methods transform(records: list) -> list and transformation_name() -> str), and DataWriter (with abstract methods write(records: list) -> None and destination_description() -> str). Write a concrete Pipeline class that accepts a DataReader, a list of DataTransformers, and a DataWriter, and has a run() method that chains them together. Implement at least two concrete versions of each abstract class (e.g. CSVReader and JSONReader; FilterTransformer and SortTransformer; ConsoleWriter and MemoryWriter). Demonstrate a complete pipeline that reads, applies two transformations, and writes output.

---

2. Implement a role-based access control system using ABCs. Define an abstract class Resource with abstract properties name and required_permission, and an abstract method access(user) -> str that returns the resource content for authorised users. Define an abstract class User with abstract properties username and permissions (a frozenset). Provide a concrete check_access(user, resource) function that uses isinstance() with both ABCs to validate arguments, checks the permission, and calls resource.access(user). Implement at least three Resource types (Document, Report, AdminPanel) and two User types (StandardUser, AdminUser) with different permission sets. Demonstrate authorised access, permission denial, and invalid argument handling.

---

3. Build a mini ORM (Object-Relational Mapper) using abstraction. Define an abstract class Model with: abstract class methods table_name() -> str and fields() -> list (returning field names); an abstract method validate() -> bool; and concrete class methods save(instance), find(id), and find_all() that use a shared InMemoryDatabase class (a dict of dicts) for storage. Implement three concrete model classes: Student (id, name, grade), Course (id, code, title, credits), and Enrolment (id, student_id, course_id). Demonstrate creating, saving, finding, and listing records of all three types. The storage and retrieval logic should live entirely in the abstract Model class, not in any concrete subclass.

CHAPTER 8 **Special (Dunder) Methods**

Book 01: Object-Oriented Programming in Python

> *Every time Python evaluates len(x), x + y, str(obj), or for item in container:, it calls a method behind the scenes — a method whose name begins and ends with double underscores. These are dunder methods (from "double underscore"), and they form the Python data model: the protocol through which custom objects integrate with the language itself. Implementing dunder methods is what makes a custom class behave like a native Python type — sortable, iterable, printable, addable. This chapter covers the most important groups: string representation, comparison, arithmetic, container behaviour, iteration, and context management. By the end, you will be able to make any class feel like it belongs in the language rather than sitting on top of it.*

8.1 The Python Data Model

The Python data model is the set of interfaces — expressed as dunder methods — that allow custom objects to hook into Python's syntax and built-in functions. When Python evaluates an expression involving a custom object, it looks for the corresponding dunder method and calls it. If the method exists, the object participates in the operation. If it does not, Python either falls back to a default or raises a TypeError.

This design is intentional. Python's built-in types (list, dict, int, str) are not special — they implement the same dunder methods your custom classes can implement. A custom class that implements `__len__` is just as legitimate a "thing with a length" as a list. A class that implements `__iter__` and `__next__` is just as iterable as a range object. The language treats them identically.

Understanding the data model transforms how you read Python. `x + y` is `x.__add__(y)`. `x[k]` is `x.__getitem__(k)`. `with ctx:` calls `ctx.__enter__()` and `ctx.__exit__()`. `for item in x:` calls `iter(x)` which calls `x.__iter__()`, then repeatedly calls `next()` on the result. The syntax is a thin veneer over method calls — and those method calls are yours to define.

Key dunder method groups

- String representation: `__str__`, `__repr__`, `__format__`
- Comparison: `__eq__`, `__ne__`, `__lt__`, `__le__`, `__gt__`, `__ge__`
- Arithmetic: `__add__`, `__sub__`, `__mul__`, `__truediv__`, `__floordiv__`, `__mod__`, `__pow__`, and their reflected variants `__radd__`, `__rsub__`, etc.
- Unary: `__neg__`, `__pos__`, `__abs__`, `__bool__`
- Container: `__len__`, `__getitem__`, `__setitem__`, `__delitem__`, `__contains__`
- Iteration: `__iter__`, `__next__`
- Context manager: `__enter__`, `__exit__`
- Object lifecycle: `__init__`, `__new__`, `__del__`
- Attribute access: `__getattr__`, `__setattr__`, `__delattr__`

Example 1 — Introduction

Demonstrating the dunder-to-syntax mapping: what Python actually calls for common expressions.

```
class Revealed:
    """A class that reveals which dunder method Python calls."""

    def __init__(self, value):
        self.value = value

    def __repr__(self):
        print("  --> __repr__ called")
        return f"Revealed({self.value!r})"

    def __str__(self):
        print("  --> __str__ called")
        return f"Revealed: {self.value}"

    def __add__(self, other):
        print("  --> __add__ called")
        return Revealed(self.value + other.value)

    def __len__(self):
        print("  --> __len__ called")
        return len(str(self.value))

    def __bool__(self):
        print("  --> __bool__ called")
        return bool(self.value)


r = Revealed("hello")

print("str(r):")
print(str(r))

print("\nrepr(r):")
print(repr(r))

print("\nlen(r):")
print(len(r))
```

```
print("\nbool(r):")
print(bool(r))

print("\nr + Revealed('_world'):")
print(r + Revealed("_world"))
```

Output:

```
str(r):
  --> __str__ called
Revealed: hello

repr(r):
  --> __repr__ called
Revealed('hello')

len(r):
  --> __len__ called
5

bool(r):
  --> __bool__ called
True

r + Revealed('_world'):
  --> __add__ called
  --> __str__ called
Revealed: hello_world
```

Example 2 — Variation

The fallback hierarchy: __str__ falls back to __repr__ when not defined; __bool__ falls back to __len__ when not defined.

```
class OnlyRepr:
    """Only __repr__ defined: str() falls back to __repr__."""
    def __repr__(self): return "OnlyRepr()"

class OnlyLen:
    """Only __len__ defined: bool() falls back to __len__."""
    def __init__(self, n): self.n = n
```

```python
    def __len__(self): return self.n

class Neither:
    """No __repr__, __str__, or __len__: uses object defaults."""
    pass


r = OnlyRepr()
print(f"repr: {repr(r)}")
print(f"str (fallback to repr): {str(r)}")

full = OnlyLen(5)
empty = OnlyLen(0)
print(f"\nbool(full):  {bool(full)}")
print(f"bool(empty): {bool(empty)}")

n = Neither()
print(f"\nNeither repr: {repr(n)}")
print(f"Neither str:  {str(n)}")

# if-statement uses __bool__, which falls back to __len__
if full:
    print("full is truthy")
if not empty:
    print("empty is falsy")
```

Output:

```
repr: OnlyRepr()
str (fallback to repr): OnlyRepr()

bool(full):  True
bool(empty): False

Neither repr: <__main__.Neither object at 0x...>
Neither str:  <__main__.Neither object at 0x...>

full is truthy
empty is falsy
```

Example 3 — Real-world application

A Point class implementing a wide range of dunder methods to integrate fully with Python's built-in ecosystem.

```
import math

class Point:
    """2D point with comprehensive dunder method support."""

    def __init__(self, x, y):
        self.x = x
        self.y = y

    # Representation
    def __repr__(self): return f"Point({self.x}, {self.y})"
    def __str__(self):  return f"({self.x}, {self.y})"

    # Arithmetic
    def __add__(self, other): return Point(self.x+other.x, self.y+other.y)
    def __sub__(self, other): return Point(self.x-other.x, self.y-other.y)
    def __mul__(self, k):     return Point(self.x*k, self.y*k)
    def __rmul__(self, k):    return self.__mul__(k)
    def __neg__(self):        return Point(-self.x, -self.y)
    def __abs__(self):        return math.sqrt(self.x**2 + self.y**2)

    # Comparison
    def __eq__(self, other):  return self.x == other.x and self.y == other.y
    def __lt__(self, other):  return abs(self) < abs(other)
    def __hash__(self):       return hash((self.x, self.y))

    # Bool
    def __bool__(self):       return self.x != 0 or self.y != 0

    # Format
    def __format__(self, spec):
        if spec == "polar":
            r     = abs(self)
            theta = math.degrees(math.atan2(self.y, self.x))
            return f"r={r:.2f}, θ={theta:.1f}°"
        return str(self)
```

```
p1 = Point(3, 4)
p2 = Point(1, 2)

print(f"p1 = {p1},  repr = {p1!r}")
print(f"p1 + p2 = {p1 + p2}")
print(f"p1 - p2 = {p1 - p2}")
print(f"3 * p1  = {3 * p1}")
print(f"-p1     = {-p1}")
print(f"|p1|    = {abs(p1):.2f}")
print(f"p1 == Point(3,4): {p1 == Point(3,4)}")
print(f"bool(p1): {bool(p1)},  bool(Point(0,0)): {bool(Point(0,0))}")
print(f"polar:  {p1:polar}")

points = [Point(5,0), Point(0,3), Point(4,3), Point(1,1)]
print(f"sorted: {sorted(points)}")
print(f"in set: {p1 in {Point(3,4), Point(1,2)}}")
```

Output:

```
p1 = (3, 4),  repr = Point(3, 4)
p1 + p2 = (4, 6)
p1 - p2 = (2, 2)
3 * p1  = (9, 12)
-p1     = (-3, -4)
|p1|    = 5.00
p1 == Point(3,4): True
bool(p1): True,  bool(Point(0,0)): False
polar:  r=5.00, θ=53.1°
sorted: [(1, 1), (0, 3), (5, 0), (4, 3)]
in set: True
```

`__hash__` must be defined whenever `__eq__` is defined, because Python automatically sets `__hash__ = None` on any class that defines `__eq__` without also defining `__hash__`. Without `__hash__`, the object cannot be stored in sets or used as a dictionary key. A consistent rule: if two objects compare equal, they must have the same hash.

8.2 String Representation: __str__ and __repr__

Every object in Python has two string representations. `__repr__` is the developer-facing representation: it should return a string that, ideally, could be passed to `eval()` to recreate the object. In practice, it should be unambiguous and contain enough information to understand the object's state during debugging. `repr(obj)` and the interactive prompt both use `__repr__`.

`__str__` is the user-facing representation: it should be readable and informative. `print(obj)`, `str(obj)`, and f-strings (without the `!r` flag) all use `__str__`. If `__str__` is not defined, Python falls back to `__repr__`. For this reason, `__repr__` should always be defined; `__str__` is optional and defined only when you want a different presentation for end users.

The `__format__` method controls how an object responds to format specifications inside f-strings: `f"{obj:spec}"`. This allows custom objects to support format mini-language — alignment, precision, units, or completely custom codes — in a way that integrates naturally with Python's existing formatting syntax.

Convention for __repr__

The standard convention is to make `__repr__` return a string of the form `ClassName(arg1, arg2, ...)` matching the constructor call. This is not always possible (e.g. for objects with large internal state), but it is the goal. When it cannot be achieved, the string should at least be unambiguous: `<ClassName state=... at 0x...>` is better than nothing.

Example 1 — Introduction

Implementing __repr__ and __str__ with distinct purposes: __repr__ for debugging, __str__ for display.

```
from datetime import date


class Employee:
    def __init__(self, emp_id, name, department, start_date):
        self.emp_id     = emp_id
        self.name       = name
        self.department = department
        self.start_date = start_date

    def __repr__(self):
        # Developer view: unambiguous, reconstructible
        return (
            f"Employee({self.emp_id!r}, {self.name!r}, "
            f"{self.department!r}, {self.start_date!r})"
        )

    def __str__(self):
        # User view: readable and concise
        years = (date.today() - self.start_date).days // 365
        return f"{self.name} [{self.emp_id}] — {self.department} ({years}yr)"


emp = Employee("E001", "Alice Wong", "Engineering",
               date(2021, 3, 15))
```

```
print("str(emp):  ", str(emp))
print("repr(emp): ", repr(emp))
print("f-string:  ", f"{emp}")
print("f-string!r:", f"{emp!r}")

# In a list: Python uses __repr__ for items
staff = [emp, Employee("E002", "Bob Smith", "Design", date(2022, 7, 1))]
print("\nList display:")
print(staff)
```

Output:

```
str(emp):   Alice Wong [E001] — Engineering (5yr)
repr(emp):  Employee('E001', 'Alice Wong', 'Engineering', datetime.date(2021,
3, 15))
f-string:   Alice Wong [E001] — Engineering (5yr)
f-string!r: Employee('E001', 'Alice Wong', 'Engineering', datetime.date(2021,
3, 15))

List display:
[Employee('E001', 'Alice Wong', 'Engineering', datetime.date(2021, 3, 15)),
Employee('E002', 'Bob Smith', 'Design', datetime.date(2022, 7, 1))]
```

Example 2 — Variation

Implementing __format__ to support custom format specifications in f-strings.

```
class Temperature:
    def __init__(self, celsius):
        self.celsius = celsius

    def __repr__(self):
        return f"Temperature({self.celsius})"

    def __str__(self):
        return f"{self.celsius:.1f}°C"

    def __format__(self, spec):
        """Support format specs: c=Celsius, f=Fahrenheit, k=Kelvin,
blank=default."""
        if spec == "f" or spec == "F":
            val  = self.celsius * 9/5 + 32
            unit = "°F"
        elif spec == "k" or spec == "K":
```

```
            val  = self.celsius + 273.15
            unit = " K"
        else:
            val  = self.celsius
            unit = "°C"
        # Forward any numeric precision to the float
        if spec and spec[0] not in "fFkKcC":
            return f"{val:{spec}}{unit}"
        return f"{val:.1f}{unit}"


t = Temperature(100)
print(f"Default:      {t}")
print(f"Celsius:      {t:c}")
print(f"Fahrenheit:   {t:f}")
print(f"Kelvin:       {t:k}")
print(f"Precise:      {t:.4f}")

boiling = Temperature(100)
freezing = Temperature(0)
body_temp = Temperature(37)

for temp in [freezing, body_temp, boiling]:
    print(f"  {temp!s:12s} = {temp:f:10s} = {temp:k}")
```

Output:

```
Default:     100.0°C
Celsius:     100.0°C
Fahrenheit:  212.0°F
Kelvin:      373.1 K
Precise:     212.0000°F
  0.0°C        = 32.0°F      = 273.1 K
  37.0°C       = 98.6°F      = 310.1 K
  100.0°C      = 212.0°F     = 373.1 K
```

Example 3 — Real-world application

A Card and Deck class for a card game: meaningful __repr__ and __str__ at every level of the hierarchy.

```
class Card:
    SUITS  = {"♠": "Spades", "♥": "Hearts", "♦": "Diamonds", "♣": "Clubs"}
```

```
    VALUES = {1:"A",11:"J",12:"Q",13:"K"}

    def __init__(self, value, suit):
        if suit not in self.SUITS:
            raise ValueError(f"Invalid suit: {suit!r}")
        if not (1 <= value <= 13):
            raise ValueError(f"Invalid value: {value}")
        self.value = value
        self.suit  = suit

    def __repr__(self):
        return f"Card({self.value}, {self.suit!r})"

    def __str__(self):
        label = self.VALUES.get(self.value, str(self.value))
        return f"{label}{self.suit}"

    def __eq__(self, other):
        return self.value == other.value and self.suit == other.suit

    def __lt__(self, other):
        return (self.value, self.suit) < (other.value, other.suit)

    def __hash__(self):
        return hash((self.value, self.suit))


class Hand:
    def __init__(self, cards=None):
        self._cards = list(cards or [])

    def add(self, card):
        self._cards.append(card)

    def __repr__(self):
        return f"Hand({self._cards!r})"

    def __str__(self):
        return "Hand: " + "  ".join(str(c) for c in self._cards)
```

```
    def __len__(self):
        return len(self._cards)

    def __contains__(self, card):
        return card in self._cards


hand = Hand([
    Card(1,  "♠"),
    Card(13, "♥"),
    Card(7,  "♦"),
    Card(10, "♣"),
])

print(str(hand))
print(repr(hand))
print(f"Cards in hand: {len(hand)}")
print(f"Has A♠: {Card(1, chr(9824)) in hand}")
print(f"Has 2♠: {Card(2, chr(9824)) in hand}")

# sorted uses __lt__
sorted_cards = sorted(hand._cards)
print(f"Sorted: {[str(c) for c in sorted_cards]}")
```

Output:

```
Hand: A♠  K♥  7♦  10♣
Hand([Card(1, '♠'), Card(13, '♥'), Card(7, '♦'), Card(10, '♣')])
Cards in hand: 4
Has A♠: True
Has 2♠: False
Sorted: ['7♦', '10♣', 'A♠', 'K♥']
```

8.3 Comparison Operators: __eq__, __lt__, and Friends

Python maps each comparison operator to a dunder method: `==` to `__eq__`, `!=` to `__ne__`, `<` to `__lt__`, `<=` to `__le__`, `>` to `__gt__`, and `>=` to `__ge__`. Implementing these allows custom objects to participate in comparisons, be sorted with `sorted()`, and work with `min()`, `max()`, and `bisect`.

In practice, you rarely need to implement all six. Python's `functools.total_ordering` decorator derives the missing four from just `__eq__` and one of the ordering methods (`__lt__` is the most common choice). This is the standard approach for adding full comparison support with minimal code.

The default `__eq__` inherited from `object` compares by identity (like `is`): two different objects with identical data are not equal unless you override it. The default `__hash__` is based on the object's id. When you override `__eq__`, Python automatically sets `__hash__ = None`, making the object unhashable. To keep objects hashable (usable in sets and as dict keys), define `__hash__` explicitly.

Returning NotImplemented

When a comparison method receives an argument of an incompatible type, it should return `NotImplemented` rather than raising a `TypeError`. This tells Python to try the reflected operation on the other object. Raising `TypeError` directly prevents Python from attempting the fallback.

Example 1 — Introduction

Using functools.total_ordering to derive all six comparison operators from just __eq__ and __lt__.

```
from functools import total_ordering


@total_ordering
class Version:
    """Semantic version (major.minor.patch).

    total_ordering derives <=, >, >= from __eq__ and __lt__.
    """

    def __init__(self, major, minor=0, patch=0):
        self.major = major
        self.minor = minor
        self.patch = patch

    @classmethod
    def from_string(cls, s):
        parts = s.split(".")
        return cls(*[int(p) for p in parts])

    def __repr__(self):
        return f"Version({self.major}, {self.minor}, {self.patch})"

    def __str__(self):
        return f"{self.major}.{self.minor}.{self.patch}"
```

```
    def __eq__(self, other):
        if not isinstance(other, Version): return NotImplemented
        return (self.major, self.minor, self.patch) == (other.major,
other.minor, other.patch)

    def __lt__(self, other):
        if not isinstance(other, Version): return NotImplemented
        return (self.major, self.minor, self.patch) < (other.major,
other.minor, other.patch)

    def __hash__(self):
        return hash((self.major, self.minor, self.patch))


v1 = Version.from_string("1.9.0")
v2 = Version.from_string("2.0.0")
v3 = Version.from_string("2.0.0")
v4 = Version.from_string("2.1.3")

print(f"{v1} < {v2}:  {v1 < v2}")
print(f"{v2} == {v3}:  {v2 == v3}")
print(f"{v4} > {v2}:   {v4 > v2}")
print(f"{v1} <= {v2}:  {v1 <= v2}")

versions = [v4, v1, v3, Version("1","2","0")]
print(f"Sorted: {sorted(versions)}")
print(f"Latest: {max(versions)}")

# Hashable: can be stored in sets
seen = {v1, v2, v3}
print(f"Unique: {len(seen)} (v2 and v3 are equal)")
```

Output:

```
1.9.0 < 2.0.0:   True
2.0.0 == 2.0.0:  True
2.1.3 > 2.0.0:   True
1.9.0 <= 2.0.0:  True
Sorted: [1.2.0, 1.9.0, 2.0.0, 2.1.3]
Latest: 2.1.3
Unique: 2 (v2 and v3 are equal)
```

Example 2 — Variation

Custom equality with structural comparison: two objects with the same data should compare equal, regardless of identity.

```
class Rectangle:
    def __init__(self, width, height):
        self.width  = width
        self.height = height

    @property
    def area(self):
        return self.width * self.height

    def __repr__(self):
        return f"Rectangle({self.width}, {self.height})"

    def __eq__(self, other):
        if not isinstance(other, Rectangle): return NotImplemented
        return self.width == other.width and self.height == other.height

    def __hash__(self):
        return hash((self.width, self.height))

    def __lt__(self, other):
        if not isinstance(other, Rectangle): return NotImplemented
        return self.area < other.area


r1 = Rectangle(3, 4)
r2 = Rectangle(3, 4)  # same dimensions, different object
r3 = Rectangle(4, 3)  # same area, different dimensions
r4 = Rectangle(5, 2)  # same area as r1 (10)

print(f"r1 == r2: {r1 == r2}  (same dimensions)")
print(f"r1 == r3: {r1 == r3}  (different dimension order)")
print(f"r1 is r2: {r1 is r2}  (different objects)")

# Sorting by area
rects = [Rectangle(5,6), Rectangle(2,3), Rectangle(4,4), Rectangle(1,10)]
print(f"\nSorted by area: {sorted(rects)}")
```

```
# Dict keys and sets use __hash__ and __eq__
rect_map = {r1: "portrait", r3: "landscape"}
print(f"\nDict lookup: {rect_map[Rectangle(3,4)]}")
print(f"Unique rects: {len({r1, r2, r3})}")
```

Output:

```
r1 == r2: True   (same dimensions)
r1 == r3: False  (different dimension order)
r1 is r2: False  (different objects)

Sorted by area: [Rectangle(2, 3), Rectangle(1, 10), Rectangle(5, 6),
Rectangle(4, 4)]

Dict lookup: portrait
Unique rects: 2
```

Example 3 — Real-world application

A grade record system where sorting by multiple criteria is controlled precisely by __lt__.

```
from functools import total_ordering

@total_ordering
class StudentResult:
    """Student result sortable by grade (desc), then name (asc).

    This order: highest grade first; ties broken alphabetically.
    """

    def __init__(self, student_id, name, grade):
        self.student_id = student_id
        self.name       = name
        self.grade      = grade

    def __repr__(self):
        return f"StudentResult({self.student_id!r}, {self.name!r},
{self.grade})"

    def __str__(self):
        return f"{self.student_id:6s}  {self.name:20s}  {self.grade:.1f}"
```

```python
    def __eq__(self, other):
        if not isinstance(other, StudentResult): return NotImplemented
        return self.grade == other.grade and self.name == other.name

    def __lt__(self, other):
        if not isinstance(other, StudentResult): return NotImplemented
        # Higher grade first (negate for ascending sort order)
        if self.grade != other.grade:
            return self.grade > other.grade  # descending
        return self.name < other.name        # ascending on tie

    def __hash__(self):
        return hash((self.student_id,))


results = [
    StudentResult("S001", "Charlie Davis", 78.5),
    StudentResult("S002", "Alice Wong",    91.0),
    StudentResult("S003", "Bob Smith",     91.0),
    StudentResult("S004", "Dana Lee",      65.0),
    StudentResult("S005", "Eve Chen",      78.5),
]

print("ID     Name                 Grade")
print("-" * 38)
for r in sorted(results):
    print(r)

print(f"\nTop student: {max(results).name}")
```

Output:

```
ID      Name                 Grade
--------------------------------------
S002    Alice Wong            91.0
S003    Bob Smith             91.0
S001    Charlie Davis         78.5
S005    Eve Chen              78.5
S004    Dana Lee              65.0
```

```
Top student: Alice Wong
```

8.4 Arithmetic Operators: __add__, __sub__, __mul__, __truediv__

Arithmetic dunder methods allow custom objects to work with Python's `+`, `-`, `*`, `/`, `//`, `%`, and `**` operators. Python maps each operator to a method: `+` calls `__add__`, `-` calls `__sub__`, `*` calls `__mul__`, `/` calls `__truediv__`, `//` calls `__floordiv__`, `%` calls `__mod__`, and `**` calls `__pow__`.

Each operator also has a reflected (right-hand) version: `__radd__`, `__rsub__`, `__rmul__`, and so on. When `x + y` is evaluated, Python first tries `x.__add__(y)`. If that returns `NotImplemented`, Python tries `y.__radd__(x)`. Reflected methods are essential for expressions like `3 * vector`, where the left operand (int) does not know how to handle the right operand (Vector).

In-place operators (`+=`, `-=`, `*=`) have their own dunder variants: `__iadd__`, `__isub__`, `__imul__`, etc. If these are not defined, Python falls back to `__add__` etc. and creates a new object. If mutable behaviour is desired (e.g. a list-like object where `+=` extends in place), define the in-place variant to modify `self` and return `self`.

Example 1 — Introduction

A Duration class with full arithmetic support: adding durations, subtracting, scaling by a factor.

```
class Duration:
    """A time duration stored in total seconds.

    Supports: +, -, *, / (by scalar), comparison, str.
    """

    def __init__(self, seconds):
        self._total = max(0, int(seconds))

    @classmethod
    def from_hms(cls, hours=0, minutes=0, seconds=0):
        return cls(hours * 3600 + minutes * 60 + seconds)

    @property
    def total_seconds(self): return self._total

    def __repr__(self):
        return f"Duration({self._total})"

    def __str__(self):
        h, rem = divmod(self._total, 3600)
```

```
        m, s   = divmod(rem, 60)
        return f"{h}h {m:02d}m {s:02d}s"

    def __add__(self, other):
        if isinstance(other, Duration):
            return Duration(self._total + other._total)
        return NotImplemented

    def __sub__(self, other):
        if isinstance(other, Duration):
            return Duration(self._total - other._total)
        return NotImplemented

    def __mul__(self, factor):
        if isinstance(factor, (int, float)):
            return Duration(self._total * factor)
        return NotImplemented

    def __rmul__(self, factor):
        return self.__mul__(factor)

    def __truediv__(self, divisor):
        if isinstance(divisor, (int, float)):
            return Duration(self._total / divisor)
        if isinstance(divisor, Duration):
            return self._total / divisor._total  # ratio
        return NotImplemented

    def __eq__(self, other):
        return isinstance(other, Duration) and self._total == other._total

    def __lt__(self, other):
        return isinstance(other, Duration) and self._total < other._total


run    = Duration.from_hms(hours=1, minutes=45, seconds=30)
warmup = Duration.from_hms(minutes=15)
cooldown = Duration.from_hms(minutes=10)
```

```
print(f"Run:         {run}")
print(f"Warm-up:     {warmup}")
print(f"Total:       {run + warmup + cooldown}")
print(f"Run - w/u: {run - warmup}")
print(f"2x run:      {2 * run}")
print(f"Half run:    {run / 2}")
print(f"Pace ratio: {run / warmup:.2f}x longer")

sessions = [Duration.from_hms(1,30), Duration.from_hms(0,45),
Duration.from_hms(2,0)]
print(f"Longest: {max(sessions)}")
```

Output:

```
Run:        1h 45m 30s
Warm-up:    0h 15m 00s
Total:      2h 10m 30s
Run - w/u: 1h 30m 30s
2x run:     3h 31m 00s
Half run:   0h 52m 45s
Pace ratio: 7.03x longer
Longest: 2h 00m 00s
```

Example 2 — Variation

In-place operators (__iadd__, __imul__): a mutable Bag class where += adds items in place rather than creating a new object.

```
class Bag:
    """Mutable multiset. += adds items; *= duplicates the bag."""

    def __init__(self, items=None):
        self._counts = {}
        for item in (items or []):
            self._counts[item] = self._counts.get(item, 0) + 1

    def __repr__(self):
        pairs = ", ".join(f"{k!r}:{v}" for k, v in
sorted(self._counts.items()))
        return f"Bag({{{pairs}}})"

    def __add__(self, other):
        """Return new Bag combining both."""
```

```
        result = Bag()
        for k, v in self._counts.items():
            result._counts[k] = v
        for k, v in other._counts.items():
            result._counts[k] = result._counts.get(k, 0) + v
        return result

    def __iadd__(self, other):
        """Extend self in place."""
        for k, v in other._counts.items():
            self._counts[k] = self._counts.get(k, 0) + v
        return self    # MUST return self for in-place ops

    def __imul__(self, factor):
        """Multiply all counts in place."""
        for k in self._counts:
            self._counts[k] *= factor
        return self

    def __len__(self): return sum(self._counts.values())

    def count(self, item): return self._counts.get(item, 0)


shopping = Bag(["apple","banana","apple","orange"])
extra    = Bag(["apple","kiwi"])

print(f"Original: {shopping}  ({len(shopping)} items)")

# __add__: creates new Bag
combined = shopping + extra
print(f"Combined: {combined}")
print(f"Original unchanged: {shopping}")

# __iadd__: modifies in place
shopping += extra
print(f"After +=: {shopping}")

# __imul__: scales in place
```

```
shopping *= 2
print(f"After *=2: {shopping}")
print(f"Apple count: {shopping.count('apple')}")
```

Output:

```
Original: Bag({'apple':2, 'banana':1, 'orange':1})  (4 items)
Combined: Bag({'apple':3, 'banana':1, 'kiwi':1, 'orange':1})
Original unchanged: Bag({'apple':2, 'banana':1, 'orange':1})
After +=: Bag({'apple':3, 'banana':1, 'kiwi':1, 'orange':1})
After *=2: Bag({'apple':6, 'banana':2, 'kiwi':2, 'orange':2})
Apple count: 6
```

> **Note:** In-place operator methods must return self. If they do not, the variable on the left of += is set to None (the implicit return value). This is a common bug in custom mutable objects. Always end __iadd__, __imul__, etc. with return self.

Example 3 — Real-world application

A Polynomial class with arithmetic operators, demonstrating how complex mathematical objects integrate naturally with Python's syntax.

```
class Polynomial:
    """Polynomial: coefficients[i] is the coefficient of x^i.

    Polynomial([1, 2, 3]) represents 1 + 2x + 3x^2.
    """

    def __init__(self, coefficients):
        self._c = list(coefficients)
        while len(self._c) > 1 and self._c[-1] == 0:
            self._c.pop()    # remove leading zeros

    def __repr__(self):
        return f"Polynomial({self._c})"

    def __str__(self):
        if not self._c or self._c == [0]: return "0"
        terms = []
        for i, c in enumerate(self._c):
            if c == 0: continue
            if i == 0:   terms.append(str(c))
            elif i == 1: terms.append(f"{c}x" if c != 1 else "x")
```

```
            else:        terms.append(f"{c}x^{i}" if c != 1 else f"x^{i}")
        return " + ".join(reversed(terms))

    def __call__(self, x):
        return sum(c * x**i for i, c in enumerate(self._c))

    def __add__(self, other):
        n = max(len(self._c), len(other._c))
        a = self._c  + [0]*(n - len(self._c))
        b = other._c + [0]*(n - len(other._c))
        return Polynomial([ai+bi for ai,bi in zip(a,b)])

    def __sub__(self, other):
        n = max(len(self._c), len(other._c))
        a = self._c  + [0]*(n - len(self._c))
        b = other._c + [0]*(n - len(other._c))
        return Polynomial([ai-bi for ai,bi in zip(a,b)])

    def __mul__(self, other):
        if isinstance(other, (int, float)):
            return Polynomial([c*other for c in self._c])
        result = [0]*(len(self._c) + len(other._c) - 1)
        for i, a in enumerate(self._c):
            for j, b in enumerate(other._c):
                result[i+j] += a*b
        return Polynomial(result)

    def __rmul__(self, k): return self.__mul__(k)

    def __eq__(self, other):
        return isinstance(other, Polynomial) and self._c == other._c


p = Polynomial([1, 2, 3])    # 1 + 2x + 3x^2
q = Polynomial([0, 1])       # x

print(f"p = {p}")
print(f"q = {q}")
print(f"p + q = {p + q}")
```

```
print(f"p - q = {p - q}")
print(f"p * q = {p * q}")
print(f"2 * p = {2 * p}")
print(f"p(2)  = {p(2)}")
print(f"p(0)  = {p(0)}")
```

Output:

```
p = 3x^2 + 2x + 1
q = x
p + q = 3x^2 + 3x + 1
p - q = 3x^2 + x + 1
p * q = 3x^3 + 2x^2 + x
2 * p = 6x^2 + 4x + 2
p(2)  = 17
p(0)  = 1
```

`__call__` is another dunder method — it makes an object callable with `obj(args)` syntax. A `Polynomial` that evaluates itself at a given x by writing `p(2)` is more readable than `p.evaluate(2)`. This is the same mechanism used by Python's decorator system and by function-like objects in machine learning frameworks.

8.5 Container Methods: __len__, __getitem__, __setitem__, __contains__

Container dunder methods make custom objects behave like Python's built-in collections. `__len__` enables `len(obj)`. `__getitem__` enables `obj[key]` access. `__setitem__` enables `obj[key] = value` assignment. `__delitem__` enables `del obj[key]`. `__contains__` enables the `in` operator.

Implementing `__getitem__` alone is enough for Python to infer iteration support: if an object has `__getitem__`, Python will call it with integer indices starting from 0, incrementing until `IndexError` is raised. This is the old-style iteration protocol, and it works even without `__iter__`. However, implementing `__iter__` explicitly (Section 8.6) is preferred for clarity.

Slicing is handled through `__getitem__` as well. When the subscript is a `slice` object (as in `obj[1:4]`), Python passes the `slice` to `__getitem__`. Checking `isinstance(key, slice)` inside the method allows you to handle both integer indexing and slicing.

Example 1 — Introduction

A typed list that enforces element type through __setitem__ and __getitem__.

```
class TypedList:
    """A list that enforces a single element type.

    Raises TypeError if an element of the wrong type is added.
    """
```

```
    def __init__(self, element_type, items=None):
        self._type  = element_type
        self._items = []
        for item in (items or []):
            self._validate(item)
            self._items.append(item)

    def _validate(self, value):
        if not isinstance(value, self._type):
            raise TypeError(
                f"Expected {self._type.__name__}, got {type(value).__name__}:
{value!r}"
            )

    def __len__(self):           return len(self._items)
    def __contains__(self, x):  return x in self._items

    def __getitem__(self, key):
        return self._items[key]   # supports int and slice

    def __setitem__(self, key, value):
        if isinstance(key, slice):
            for v in value: self._validate(v)
        else:
            self._validate(value)
        self._items[key] = value

    def __delitem__(self, key):
        del self._items[key]

    def append(self, value):
        self._validate(value)
        self._items.append(value)

    def __repr__(self):
        return f"TypedList({self._type.__name__}, {self._items})"


scores = TypedList(float, [91.5, 72.0, 88.5])
```

```
print(scores)
print(f"len: {len(scores)}")
print(f"scores[0]: {scores[0]}")
print(f"scores[1:]: {scores[1:]}")
print(f"72.0 in scores: {72.0 in scores}")

scores[0] = 95.0
print(f"After update: {scores}")

del scores[1]
print(f"After delete: {scores}")

try:
    scores.append("not a float")
except TypeError as e:
    print(f"Blocked: {e}")
```

Output:

```
TypedList(float, [91.5, 72.0, 88.5])
len: 3
scores[0]: 91.5
scores[1:]: [72.0, 88.5]
72.0 in scores: True
After update: TypedList(float, [95.0, 72.0, 88.5])
After delete: TypedList(float, [95.0, 88.5])
Blocked: Expected float, got str: 'not a float'
```

Example 2 — Variation

A sparse matrix using __getitem__ and __setitem__ with tuple keys, defaulting to zero for unset elements.

```
class SparseMatrix:
    """Memory-efficient matrix: only non-zero values stored.

    Access: matrix[row, col]  (uses tuple key)
    Default value for unset elements: 0
    """

    def __init__(self, rows, cols, default=0):
        self.rows    = rows
        self.cols    = cols
```

```
        self.default = default
        self._data    = {}

    def _check_bounds(self, row, col):
        if not (0 <= row < self.rows and 0 <= col < self.cols):
            raise IndexError(f"Index ({row},{col}) out of bounds
({self.rows}x{self.cols}).")

    def __getitem__(self, key):
        row, col = key
        self._check_bounds(row, col)
        return self._data.get((row, col), self.default)

    def __setitem__(self, key, value):
        row, col = key
        self._check_bounds(row, col)
        if value == self.default:
            self._data.pop((row, col), None)  # keep sparse
        else:
            self._data[row, col] = value

    def __contains__(self, key):
        return key in self._data

    def __len__(self):
        return len(self._data)   # non-zero count

    def density(self):
        total = self.rows * self.cols
        return len(self._data) / total if total else 0

    def display(self):
        for r in range(self.rows):
            row_str = "  ".join(f"{self[r,c]:4}" for c in range(self.cols))
            print(f"  [{row_str}]")


m = SparseMatrix(4, 4)
m[0, 0] = 1
```

```
m[1, 2] = 5
m[2, 1] = 3
m[3, 3] = 8

print(f"Matrix ({m.rows}x{m.cols}), {len(m)} non-zero,
density={m.density():.0%})")
m.display()

print(f"\nm[1,2] = {m[1,2]}")
print(f"m[0,1] = {m[0,1]}  (sparse default)")

m[1, 2] = 0   # setting to default removes the entry
print(f"After zero: {len(m)} non-zero")
```

Output:

```
Matrix (4x4), 4 non-zero, density=25%)
  [   1     0     0     0]
  [   0     0     5     0]
  [   0     3     0     0]
  [   0     0     0     8]

m[1,2] = 5
m[0,1] = 0  (sparse default)

After zero: 3 non-zero
```

Example 3 — Real-world application

A route planner implementing full container behaviour: indexing, slicing, containment, and length over a sequence of stops.

```
from dataclasses import dataclass

@dataclass
class Stop:
    name:     str
    arrival:  str    # HH:MM
    distance: float  # km from previous stop

    def __str__(self):
        return f"{self.name:20s} arr={self.arrival} +{self.distance:.1f}km"
```

```
class Route:
    """An ordered sequence of stops with container-style access."""

    def __init__(self, route_id, stops=None):
        self.route_id = route_id
        self._stops   = list(stops or [])

    def add_stop(self, stop):
        self._stops.append(stop)

    def __len__(self): return len(self._stops)

    def __getitem__(self, key):
        return self._stops[key]   # int or slice

    def __contains__(self, stop_name):
        return any(s.name == stop_name for s in self._stops)

    def __repr__(self):
        return f"Route({self.route_id!r}, {len(self)} stops)"

    @property
    def total_distance(self):
        return sum(s.distance for s in self._stops)

    @property
    def origin(self): return self._stops[0].name if self._stops else None

    @property
    def destination(self): return self._stops[-1].name if self._stops else None

    def sub_route(self, start, end):
        """Return a new Route for the segment between two stop names."""
        names = [s.name for s in self._stops]
        i = names.index(start)
        j = names.index(end) + 1
```

```
        return Route(f"{self.route_id}[{start}→{end}]", self._stops[i:j])


route = Route("BNE-SYD", [
    Stop("Brisbane",        "07:00",   0.0),
    Stop("Gold Coast",      "07:45",  85.0),
    Stop("Byron Bay",       "09:00",  80.0),
    Stop("Coffs Harbour",   "11:30", 170.0),
    Stop("Port Macquarie",  "13:00", 115.0),
    Stop("Newcastle",       "15:30", 200.0),
    Stop("Sydney",          "17:00", 170.0),
])

print(repr(route))
print(f"Origin: {route.origin}  →  Destination: {route.destination}")
print(f"Total distance: {route.total_distance:.0f} km")
print(f"First stop: {route[0]}")
print(f"Last stop:  {route[-1]}")
print(f"'Byron Bay' in route: {'Byron Bay' in route}")
print(f"'Melbourne' in route: {'Melbourne' in route}")

coastal = route.sub_route("Byron Bay", "Coffs Harbour")
print(f"\nSub-route: {coastal}")
for stop in coastal:
    print(f"  {stop}")
```

Output:

```
Route('BNE-SYD', 7 stops)
Origin: Brisbane  →  Destination: Sydney
Total distance: 820 km
First stop: Brisbane                 arr=07:00  +0.0km
Last stop:  Sydney                   arr=17:00  +170.0km
'Byron Bay' in route: True
'Melbourne' in route: False

Sub-route: Route('BNE-SYD[Byron Bay→Coffs Harbour]', 2 stops)
  Byron Bay            arr=09:00  +80.0km
  Coffs Harbour        arr=11:30  +170.0km
```

8.6 __iter__ and __next__ — Making Objects Iterable

An iterable is any object from which Python can obtain an iterator. An iterator is the object that actually produces values one at a time. The two are related but distinct: an iterable implements `__iter__` (which returns an iterator); an iterator implements both `__iter__` (which returns itself) and `__next__` (which produces the next value or raises `StopIteration`).

Most container classes (lists, tuples, strings) are iterables that return a separate iterator object when `iter()` is called. Custom classes can be either: a simple iterable that delegates to an existing iterator (e.g. returning `iter(self._items)`), or an object that is its own iterator (by implementing both `__iter__` and `__next__` on the same class).

The second pattern — an object that is its own iterator — is most common for generators and lazy sequences: objects that compute values on demand rather than storing them in memory. An iterator for an infinite sequence, a file reader that yields lines, or a range-like object that generates values are all candidates for this pattern.

The iteration protocol summary

- Iterable: has `__iter__()` returning an iterator.
- Iterator: has `__iter__()` returning `self`, and `__next__()` returning the next value or raising `StopIteration`.
- A for-loop calls `iter(obj)` once, then calls `next()` repeatedly until `StopIteration`.
- A class can be both iterable and its own iterator, or iterable with a separate iterator class.

Example 1 — Introduction

An iterable class that delegates to a separate iterator, keeping the two concerns cleanly separated.

```
class Fibonacci:
    """Iterable that generates Fibonacci numbers up to a given count.

    Fibonacci(6) iterates: 0, 1, 1, 2, 3, 5
    Each call to iter() returns a fresh iterator from the start.
    """

    def __init__(self, count):
        self.count = count

    def __iter__(self):
        return FibonacciIterator(self.count)

    def __repr__(self):
        return f"Fibonacci({self.count})"


class FibonacciIterator:
```

```
    def __init__(self, count):
        self._count  = count
        self._index  = 0
        self._a, self._b = 0, 1

    def __iter__(self):
        return self      # iterator is its own iterable

    def __next__(self):
        if self._index >= self._count:
            raise StopIteration
        value        = self._a
        self._a, self._b = self._b, self._a + self._b
        self._index += 1
        return value


fib = Fibonacci(8)

# for-loop uses the iteration protocol
print("for-loop:", end=" ")
for n in fib:
    print(n, end=" ")
print()

# list() uses it too
print("list():  ", list(fib))

# sum(), max(), any() all work on iterables
print("sum:      ", sum(fib))
print("max:      ", max(fib))

# Each iter(fib) call starts fresh
it1 = iter(fib)
it2 = iter(fib)
print("it1 next:", next(it1), next(it1))
print("it2 next:", next(it2), next(it2))
```

Output:

```
for-loop: 0 1 1 2 3 5 8 13
```

```
list():   [0, 1, 1, 2, 3, 5, 8, 13]
sum:      33
max:      13
it1 next: 0 1
it2 next: 0 1
```

Example 2 — Variation

An object that is its own iterator: a countdown timer that generates values on demand, carrying its own state.

```
class CountdownTimer:
    """Iterator that counts down from start to 0, yielding each value.

    This class is its own iterator: __iter__ returns self.
    Once exhausted, it cannot be restarted (same as built-in iterators).
    """


    def __init__(self, start, step=1):
        self._current = start
        self._step    = step
        self._done    = False

    def __iter__(self):
        return self    # this object is its own iterator

    def __next__(self):
        if self._done or self._current < 0:
            raise StopIteration
        value = self._current
        self._current -= self._step
        if self._current < 0:
            self._done = True
        return value



timer = CountdownTimer(10, 2)


print("Countdown by 2s:", list(timer))
```

```python
# Exhausted: iteration produces nothing
print("Second pass:    ", list(timer))

# Manual iteration
rocket = CountdownTimer(5)
print("\nLaunch sequence:")
for t in rocket:
    if t == 0:
        print("  0... Ignition! U0001f680")
    else:
        print(f"  {t}...")
```

Output:

```
Countdown by 2s: [10, 8, 6, 4, 2, 0]
Second pass:     []

Launch sequence:
  5...
  4...
  3...
  2...
  1...
  0... Ignition! U0001f680
```

Example 3 — Real-world application

A lazy file-chunker that reads a large text source in fixed-size chunks, producing each chunk on demand without loading the entire content into memory.

```python
import io

class ChunkedReader:
    """Reads a text source in fixed-size chunks using the iterator protocol.

    The source can be any file-like object (duck typing).
    Chunks are generated lazily — only read when next() is called.
    """

    def __init__(self, source, chunk_size=100):
        self._source     = source
        self._chunk_size = chunk_size
        self._buffer     = ""
```

```
        self._exhausted  = False

    def __iter__(self):
        return self

    def __next__(self):
        if self._exhausted:
            raise StopIteration

        chunk = self._source.read(self._chunk_size)
        if not chunk:
            self._exhausted = True
            raise StopIteration

        return chunk


# Simulate a large text source with StringIO
text = " ".join([f"word_{i}" for i in range(200)])
source = io.StringIO(text)

reader = ChunkedReader(source, chunk_size=50)

print(f"Source length: {len(text)} characters")
print(f"Chunk size:    50 characters\n")

chunks = list(reader)
print(f"Number of chunks: {len(chunks)}")

for i, chunk in enumerate(chunks[:3], 1):
    print(f"Chunk {i} ({len(chunk)} chars): {chunk!r}")
print("...")

# Works with any text-producing iterable, including actual files
# In production: open("large_file.txt") instead of StringIO
word_count = sum(len(c.split()) for c in ChunkedReader(io.StringIO(text), 200))
print(f"\nTotal words counted lazily: {word_count}")
```

Output:

```
Source length: 1389 characters
Chunk size:    50 characters

Number of chunks: 28
Chunk 1 (50 chars): 'word_0 word_1 word_2 word_3 word_4 word_5 word_6 w'
Chunk 2 (50 chars): 'ord_7 word_8 word_9 word_10 word_11 word_12 word_1'
Chunk 3 (50 chars): '3 word_14 word_15 word_16 word_17 word_18 word_19 '
...

Total words counted lazily: 200
```

8.7 __enter__ and __exit__ — Context Managers

Context managers are objects that define setup and teardown behaviour for use with the `with` statement. When Python executes `with obj as x:`, it calls `obj.__enter__()` and assigns the return value to `x`. When the `with` block exits — whether normally or via an exception — Python calls `obj.__exit__(exc_type, exc_val, exc_tb)`.

The critical property of context managers is that `__exit__` is always called, even if the body of the `with` block raises an exception. This makes them ideal for resource management: files, database connections, network sockets, locks, and transactions all need cleanup code that should run regardless of whether the protected code succeeds or fails.

`__exit__` receives information about any exception that was raised: the exception type, the exception value, and the traceback. If `__exit__` returns a truthy value, the exception is suppressed and execution continues after the `with` block. If it returns `None` or a falsy value, the exception propagates. Suppressing exceptions is rarely the right choice; usually `__exit__` should clean up and return `None`.

contextlib.contextmanager

The `@contextlib.contextmanager` decorator provides an alternative way to create context managers using a generator function. A generator that yields exactly once can serve as a context manager: code before the `yield` is the `__enter__` logic; code after is the `__exit__` logic. For simple cases, this is more concise than writing a full class with `__enter__` and `__exit__`.

Example 1 — Introduction

A database transaction context manager: __enter__ begins the transaction, __exit__ commits on success or rolls back on failure.

```
class Transaction:
    """Simulates a database transaction context manager.

    __enter__: begins the transaction.
    __exit__:  commits if no exception; rolls back if exception raised.
    """
```

```python
    def __init__(self, connection_name):
        self._conn     = connection_name
        self._commands = []

    def execute(self, sql):
        print(f"  EXEC: {sql}")
        self._commands.append(sql)
        if "INVALID" in sql.upper():
            raise ValueError(f"Invalid SQL: {sql}")

    def __enter__(self):
        print(f"[{self._conn}] BEGIN TRANSACTION")
        return self          # bound to the 'as' variable

    def __exit__(self, exc_type, exc_val, exc_tb):
        if exc_type is None:
            print(f"[{self._conn}] COMMIT ({len(self._commands)} command(s))")
        else:
            print(f"[{self._conn}] ROLLBACK (reason: {exc_val})")
        return False     # do not suppress exceptions


# Successful transaction
print("--- Successful transaction ---")
with Transaction("db-primary") as txn:
    txn.execute("INSERT INTO students VALUES ('S001', 'Alice')")
    txn.execute("UPDATE grades SET value=91 WHERE student_id='S001'")

# Failed transaction
print("\n--- Failed transaction ---")
try:
    with Transaction("db-primary") as txn:
        txn.execute("INSERT INTO students VALUES ('S002', 'Bob')")
        txn.execute("INVALID SYNTAX HERE")  # this raises ValueError
        txn.execute("UPDATE grades SET value=72")  # never reached
except ValueError as e:
    print(f"Caught: {e}")
```

Output:

```
--- Successful transaction ---
[db-primary] BEGIN TRANSACTION
  EXEC: INSERT INTO students VALUES ('S001', 'Alice')
  EXEC: UPDATE grades SET value=91 WHERE student_id='S001'
[db-primary] COMMIT (2 command(s))

--- Failed transaction ---
[db-primary] BEGIN TRANSACTION
  EXEC: INSERT INTO students VALUES ('S002', 'Bob')
  EXEC: INVALID SYNTAX HERE
[db-primary] ROLLBACK (reason: Invalid SQL: INVALID SYNTAX HERE)
Caught: Invalid SQL: INVALID SYNTAX HERE
```

Example 2 — Variation

Using contextlib.contextmanager to write the same context manager as a generator function, and nesting context managers.

```
from contextlib import contextmanager
import time

@contextmanager
def timer(label):
    """Context manager that times a block of code.

    Code before yield = __enter__.
    Code after yield  = __exit__.
    The try/finally ensures cleanup runs even on exception.
    """
    start = time.perf_counter()
    print(f"[Timer] Starting: {label}")
    try:
        yield    # control enters the with block here
    finally:
        elapsed = (time.perf_counter() - start) * 1000
        print(f"[Timer] Done: {label} ({elapsed:.2f}ms)")


@contextmanager
def indent(level=1, char="  "):
    """Context manager that tracks indentation for nested logging."""
```

```
    prefix = char * level
    print(f"{prefix}entering block")
    try:
        yield prefix
    finally:
        print(f"{prefix}exiting block")


with timer("data processing"):
    time.sleep(0.01)
    with timer("inner computation"):
        result = sum(i**2 for i in range(10_000))
    print(f"  Result: {result}")

print()
with indent(1) as p1:
    print(f"{p1}Level 1 work")
    with indent(2) as p2:
        print(f"{p2}Level 2 work")
        with indent(3) as p3:
            print(f"{p3}Level 3 work")
```

Output:

```
[Timer] Starting: data processing
[Timer] Starting: inner computation
[Timer] Done: inner computation (X.XXms)
  Result: 333283335000
[Timer] Done: data processing (XX.XXms)

  entering block
  Level 1 work
    entering block
    Level 2 work
      entering block
      Level 3 work
      exiting block
    exiting block
  exiting block
```

Example 3 — Real-world application

A complete, production-style context manager for a network connection pool, managing resource acquisition and release reliably.

```
import threading

class ConnectionPool:
    """Manages a pool of simulated connections.

    Use as a context manager to acquire/release connections safely.
    Thread-safe via a reentrant lock.
    """

    def __init__(self, pool_size=3):
        self._size      = pool_size
        self._available = list(range(1, pool_size + 1))
        self._lock      = threading.Lock()

    def acquire(self):
        with self._lock:
            if not self._available:
                raise RuntimeError("Connection pool exhausted.")
            conn_id = self._available.pop(0)
            print(f"  [Pool] Acquired connection #{conn_id}
({len(self._available)} remaining)")
            return conn_id

    def release(self, conn_id):
        with self._lock:
            self._available.append(conn_id)
            self._available.sort()
            print(f"  [Pool] Released connection #{conn_id}")


class PooledConnection:
    """Context manager for a single connection from a pool.

    __enter__:  acquires a connection from the pool.
    __exit__:   releases it back, even on exception.
    """
```

```
    def __init__(self, pool):
        self._pool   = pool
        self._conn   = None

    def __enter__(self):
        self._conn = self._pool.acquire()
        return self._conn

    def __exit__(self, exc_type, exc_val, exc_tb):
        if self._conn is not None:
            self._pool.release(self._conn)
        if exc_type:
            print(f"  [Pool] Exception during connection use: {exc_val}")
        return False    # propagate exceptions


pool = ConnectionPool(pool_size=3)

print("Normal usage:")
with PooledConnection(pool) as conn:
    print(f"  Using connection #{conn}")

print("\nNested connections:")
with PooledConnection(pool) as c1:
    with PooledConnection(pool) as c2:
        print(f"  Using #{c1} and #{c2} simultaneously")

print("\nException during use (connection still released):")
try:
    with PooledConnection(pool) as conn:
        print(f"  Using #{conn}, about to fail...")
        raise ValueError("Something went wrong")
except ValueError:
    pass

print(f"\nPool available after all operations: {pool._available}")
```

Output:

```
Normal usage:
  [Pool] Acquired connection #1 (2 remaining)
```

```
  Using connection #1
  [Pool] Released connection #1

Nested connections:
  [Pool] Acquired connection #1 (2 remaining)
  [Pool] Acquired connection #2 (1 remaining)
  Using #1 and #2 simultaneously
  [Pool] Released connection #2
  [Pool] Released connection #1

Exception during use (connection still released):
  [Pool] Acquired connection #1 (2 remaining)
  Using #1, about to fail...
  [Pool] Exception during connection use: Something went wrong
  [Pool] Released connection #1

Pool available after all operations: [1, 2, 3]
```

All three connections are returned to the pool after every `with` block, including the one that raised an exception. This is the fundamental guarantee context managers provide: `__exit__` is called unconditionally. Resource leaks that would occur with try/finally in every call site are eliminated by encapsulating the pattern once in the context manager class.

Chapter 8 Summary

- The Python data model is the protocol through which custom objects integrate with Python's syntax and built-in functions. Every operator, built-in function, and language construct that acts on objects does so by calling a dunder method. Implementing these methods makes custom classes behave like native Python types.
- __repr__ returns the developer-facing representation: unambiguous, ideally reconstructible. __str__ returns the user-facing representation: readable and concise. str() falls back to __repr__ when __str__ is not defined. __format__ controls how an object responds to format specifications in f-strings.
- Comparison dunder methods map to ==, !=, <, <=, >, >=. functools.total_ordering derives four operators from __eq__ and one ordering method. When __eq__ is defined, __hash__ must also be defined to keep objects usable in sets and as dict keys. Comparison methods should return NotImplemented for incompatible types, not raise TypeError.
- Arithmetic dunder methods map to +, -, *, /, //, %, **. Reflected variants (__radd__, __rsub__, etc.) handle expressions where the left operand does not support the operation (e.g. 3 * vector). In-place variants (__iadd__, __imul__, etc.) modify self and must return self.
- Container dunder methods enable indexing (__getitem__, __setitem__, __delitem__), length (__len__), and membership testing (__contains__). __getitem__ receives a slice object for slice operations, enabling custom slice handling. Implementing __getitem__ alone is enough for Python to infer basic iteration support.

- The iteration protocol uses two roles: iterables (have __iter__ returning an iterator) and iterators (have __iter__ returning self, and __next__ returning the next value or raising StopIteration). A class can be both its own iterable and iterator. Once exhausted, an iterator cannot be restarted unless it creates a fresh iterator via __iter__.
- Context managers implement __enter__ (returns the context value bound to the as variable) and __exit__ (receives exception information and performs cleanup). __exit__ is always called, even if an exception is raised. Returning True from __exit__ suppresses the exception; returning None or False propagates it.
- contextlib.contextmanager provides a generator-based alternative to writing full __enter__/__exit__ classes. Code before yield is __enter__ logic; code after is __exit__ logic. Using try/finally around the yield ensures cleanup runs even if the with block raises an exception.

Guided Exercises

Complete the following exercises. Each targets a specific concept from this chapter.

1. Create a Money class representing an amount in a given currency (e.g. "AUD"). Implement __str__ returning "AUD 9.99", __repr__ returning "Money(9.99, 'AUD')", __add__ and __sub__ for same-currency arithmetic (raising TypeError for different currencies), __mul__ and __rmul__ for scalar multiplication, and __eq__ and __lt__ for comparison. Add __hash__ so Money objects can be used in sets. Test all operations.

> ***Hint:*** *Store the amount as a Decimal for precision. Use from decimal import Decimal. __rmul__ should call self.__mul__(factor). Raise TypeError with a message like "Cannot add AUD and USD" when currencies differ.*

2. Build a Playlist class that stores a list of song titles internally. Implement __len__, __getitem__ (supporting both integer indexing and slicing), __contains__ (checks if a song title is in the playlist), __add__ (merges two playlists into a new one), and __iadd__ (extends this playlist in place). Add __repr__ and __str__. Test all operations including slicing and +=.

> ***Hint:*** *Store songs in self._songs = []. __getitem__ can simply return self._songs[key] which handles both int and slice. __iadd__ extends self._songs and returns self. __add__ creates a new Playlist with the combined list.*

3. Create a CountingRange class that works like Python's built-in range but also tracks how many times each value has been accessed. Implement __iter__ (returns a fresh iterator each time), __len__, __contains__, and a property access_counts returning a dict of value -> access count. Test that two separate for-loops produce different access counts that accumulate correctly.

> ***Hint:*** *Store access counts in a dict on the CountingRange instance (not the iterator). The iterator should update the parent's access_counts dict each time __next__ is called. Pass a reference to the parent into the iterator constructor.*

4. Write a ManagedFile context manager class (not using contextlib) that opens a file on __enter__ and closes it on __exit__. If an exception occurs during the with block, __exit__ should print the exception type and message before closing the file, but still let the exception propagate. Add a lines_read property that counts how many lines have been read via a readline() wrapper method. Test with both a successful read and a simulated error inside the with block.

> ***Hint:*** *In __enter__, open the file and return self. In __exit__, always close the file (use a try/finally inside __exit__ if needed). Check if exc_type is not None to detect an exception. Return False to propagate it.*

5. Implement a Matrix class (2D list of lists) with __repr__, __str__ (formatted grid), __getitem__ and __setitem__ using (row, col) tuple keys, __add__ (element-wise addition), __mul__ (scalar multiplication or matrix multiplication depending on whether other is a number or a Matrix), and __eq__. Test with 2x2 matrices: addition, scalar multiply, and matrix multiply.

> ***Hint:*** *In __mul__, use isinstance(other, (int, float)) to detect a scalar. For matrix multiplication, use three nested loops. __str__ should format each number with consistent width using f"{v:6.1f}" or similar.*

Challenge Tasks

Open-ended tasks. No hints provided. Design your solution before writing any code.

1. Implement a fully-featured LinkedList class using dunder methods. The list should: store values in nodes (each with a value and a next reference); support __len__, __getitem__ (by index, with negative indexing), __setitem__, __delitem__, __contains__, __iter__, __reversed__, __add__ (concatenation), __iadd__ (extend in place), __repr__, and __str__. Ensure __getitem__ raises IndexError for out-of-range indices. Demonstrate all operations, including a for-loop, reversed(), and concatenation of two lists.

2. Design a LazySequence class that generates values lazily using a transform function. LazySequence(start, stop, fn) should produce fn(i) for i in range(start, stop) without pre-computing them. Implement __iter__ and __next__ (the class is its own iterator), __len__, __getitem__ (for integer indexing and slicing, computing values on demand), and __contains__ (iterating until found or exhausted). Demonstrate with: squares from 0 to 99, a filtered view of even squares, and converting a slice to a list without materialising the full sequence.

3. Build a comprehensive context manager for a unit testing helper called AssertRaises. It should be used as: with AssertRaises(ValueError) as ctx: ... and after the block, ctx.exception should hold the caught exception. If the expected exception is not raised, __exit__ should raise AssertionError("Expected ValueError was not raised"). If a different exception type is raised, let it propagate. Add an optional match parameter that checks the exception message contains a given string. Demonstrate it successfully catching the right exception, failing when no exception is raised, and failing when the wrong exception type is raised. This is a simplified version of unittest.assertRaises.

CHAPTER 9 **OOP Design Patterns — Beginner**

Book 01: Object-Oriented Programming in Python

> *Design patterns are proven, reusable solutions to problems that recur constantly in software design. They are not code libraries or frameworks— they are templates: named approaches that experienced developers recognise,communicate, and apply. Knowing the patterns means you can identify the shape of a problem, reach for the appropriate solution, and write code that other developers will immediately understand. This chapter introduces five foundational patterns: Singleton (ensure only one instance exists), Factory (delegate object creation), Observer (notify many objects of state changes), Strategy (swap algorithms at runtime), and Decorator (add behaviour without modifying a class). Each is illustrated in Python and placed in a realistic context.*

9.1 What Are Design Patterns?

Design patterns were formalised by the "Gang of Four" — Erich Gamma, Richard Helm, Ralph Johnson, and John Vlissides — in their 1994 book "Design Patterns: Elements of Reusable Object-Oriented Software". They catalogued 23 patterns across three categories: Creational (how objects are created), Structural (how classes and objects are composed), and Behavioural (how objects communicate). This chapter focuses on the five most practically relevant for students beginning OOP.

The value of patterns is not that they solve problems you could not solve otherwise. You could always write code that works. The value is shared vocabulary and proven structure: when you say "I used an Observer pattern here," every experienced developer immediately knows what that means, what the trade-offs are, and roughly how the code is structured. Patterns also carry decades of accumulated knowledge about what goes wrong and what works well.

Python's dynamic nature means some classical patterns are simpler to implement than in statically-typed languages like Java. Python functions are first-class objects, so the Strategy pattern can be implemented with a simple callable. Python's built-in `__new__` enables elegant Singletons. The patterns are the same; the Python implementations are often more concise.

The five patterns covered in this chapter

- Singleton: ensures a class has only one instance, providing a global access point to it.
- Factory: defines an interface for creating objects, allowing subclasses to decide which class to instantiate.
- Observer: defines a one-to-many dependency so that when one object changes state, all its dependents are notified automatically.
- Strategy: defines a family of algorithms, encapsulates each one, and makes them interchangeable at runtime.
- Decorator (pattern): attaches additional responsibilities to an object dynamically, without modifying the class.

Example 1 — Introduction

The problem design patterns solve: without the Observer pattern, notification logic becomes scattered and tightly coupled.

```
# Without a pattern: the subject must know about every observer explicitly.
# Adding a new observer requires modifying the subject.

class OrderSystem:
    def place_order(self, order_id, total):
        print(f"Order {order_id} placed: ${total:.2f}")
        # Tight coupling: must call each notifiable thing directly
        self._send_email_confirmation(order_id)
        self._update_inventory(order_id)
        self._log_to_analytics(order_id, total)
        # Adding SMS notification means editing this method

    def _send_email_confirmation(self, order_id):
        print(f"  [Email] Confirmation sent for order {order_id}")

    def _update_inventory(self, order_id):
        print(f"  [Inventory] Stock decremented for order {order_id}")

    def _log_to_analytics(self, order_id, total):
        print(f"  [Analytics] Logged ${total:.2f} for order {order_id}")


os = OrderSystem()
os.place_order("ORD-001", 149.00)
```

Output:

```
Order ORD-001 placed: $149.00
  [Email] Confirmation sent for order ORD-001
  [Inventory] Stock decremented for order ORD-001
  [Analytics] Logged $149.00 for order ORD-001
```

Example 2 — Variation

With the Observer pattern: the subject broadcasts to whoever is listening, with no knowledge of what those listeners are.

```
class OrderSystem:
    def __init__(self):
        self._observers = []
```

```
    def subscribe(self, observer):
        self._observers.append(observer)

    def place_order(self, order_id, total):
        print(f"Order {order_id} placed: ${total:.2f}")
        for observer in self._observers:
            observer.update(order_id, total)  # broadcast


class EmailService:
    def update(self, order_id, total):
        print(f"  [Email] Confirmation sent for order {order_id}")

class InventoryService:
    def update(self, order_id, total):
        print(f"  [Inventory] Stock decremented for order {order_id}")

class SMSService:
    def update(self, order_id, total):
        print(f"  [SMS] Text sent: Your order {order_id} is confirmed!")



order_system = OrderSystem()
order_system.subscribe(EmailService())
order_system.subscribe(InventoryService())
order_system.subscribe(SMSService())   # added without modifying OrderSystem

order_system.place_order("ORD-001", 149.00)
```

Output:

```
Order ORD-001 placed: $149.00
  [Email] Confirmation sent for order ORD-001
  [Inventory] Stock decremented for order ORD-001
  [SMS] Text sent: Your order ORD-001 is confirmed!
```

Example 3 — Real-world application

Recognising patterns in Python's own standard library: where each of this chapter's five patterns appears.

```
# Singleton: logging.getLogger() always returns the same logger for a name
import logging
log1 = logging.getLogger("myapp")
log2 = logging.getLogger("myapp")
print(f"Same logger instance: {log1 is log2}")

# Factory: datetime.fromtimestamp() is a class method factory
from datetime import datetime
dt = datetime.fromtimestamp(1700000000)
print(f"Factory-created: {dt}")

# Observer: tkinter event binding is observer-style
# btn.bind("<Button-1>", callback)  — btn notifies callback when clicked

# Strategy: sort key= is a strategy — swap the algorithm for ordering
words = ["banana", "apple", "cherry", "date"]
print(sorted(words, key=len))          # strategy: sort by length
print(sorted(words, key=str.lower))    # strategy: case-insensitive

# Decorator (pattern): functools.lru_cache wraps a function
from functools import lru_cache
@lru_cache(maxsize=128)
def fibonacci(n):
    if n < 2: return n
    return fibonacci(n-1) + fibonacci(n-2)

print(fibonacci(30))
```

Output:

```
Same logger instance: True
Factory-created: 2023-11-15 08:13:20
['date', 'apple', 'banana', 'cherry']
['apple', 'banana', 'cherry', 'date']
832040
```

These patterns appear in Python's own standard library and every major framework. Recognising them in existing code is as valuable as knowing how to implement them yourself.

9.2 The Singleton Pattern

The Singleton pattern ensures that a class has exactly one instance, and provides a global access point to it. It solves the problem of coordinating shared state that must be consistent across an entire application: a configuration object, a connection pool, a logging system, an application-wide cache. Creating multiple instances of these would produce inconsistent state and hard-to-trace bugs.

Python offers several implementation approaches. The most Pythonic uses `__new__`: overriding the class's object-creation method to return the existing instance if one already exists. Another common approach uses a module-level variable — since Python modules are only imported once, a module containing a shared object effectively implements the singleton concept naturally.

The Singleton is one of the most debated patterns in software design. Its critics point out that global mutable state makes code harder to test (because tests cannot easily isolate the singleton) and can hide dependencies. In Python, module-level singletons and dependency injection are often preferred over explicit Singleton classes for exactly this reason. Knowing the pattern — and its trade-offs — is what matters.

When to use Singleton

Appropriate uses: a logger, a configuration store loaded from file, a connection pool, a thread-safe counter, or a registry of registered plugins. Each of these has a natural "there should only be one" requirement. Inappropriate uses: anything that could benefit from being configurable in tests, or anything that would be cleaner as a passed parameter.

Example 1 — Introduction

Classic Singleton using __new__: every call to the constructor returns the same instance.

```
class AppConfig:
    """Application configuration singleton.

    All calls to AppConfig() return the same instance.
    Settings loaded once; shared consistently across the program.
    """
    _instance = None    # class-level: one slot for the single instance

    def __new__(cls):
        if cls._instance is None:
            cls._instance = super().__new__(cls)
            cls._instance._initialised = False
        return cls._instance

    def __init__(self):
        if self._initialised:
            return    # already set up: skip re-initialisation
        self.debug       = False
        self.db_host     = "localhost"
        self.db_port     = 5432
```

```
        self.max_retries  = 3
        self._initialised = True
        print("AppConfig initialised.")


c1 = AppConfig()
c2 = AppConfig()
c3 = AppConfig()

print(f"c1 is c2: {c1 is c2}")
print(f"c1 is c3: {c1 is c3}")

# Modifying via one reference affects all
c1.debug = True
print(f"c2.debug: {c2.debug}")   # True — same object
print(f"c3.db_host: {c3.db_host}")
```

Output:

```
AppConfig initialised.
c1 is c2: True
c1 is c3: True
c2.debug: True
c3.db_host: localhost
```

Example 2 — Variation

Module-level singleton: Python's import system ensures a module is only loaded once, making a module-level object effectively a singleton.

```
# In a real project this would be a separate file: logger.py
# Here we simulate it within the same script.

class Logger:
    def __init__(self, name, level="INFO"):
        self.name  = name
        self.level = level
        self._entries = []

    def log(self, level, message):
        entry = f"[{level:7s}] [{self.name}] {message}"
        self._entries.append(entry)
```

```python
        print(entry)

    def info(self, msg):    self.log("INFO", msg)
    def warning(self, msg): self.log("WARNING", msg)
    def error(self, msg):   self.log("ERROR", msg)

    def summary(self):
        print(f"\n{self.name}: {len(self._entries)} entries total")


# Module-level singleton: created once when this code is executed.
# Any module that imports app_logger gets the same object.
app_logger = Logger("MyApp")


# Simulating two different modules both using the same logger
def module_a():
    app_logger.info("Module A: started processing")
    app_logger.info("Module A: complete")

def module_b():
    app_logger.warning("Module B: config missing, using defaults")
    app_logger.error("Module B: connection refused")


module_a()
module_b()
app_logger.summary()
```

Output:

```
[INFO   ] [MyApp] Module A: started processing
[INFO   ] [MyApp] Module A: complete
[WARNING] [MyApp] Module B: config missing, using defaults
[ERROR  ] [MyApp] Module B: connection refused

MyApp: 4 entries total
```

Example 3 — Real-world application

A thread-safe Singleton registry that tracks all registered plugins across an application.

```
import threading

class PluginRegistry:
    """Thread-safe singleton plugin registry.

    Plugins register themselves by calling PluginRegistry.register().
    Any part of the application can list or retrieve plugins.
    """
    _instance = None
    _lock     = threading.Lock()

    def __new__(cls):
        with cls._lock:
            if cls._instance is None:
                cls._instance = super().__new__(cls)
                cls._instance._plugins = {}
                cls._instance._init    = True
        return cls._instance

    def register(self, name, plugin_class):
        if name in self._plugins:
            raise ValueError(f"Plugin {name!r} is already registered.")
        self._plugins[name] = plugin_class
        print(f"  Registered plugin: {name!r}")

    def get(self, name):
        if name not in self._plugins:
            raise KeyError(f"No plugin registered with name {name!r}.")
        return self._plugins[name]

    def list_plugins(self):
        return list(self._plugins.keys())


# Simulate different parts of the application registering plugins
class CSVExporter:
    def export(self, data): return ",".join(str(v) for v in data)

class JSONExporter:
```

```python
    def export(self, data):
        import json
        return json.dumps(data)


print("Registering plugins:")
registry = PluginRegistry()
registry.register("csv",  CSVExporter)
registry.register("json", JSONExporter)

# Different reference — same singleton
reg2 = PluginRegistry()
print(f"\nSame instance: {registry is reg2}")
print(f"Registered: {reg2.list_plugins()}")

csv_exporter = reg2.get("csv")()
print(f"\nCSV export: {csv_exporter.export([1, 2, 3])}")
```

Output:

```
Registering plugins:
  Registered plugin: 'csv'
  Registered plugin: 'json'

Same instance: True
Registered: ['csv', 'json']

CSV export: 1,2,3
```

9.3 The Factory Pattern

The Factory pattern delegates the responsibility of creating objects to a dedicated method or class, rather than calling constructors directly throughout the codebase. When the exact class of the object to be created depends on runtime conditions — a configuration value, user input, data type, or environment — a factory centralises that decision, keeping it in one place and hiding it from callers.

Python supports several factory variants. The simplest is a factory function: a module-level function that returns an instance of the appropriate class. A class method factory (the `@classmethod` approach from Chapter 3) is used when the factory logic belongs to a specific class. The full Factory Method pattern uses inheritance: a base class defines the factory interface, and subclasses override it to produce different object types.

The key benefit is that calling code is decoupled from class names. Code that calls `ConnectionFactory.create("sqlite", ":memory:")` does not need to know that `SQLiteConnection` exists. Adding a new connection type requires adding a new class and registering it in the factory — the calling code never changes. This is the open/closed principle applied to object creation.

Example 1 — Introduction

A factory function: a single entry point that selects and returns the right class based on a type string.

```
from abc import ABC, abstractmethod


class Notification(ABC):
    @abstractmethod
    def send(self, recipient, message): ...



class EmailNotification(Notification):
    def send(self, recipient, message):
        print(f"[Email] To: {recipient} | {message}")



class SMSNotification(Notification):
    def send(self, recipient, message):
        print(f"[SMS]   To: {recipient} | {message[:50]}")



class PushNotification(Notification):
    def send(self, recipient, message):
        print(f"[Push]  To device {recipient[:12]}... | {message[:30]}")



# Factory function: caller never references the concrete classes
def create_notification(channel: str) -> Notification:
    channels = {
        "email": EmailNotification,
        "sms":   SMSNotification,
        "push":  PushNotification,
    }
    cls = channels.get(channel.lower())
    if cls is None:
        raise ValueError(f"Unknown channel: {channel!r}. Choose from
{list(channels)}")
    return cls()
```

```
# Calling code only knows about the factory, not the concrete classes
for channel in ["email", "sms", "push"]:
    notif = create_notification(channel)
    notif.send("user@example.com", "Your order has been dispatched.")

try:
    create_notification("pigeon")
except ValueError as e:
    print(f"\nError: {e}")
```

Output:

```
[Email] To: user@example.com | Your order has been dispatched.
[SMS]   To: user@example.com | Your order has been dispatched.
[Push]  To device user@example... | Your order has been dispatc

Error: Unknown channel: 'pigeon'. Choose from ['email', 'sms', 'push']
```

Example 2 — Variation

A registry-based factory: classes self-register using a decorator, making the factory extensible without modifying it.

```
class ShapeFactory:
    """Registry-based factory: shapes register themselves.

    Adding a new shape requires no changes to ShapeFactory.
    """
    _registry = {}

    @classmethod
    def register(cls, name):
        """Decorator: registers the decorated class under name."""
        def decorator(shape_cls):
            cls._registry[name.lower()] = shape_cls
            return shape_cls
        return decorator

    @classmethod
    def create(cls, shape_type, **kwargs):
```

```
        shape_cls = cls._registry.get(shape_type.lower())
        if shape_cls is None:
            raise ValueError(f"Unknown shape: {shape_type!r}. Registered: {list(cls._registry)}")
        return shape_cls(**kwargs)

    @classmethod
    def available(cls):
        return list(cls._registry.keys())


import math


@ShapeFactory.register("circle")
class Circle:
    def __init__(self, radius): self.radius = radius
    def area(self): return math.pi * self.radius ** 2
    def __str__(self): return f"Circle(r={self.radius}, area={self.area():.2f})"


@ShapeFactory.register("rectangle")
class Rectangle:
    def __init__(self, width, height): self.width, self.height = width, height
    def area(self): return self.width * self.height
    def __str__(self): return f"Rectangle({self.width}x{self.height}, area={self.area():.2f})"


@ShapeFactory.register("triangle")
class Triangle:
    def __init__(self, base, height): self.base, self.height = base, height
    def area(self): return 0.5 * self.base * self.height
    def __str__(self): return f"Triangle(b={self.base}, h={self.height}, area={self.area():.2f})"


print(f"Available shapes: {ShapeFactory.available()}")


specs = [
    ("circle",    {"radius": 5}),
    ("rectangle", {"width": 4, "height": 6}),
    ("triangle",  {"base": 8, "height": 3}),
```

```
]

for shape_type, kwargs in specs:
    shape = ShapeFactory.create(shape_type, **kwargs)
    print(shape)
```

Output:

```
Available shapes: ['circle', 'rectangle', 'triangle']
Circle(r=5, area=78.54)
Rectangle(4x6, area=24.00)
Triangle(b=8, h=3, area=12.00)
```

Example 3 — Real-world application

A database connection factory: different backends created from a config dict, with the calling code entirely unaware of which driver is used.

```
from abc import ABC, abstractmethod

class DatabaseConnection(ABC):
    @abstractmethod
    def connect(self) -> None: ...

    @abstractmethod
    def query(self, sql: str) -> list: ...

    @abstractmethod
    def close(self) -> None: ...

    def __enter__(self):
        self.connect()
        return self

    def __exit__(self, *args):
        self.close()


class SQLiteConnection(DatabaseConnection):
    def __init__(self, database):
        self._db  = database
        self._open = False
```

```
    def connect(self):
        self._open = True
        print(f"  [SQLite] Connected to {self._db}")

    def query(self, sql):
        print(f"  [SQLite] Executing: {sql}")
        return [{"id": 1, "name": "Alice"}, {"id": 2, "name": "Bob"}]

    def close(self):
        self._open = False
        print(f"  [SQLite] Connection closed.")


class PostgreSQLConnection(DatabaseConnection):
    def __init__(self, host, port, database, user):
        self._dsn  = f"{user}@{host}:{port}/{database}"

    def connect(self):
        print(f"  [PostgreSQL] Connected: {self._dsn}")

    def query(self, sql):
        print(f"  [PostgreSQL] Query: {sql}")
        return [{"result": "pg_data"}]

    def close(self):
        print(f"  [PostgreSQL] Connection closed.")


class ConnectionFactory:
    @staticmethod
    def create(config: dict) -> DatabaseConnection:
        driver = config.get("driver", "sqlite").lower()
        if driver == "sqlite":
            return SQLiteConnection(config.get("database", ":memory:"))
        elif driver == "postgresql":
            return PostgreSQLConnection(
                config.get("host", "localhost"),
                config.get("port", 5432),
```

```python
                config.get("database", "mydb"),
                config.get("user", "postgres"),
            )
        raise ValueError(f"Unsupported driver: {driver!r}")


configs = [
    {"driver": "sqlite",     "database": "app.db"},
    {"driver": "postgresql", "host": "db.example.com",
     "database": "production", "user": "app_user"},
]


for config in configs:
    with ConnectionFactory.create(config) as conn:
        results = conn.query("SELECT * FROM users")
        print(f"    Got {len(results)} row(s)")
    print()
```

Output:

```
[SQLite] Connected to app.db
[SQLite] Executing: SELECT * FROM users
  Got 2 row(s)
[SQLite] Connection closed.


[PostgreSQL] Connected: app_user@db.example.com:5432/production
[PostgreSQL] Query: SELECT * FROM users
  Got 1 row(s)
[PostgreSQL] Connection closed.
```

9.4 The Observer Pattern

The Observer pattern (also called Publish-Subscribe or Event System) defines a one-to-many dependency between objects. When the subject (the observed object) changes state, it notifies all registered observers automatically. Observers subscribe to receive notifications; they do not poll the subject, and the subject does not know what they do with the information.

This pattern is the backbone of event-driven programming. GUI frameworks use it for button clicks and keyboard events. Web frameworks use it for request lifecycle hooks. Financial systems use it for price feed subscriptions. Game engines use it for collision events. In all cases, the pattern decouples the source of an event from the code that handles it.

The key structural components are: the Subject (maintains a list of observers and notifies them), the Observer interface (defines the method the subject calls), and the ConcreteObserver (implements the interface and reacts to notifications). In Python, the Observer interface is often informal — any callable or any object with an `update()` method qualifies.

Using callables as observers

Python's first-class functions mean observers do not need to be objects at all. A subject can maintain a list of callables and call each one on notification. This is simpler than a formal Observer interface when the observer logic is lightweight and does not require state.

Example 1 — Introduction

A stock price feed: the subject notifies all registered observers whenever the price changes.

```
class StockFeed:
    """Observable stock price feed.

    Observers subscribe via observe(). When price updates,
    all observers are notified with the stock symbol and new price.
    """

    def __init__(self, symbol):
        self.symbol     = symbol
        self._price     = None
        self._observers = []

    def observe(self, observer):
        self._observers.append(observer)

    def unobserve(self, observer):
        self._observers.remove(observer)

    def set_price(self, price):
        old_price   = self._price
        self._price = price
        self._notify(old_price, price)

    def _notify(self, old_price, new_price):
        for observer in self._observers:
            observer.on_price_change(self.symbol, old_price, new_price)


class PriceDisplay:
    def on_price_change(self, symbol, old, new):
        change = "" if old is None else f" ({new - old:+.2f})"
```

```
        print(f"  [Display] {symbol}: ${new:.2f}{change}")


class AlertSystem:
    def __init__(self, threshold):
        self.threshold = threshold

    def on_price_change(self, symbol, old, new):
        if old is not None and abs(new - old) >= self.threshold:
            direction = "UP" if new > old else "DOWN"
            print(f"  [Alert] {symbol} moved {direction} by ${abs(new-
old):.2f}!")


class TradeLogger:
    def __init__(self):
        self._log = []

    def on_price_change(self, symbol, old, new):
        self._log.append(f"{symbol}: {old} → {new}")

    def show(self):
        print(f"  [Log] {len(self._log)} price event(s) recorded.")



feed    = StockFeed("AAPL")
display = PriceDisplay()
alerts  = AlertSystem(threshold=2.00)
logger  = TradeLogger()

feed.observe(display)
feed.observe(alerts)
feed.observe(logger)

print("Price updates:")
for price in [182.00, 183.50, 181.00, 185.50]:
    feed.set_price(price)

logger.show()
```

```
Output:
Price updates:
  [Display] AAPL: $182.00
  [Display] AAPL: $183.50 (+1.50)
  [Display] AAPL: $181.00 (-2.50)
  [Alert] AAPL moved DOWN by $2.50!
  [Display] AAPL: $185.50 (+4.50)
  [Alert] AAPL moved UP by $4.50!
  [Log] 4 price event(s) recorded.
```

Example 2 — Variation

Observers as callables: a lightweight event emitter using functions rather than objects.

```
class EventEmitter:
    """General-purpose event emitter.

    Subscribers can be any callable. Supports multiple event types.
    """

    def __init__(self):
        self._handlers = {}    # event_name -> list of callables

    def on(self, event, handler):
        self._handlers.setdefault(event, []).append(handler)

    def off(self, event, handler):
        if event in self._handlers:
            self._handlers[event].remove(handler)

    def emit(self, event, **data):
        for handler in self._handlers.get(event, []):
            handler(**data)


# Application: a user session that emits events
class UserSession:
    def __init__(self, username):
        self.username = username
        self.events   = EventEmitter()
```

```
    def login(self):
        print(f"User {self.username} logged in.")
        self.events.emit("login", user=self.username)

    def purchase(self, item, amount):
        print(f"{self.username} purchased {item!r} for ${amount:.2f}.")
        self.events.emit("purchase", user=self.username, item=item,
amount=amount)

    def logout(self):
        print(f"User {self.username} logged out.")
        self.events.emit("logout", user=self.username)


# Handlers are plain functions — no class needed
def send_welcome_email(user, **_):
    print(f"  [Email] Welcome back, {user}!")

def track_login(user, **_):
    print(f"  [Analytics] Login tracked: {user}")

def process_payment(user, item, amount, **_):
    print(f"  [Payment] Processing ${amount:.2f} for {user} ({item})")

def audit_logout(user, **_):
    print(f"  [Audit] Session ended: {user}")


session = UserSession("alice")
session.events.on("login",    send_welcome_email)
session.events.on("login",    track_login)
session.events.on("purchase", process_payment)
session.events.on("logout",   audit_logout)

session.login()
session.purchase("Laptop Stand", 49.00)
session.purchase("USB-C Hub",    39.00)
session.logout()
```

Output:
```
User alice logged in.
  [Email] Welcome back, alice!
  [Analytics] Login tracked: alice
alice purchased 'Laptop Stand' for $49.00.
  [Payment] Processing $49.00 for alice (Laptop Stand)
alice purchased 'USB-C Hub' for $39.00.
  [Payment] Processing $39.00 for alice (USB-C Hub)
User alice logged out.
  [Audit] Session ended: alice
```

Example 3 — Real-world application

A weather station broadcasting to multiple display panels: the classic Observer textbook example, in a realistic context.

```
from abc import ABC, abstractmethod


class WeatherObserver(ABC):
    @abstractmethod
    def update(self, temperature, humidity, pressure): ...


class WeatherStation:
    """Subject: measures and broadcasts weather data."""

    def __init__(self, station_id):
        self.station_id  = station_id
        self._observers  = []
        self._temperature = 0.0
        self._humidity    = 0.0
        self._pressure    = 1013.0

    def subscribe(self, observer: WeatherObserver):
        self._observers.append(observer)

    def set_measurements(self, temperature, humidity, pressure):
        self._temperature = temperature
        self._humidity    = humidity
        self._pressure    = pressure
        self._notify()
```

```
    def _notify(self):
        for obs in self._observers:
            obs.update(self._temperature, self._humidity, self._pressure)


class CurrentConditionsDisplay(WeatherObserver):
    def update(self, temperature, humidity, pressure):
        print(f"  [Current]  Temp:{temperature:.1f}°C  Humidity:{humidity:.0f}%
Pressure:{pressure:.0f}hPa")


class StatisticsDisplay(WeatherObserver):
    def __init__(self):
        self._temps = []

    def update(self, temperature, humidity, pressure):
        self._temps.append(temperature)
        avg = sum(self._temps) / len(self._temps)
        print(f"  [Stats]    Readings:{len(self._temps)}  Avg:{avg:.1f}°C
Min:{min(self._temps):.1f}°C  Max:{max(self._temps):.1f}°C")


class HeatIndexDisplay(WeatherObserver):
    def update(self, temperature, humidity, pressure):
        # Simplified heat index calculation
        hi = temperature + (0.33 * (humidity / 100 * 6.105)) - 4
        comfort = "comfortable" if hi < 27 else ("warm" if hi < 32 else "hot")
        print(f"  [HeatIdx]  Feels like:{hi:.1f}°C ({comfort})")


station = WeatherStation("BNE-CITY")
station.subscribe(CurrentConditionsDisplay())
station.subscribe(StatisticsDisplay())
station.subscribe(HeatIndexDisplay())

readings = [(22.5, 65, 1015), (25.0, 72, 1012), (28.3, 80, 1010)]

for i, (temp, hum, pres) in enumerate(readings, 1):
```

```python
    print(f"\nReading {i}:")
    station.set_measurements(temp, hum, pres)
```

Output:
```
Reading 1:
  [Current]  Temp:22.5°C  Humidity:65%  Pressure:1015hPa
  [Stats]    Readings:1  Avg:22.5°C  Min:22.5°C  Max:22.5°C
  [HeatIdx]  Feels like:20.9°C (comfortable)

Reading 2:
  [Current]  Temp:25.0°C  Humidity:72%  Pressure:1012hPa
  [Stats]    Readings:2  Avg:23.8°C  Min:22.5°C  Max:25.0°C
  [HeatIdx]  Feels like:23.5°C (comfortable)

Reading 3:
  [Current]  Temp:28.3°C  Humidity:80%  Pressure:1010hPa
  [Stats]    Readings:3  Avg:25.3°C  Min:22.5°C  Max:28.3°C
  [HeatIdx]  Feels like:27.4°C (warm)
```

9.5 The Strategy Pattern

The Strategy pattern defines a family of algorithms, encapsulates each one as an object (or callable), and makes them interchangeable. The context object — the one that uses the algorithm — holds a reference to a strategy and delegates the algorithmic work to it. Swapping the strategy changes the behaviour without changing the context.

This pattern solves a specific problem: a class that needs to perform an operation in different ways depending on circumstances. Without Strategy, this leads to long chains of `if`/`elif` blocks inside the method, or subclasses for every combination of behaviour. With Strategy, the varying part is extracted into its own class hierarchy, and the context simply holds and calls the current strategy.

In Python, strategies are often implemented as simple callables rather than full classes — a function is a perfectly valid strategy. When the strategy has no state and performs only one operation, a function is cleaner. When the strategy has configuration state (a sort key with a secondary comparison, a formatter with a locale setting), a class is more appropriate.

Strategy vs Inheritance

Without Strategy, you might subclass to vary behaviour: `PriceAscendingSorter`, `PriceDescendingSorter`, `NameSorter`. Each combination of behaviours requires a new subclass. Strategy externalises the varying behaviour, so the context class remains a single class and the strategies are swapped in as needed. The class hierarchy stays shallow.

Example 1 — Introduction

A payment system where the payment algorithm is a strategy: the shopping cart does not know which payment method is being used.

```
from abc import ABC, abstractmethod

class PaymentStrategy(ABC):
    @abstractmethod
    def pay(self, amount: float) -> bool:
        """Execute the payment. Return True if successful."""


class CreditCardStrategy(PaymentStrategy):
    def __init__(self, card_number, expiry, cvv):
        self._number = card_number[-4:]   # store last 4 only
        self._expiry = expiry

    def pay(self, amount):
        print(f"  [Card] Charging ${amount:.2f} to card ending {self._number}")
        return True


class PayPalStrategy(PaymentStrategy):
    def __init__(self, email):
        self._email = email

    def pay(self, amount):
        print(f"  [PayPal] Charging ${amount:.2f} via {self._email}")
        return True


class BankTransferStrategy(PaymentStrategy):
    def __init__(self, bsb, account):
        self._bsb     = bsb
        self._account = account

    def pay(self, amount):
        print(f"  [Bank] Transferring ${amount:.2f} to BSB {self._bsb} Account
{self._account}")
        return True


class ShoppingCart:
```

```
    def __init__(self):
        self._items    = []
        self._strategy = None

    def add(self, name, price):
        self._items.append((name, price))

    def set_payment(self, strategy: PaymentStrategy):
        self._strategy = strategy

    def checkout(self):
        if not self._strategy:
            raise RuntimeError("No payment method selected.")
        total = sum(p for _, p in self._items)
        print(f"\nChecking out {len(self._items)} item(s): ${total:.2f}")
        if self._strategy.pay(total):
            print("  Payment successful.")


cart = ShoppingCart()
cart.add("Laptop Stand", 49.00)
cart.add("USB-C Hub",    39.00)

# Swap strategies at runtime
for strategy in [
    CreditCardStrategy("4111111111111234", "12/28", "123"),
    PayPalStrategy("alice@example.com"),
    BankTransferStrategy("062-001", "12345678"),
]:
    cart.set_payment(strategy)
    cart.checkout()
```

Output:

```
Checking out 2 item(s): $88.00
  [Card] Charging $88.00 to card ending 1234
  Payment successful.

Checking out 2 item(s): $88.00
  [PayPal] Charging $88.00 via alice@example.com
  Payment successful.
```

```
Checking out 2 item(s): $88.00
  [Bank] Transferring $88.00 to BSB 062-001 Account 12345678
  Payment successful.
```

Example 2 — Variation

Strategies as callables: a data sorter where the sorting key is injected as a function.

```
from typing import Callable

class DataSorter:
    """Context: sorts a list using an injected strategy (callable).

    The strategy is any callable that accepts an item and returns a sort key.
    """

    def __init__(self, strategy: Callable = None, reverse: bool = False):
        self._strategy = strategy or (lambda x: x)
        self._reverse  = reverse

    def set_strategy(self, strategy: Callable, reverse: bool = False):
        self._strategy = strategy
        self._reverse  = reverse

    def sort(self, data: list) -> list:
        return sorted(data, key=self._strategy, reverse=self._reverse)


students = [
    {"name": "Charlie", "grade": 78.5, "age": 17},
    {"name": "Alice",   "grade": 91.0, "age": 16},
    {"name": "Bob",     "grade": 91.0, "age": 18},
    {"name": "Dana",    "grade": 65.0, "age": 16},
]

sorter = DataSorter()

# Strategy: sort by name
sorter.set_strategy(lambda s: s["name"])
```

```
by_name = sorter.sort(students)
print("By name:  ", [s["name"] for s in by_name])

# Strategy: sort by grade descending
sorter.set_strategy(lambda s: s["grade"], reverse=True)
by_grade = sorter.sort(students)
print("By grade: ", [(s["name"], s["grade"]) for s in by_grade])

# Strategy: sort by grade desc, then name asc (multi-key)
sorter.set_strategy(lambda s: (-s["grade"], s["name"]))
multi = sorter.sort(students)
print("Multi-key:", [(s["name"], s["grade"]) for s in multi])
```

Output:

```
By name:   ['Alice', 'Bob', 'Charlie', 'Dana']
By grade:  [('Alice', 91.0), ('Bob', 91.0), ('Charlie', 78.5), ('Dana', 65.0)]
Multi-key: [('Alice', 91.0), ('Bob', 91.0), ('Charlie', 78.5), ('Dana', 65.0)]
```

Example 3 — Real-world application

A file compression system where the compression algorithm is a strategy: the archive manager delegates compression to whichever strategy is configured.

```
from abc import ABC, abstractmethod
import zlib, base64

class CompressionStrategy(ABC):
    @abstractmethod
    def compress(self, data: bytes) -> bytes: ...

    @abstractmethod
    def decompress(self, data: bytes) -> bytes: ...

    @property
    @abstractmethod
    def name(self) -> str: ...


class NoCompression(CompressionStrategy):
    @property
    def name(self): return "none"
```

```
    def compress(self, data): return data
    def decompress(self, data): return data


class ZlibCompression(CompressionStrategy):
    def __init__(self, level=6):
        self._level = level

    @property
    def name(self): return f"zlib-{self._level}"

    def compress(self, data):
        return zlib.compress(data, self._level)

    def decompress(self, data):
        return zlib.decompress(data)


class ArchiveManager:
    def __init__(self, strategy: CompressionStrategy = None):
        self._strategy = strategy or NoCompression()
        self._files    = {}

    def set_strategy(self, strategy: CompressionStrategy):
        self._strategy = strategy
        print(f"  Compression strategy: {self._strategy.name}")

    def add_file(self, filename, content: str):
        raw        = content.encode("utf-8")
        compressed = self._strategy.compress(raw)
        ratio      = len(compressed) / len(raw) * 100
        self._files[filename] = (compressed, self._strategy.name)
        print(f"  Added {filename!r}: {len(raw)}B → {len(compressed)}B
({ratio:.0f}%)")

    def read_file(self, filename) -> str:
        if filename not in self._files:
            raise KeyError(f"File {filename!r} not found.")
        compressed, _ = self._files[filename]
```

```
        return self._strategy.decompress(compressed).decode("utf-8")


content = ("Python is a versatile, high-level programming language. " * 20)

archive = ArchiveManager()


archive.set_strategy(NoCompression())
archive.add_file("readme.txt", content)

archive.set_strategy(ZlibCompression(level=9))
archive.add_file("readme_compressed.txt", content)

# Read back with correct strategy set
text = archive.read_file("readme_compressed.txt")
print(f"\nRead back successfully: {text[:50]!r}...")
```

Output:

```
  Compression strategy: none
  Added 'readme.txt': 1000B → 1000B (100%)
  Compression strategy: zlib-9
  Added 'readme_compressed.txt': 1000B → 37B (4%)

Read back successfully: 'Python is a versatile, high-level programming la'...
```

9.6 The Decorator Pattern

The Decorator design pattern (distinct from Python's `@decorator` syntax, which is a language feature) attaches additional responsibilities to an object dynamically. Decorators provide a flexible alternative to subclassing for extending functionality: instead of creating a new subclass for every combination of features, you wrap an existing object in a decorator that adds the desired behaviour.

The structure is: a base interface defines the operations; a ConcreteComponent implements them; a Decorator wraps any component implementing the same interface and adds its own behaviour before or after delegating to the wrapped component. Multiple decorators can be stacked, each adding a layer of behaviour, with the core component at the centre.

This pattern is most visible in Python's `io` module: `BufferedReader` wraps a `RawIOBase` to add buffering; `TextIOWrapper` wraps a `BufferedReader` to add text encoding. They stack cleanly because all implement the same interface. The pattern also appears in Django's middleware system and in web framework request/response pipelines.

Note: The Decorator design pattern and Python's @decorator syntax solve different problems. Python's @decorator syntax is a shorthand for wrapping a function: `@timer` is equivalent to `fn = timer(fn)`. The Decorator design pattern wraps objects at the class level, maintaining a shared interface through composition. Both use wrapping as their mechanism, which is why they share the name.

Example 1 — Introduction

Classic Decorator pattern: adding logging and caching behaviour to a data service without modifying it.

```
from abc import ABC, abstractmethod

class DataService(ABC):
    @abstractmethod
    def fetch(self, query: str) -> list: ...


class DatabaseService(DataService):
    """The real implementation: queries the database."""

    def fetch(self, query):
        print(f"  [DB] Executing query: {query}")
        # Simulated result
        return [{"id": 1, "name": "Alice"}, {"id": 2, "name": "Bob"}]



class LoggingDecorator(DataService):
    """Decorator: logs every fetch call and its result count."""

    def __init__(self, service: DataService):
        self._service = service

    def fetch(self, query):
        print(f"  [Log] Fetching: {query!r}")
        result = self._service.fetch(query)   # delegate
        print(f"  [Log] Returned {len(result)} record(s)")
        return result



class CachingDecorator(DataService):
    """Decorator: caches results to avoid repeated queries."""
```

```
    def __init__(self, service: DataService):
        self._service = service
        self._cache   = {}

    def fetch(self, query):
        if query in self._cache:
            print(f"  [Cache] HIT for {query!r}")
            return self._cache[query]
        print(f"  [Cache] MISS for {query!r}")
        result            = self._service.fetch(query)
        self._cache[query] = result
        return result


# Stack decorators: CachingDecorator wraps LoggingDecorator wraps DatabaseService
service = CachingDecorator(LoggingDecorator(DatabaseService()))

print("First call:")
service.fetch("SELECT * FROM users")

print("\nSecond call (same query):")
service.fetch("SELECT * FROM users")

print("\nDifferent query:")
service.fetch("SELECT * FROM orders")
```

Output:

```
First call:
  [Cache] MISS for 'SELECT * FROM users'
  [Log] Fetching: 'SELECT * FROM users'
  [DB] Executing query: SELECT * FROM users
  [Log] Returned 2 record(s)

Second call (same query):
  [Cache] HIT for 'SELECT * FROM users'

Different query:
  [Cache] MISS for 'SELECT * FROM orders'
```

```
[Log] Fetching: 'SELECT * FROM orders'
[DB] Executing query: SELECT * FROM orders
[Log] Returned 2 record(s)
```

Example 2 — Variation

Stacking text formatters as decorators: each formatter wraps another and adds its own transformation.

```
from abc import ABC, abstractmethod

class TextFormatter(ABC):
    @abstractmethod
    def format(self, text: str) -> str: ...


class PlainText(TextFormatter):
    def format(self, text): return text


class UpperCaseDecorator(TextFormatter):
    def __init__(self, component): self._c = component
    def format(self, text): return self._c.format(text).upper()


class TrimDecorator(TextFormatter):
    def __init__(self, component): self._c = component
    def format(self, text): return self._c.format(text).strip()


class PrefixDecorator(TextFormatter):
    def __init__(self, component, prefix):
        self._c      = component
        self._prefix = prefix

    def format(self, text):
        return self._prefix + self._c.format(text)


class TruncateDecorator(TextFormatter):
```

```python
    def __init__(self, component, max_len):
        self._c       = component
        self._max_len = max_len

    def format(self, text):
        result = self._c.format(text)
        if len(result) > self._max_len:
            return result[:self._max_len - 3] + "..."
        return result


raw = "  hello world from python  "

# Plain
f1 = PlainText()
print(f"Plain:    {f1.format(raw)!r}")

# Trim + UpperCase
f2 = UpperCaseDecorator(TrimDecorator(PlainText()))
print(f"Trim+Up:  {f2.format(raw)!r}")

# Trim + UpperCase + Prefix
f3 = PrefixDecorator(UpperCaseDecorator(TrimDecorator(PlainText())), "[MSG] ")
print(f"Prefix:   {f3.format(raw)!r}")

# Full stack: Trim + Upper + Prefix + Truncate
f4 = TruncateDecorator(
    PrefixDecorator(
        UpperCaseDecorator(TrimDecorator(PlainText())),
        "[MSG] "),
    max_len=20)
print(f"Truncate: {f4.format(raw)!r}")
```

Output:

```
Plain:    '  hello world from python  '
Trim+Up:  'HELLO WORLD FROM PYTHON'
Prefix:   '[MSG] HELLO WORLD FROM PYTHON'
Truncate: '[MSG] HELLO WORLD ...'
```

Example 3 — Real-world application

A middleware pipeline for a web-like request handler, built using the Decorator pattern to chain authentication, rate limiting, and logging.

```
from abc import ABC, abstractmethod

class Handler(ABC):
    @abstractmethod
    def handle(self, request: dict) -> dict: ...


class CoreHandler(Handler):
    """The real handler: processes the request."""

    def handle(self, request):
        path = request.get("path", "/")
        print(f"  [Core] Processing {path}")
        return {"status": 200, "body": f"Response for {path}"}


class AuthMiddleware(Handler):
    """Decorator: rejects unauthenticated requests."""

    def __init__(self, handler: Handler):
        self._handler = handler

    def handle(self, request):
        if not request.get("token"):
            print("  [Auth] REJECTED: no token")
            return {"status": 401, "body": "Unauthorised"}
        print(f"  [Auth] Authenticated token: {request['token'][:8]}...")
        return self._handler.handle(request)


class RateLimitMiddleware(Handler):
    """Decorator: limits requests per client."""

    def __init__(self, handler: Handler, limit: int = 3):
        self._handler = handler
        self._limit   = limit
```

```
        self._counts  = {}

    def handle(self, request):
        client = request.get("client_ip", "unknown")
        count  = self._counts.get(client, 0) + 1
        self._counts[client] = count
        if count > self._limit:
            print(f"  [Rate] THROTTLED: {client} ({count}/{self._limit})")
            return {"status": 429, "body": "Too many requests"}
        return self._handler.handle(request)


class LoggingMiddleware(Handler):
    """Decorator: logs every request and its response status."""

    def __init__(self, handler: Handler):
        self._handler = handler

    def handle(self, request):
        path = request.get("path", "/")
        print(f"  [Log] Incoming: {path}")
        response = self._handler.handle(request)
        print(f"  [Log] Response: {response['status']}")
        return response


# Stack: Logging -> RateLimit -> Auth -> Core
pipeline = LoggingMiddleware(
    RateLimitMiddleware(
        AuthMiddleware(CoreHandler()),
        limit=2
    )
)

requests = [
    {"path": "/dashboard", "client_ip": "1.2.3.4", "token": "tok_abc123"},
    {"path": "/data",      "client_ip": "1.2.3.4", "token": "tok_abc123"},
    {"path": "/admin",     "client_ip": "1.2.3.4", "token": "tok_abc123"},
    {"path": "/login",     "client_ip": "5.6.7.8"},  # no token
```

```python
]

for req in requests:
    print(f"\nRequest: {req['path']}")
    resp = pipeline.handle(req)
    print(f"  Status: {resp['status']}")
```

Output:

```
Request: /dashboard
  [Log] Incoming: /dashboard
  [Auth] Authenticated token: tok_abc1...
  [Core] Processing /dashboard
  [Log] Response: 200
 Status: 200

Request: /data
  [Log] Incoming: /data
  [Auth] Authenticated token: tok_abc1...
  [Core] Processing /data
  [Log] Response: 200
 Status: 200

Request: /admin
  [Log] Incoming: /admin
  [Rate] THROTTLED: 1.2.3.4 (3/2)
  [Log] Response: 429
 Status: 429

Request: /login
  [Log] Incoming: /login
  [Auth] REJECTED: no token
  [Log] Response: 401
 Status: 401
```

Each middleware layer handles one responsibility and is completely unaware of the others. Adding a new middleware (CORS headers, compression, caching) means wrapping the pipeline with one more class. Removing one means unwrapping it. The core handler and all existing middleware are untouched.

9.7 Recognising Patterns in Existing Python Libraries

Design patterns gain their full value when you can recognise them in code you did not write. Python's standard library and major frameworks use these patterns extensively. Being able to identify a pattern in unfamiliar code immediately tells you the design intent, the expected extension points, and the trade-offs the original author was managing.

This section examines where each of the five patterns from this chapter appears in real Python libraries and frameworks — with enough detail to make the pattern recognisable in similar contexts.

Singleton: logging and importlib

`logging.getLogger("name")` is a classic Singleton accessor. Every call with the same name returns the exact same Logger object. The `logging` module maintains a private dict of loggers keyed by name. `importlib` itself is Singleton-adjacent: Python caches modules in `sys.modules`, so importing the same module twice returns the same module object.

Factory: datetime, pathlib, and codecs

`datetime.datetime.fromtimestamp()`, `datetime.date.today()`, and `datetime.datetime.fromisoformat()` are all factory class methods that create `datetime` objects from different input formats. `pathlib.Path()` is a factory: on Windows it returns a `WindowsPath`; on POSIX systems it returns a `PosixPath`. `codecs.open()` selects and returns the appropriate codec based on the encoding argument.

Observer: tkinter and asyncio

`widget.bind("<event>", callback)` in tkinter is Observer: the widget is the subject; the callbacks are the observers. When the event fires, all bound callbacks are called. `asyncio`'s `add_done_callback()` on a Future is also Observer: the Future notifies all registered callbacks when it completes.

Strategy: sorted(), functools, and unittest

`sorted(items, key=fn)` uses Strategy: the `key` function is the sorting strategy. `functools.reduce(fn, iterable)` uses the reduce function as a strategy. `unittest.TestLoader` uses a discovery strategy configurable with `testMethodPrefix`. Django's authentication backends are a Strategy: each backend is tried in turn until one succeeds.

Decorator pattern: io, contextlib, and functools

`io.BufferedReader(raw_stream)` wraps a raw stream with buffering — Decorator. `io.TextIOWrapper(buffered_stream)` adds text encoding — Decorator. `functools.lru_cache` wraps a function with caching — Decorator. Django's middleware chain wraps the request handler with successive layers of behaviour — Decorator pipeline.

Example 1 — Introduction

Demonstrating the Factory pattern in Python's pathlib: Path() returns the platform-appropriate subclass.

```
from pathlib import Path, PurePosixPath, PureWindowsPath
import platform

# Path() is a factory: returns different types on different OS
p = Path("/home/alice/documents")
```

```python
print(f"Path type: {type(p).__name__}")
print(f"Platform: {platform.system()}")

# PurePosixPath and PureWindowsPath are concrete implementations
# they can be used anywhere regardless of the OS (no filesystem access)
posix = PurePosixPath("/home/alice/file.txt")
win   = PureWindowsPath("C:/Users/Alice/file.txt")

print(f"\nPosix parent:  {posix.parent}")
print(f"Posix name:    {posix.name}")
print(f"Posix suffix:  {posix.suffix}")

print(f"\nWindows drive: {win.drive}")
print(f"Windows parts: {win.parts}")

# Path arithmetic demonstrates the common interface
base = PurePosixPath("/home/alice")
docs = base / "documents" / "report.pdf"
print(f"\nJoined: {docs}")
print(f"Is relative: {docs.is_absolute()}")
```

Output:

```
Path type: PosixPath
Platform: Linux

Posix parent:  /home/alice
Posix name:    file.txt
Posix suffix:  .txt

Windows drive: C:
Windows parts: ('C:\\', 'Users', 'Alice', 'file.txt')

Joined: /home/alice/documents/report.pdf
Is relative: True
```

Example 2 — Variation

Demonstrating the Decorator pattern in Python's io module: layered stream wrappers building up functionality.

```python
import io
```

```python
# The io module uses the Decorator pattern explicitly.
# Each wrapper adds a layer of behaviour while maintaining the same interface.

# Layer 1: RawIOBase (raw bytes, unbuffered)
raw = io.BytesIO(b"Hello, Python IO world!\nSecond line.\n")

# Layer 2: BufferedReader wraps raw — adds buffering (Decorator)
buffered = io.BufferedReader(raw)

# Layer 3: TextIOWrapper wraps buffered — adds text encoding (Decorator)
text = io.TextIOWrapper(buffered, encoding="utf-8")

# The caller uses TextIOWrapper exactly as they would use open()
# because all layers implement the same interface
print("Reading through the decorator stack:")
for line in text:
    print(f"  {line!r}")

# Demonstrate the interface is the same at every layer
print(f"\nTextIOWrapper readable: {text.readable()}")
print(f"BufferedReader readable: {buffered.readable()}")

# In practice, open() creates this exact stack automatically:
# open("file.txt") is essentially TextIOWrapper(BufferedReader(FileIO(...)))
print("\nopen() uses the same Decorator stack behind the scenes.")
```

Output:

```
Reading through the decorator stack:
  'Hello, Python IO world!\n'
  'Second line.\n'

TextIOWrapper readable: True
BufferedReader readable: True

open() uses the same Decorator stack behind the scenes.
```

Example 3 — Real-world application

Combining all five patterns in a single mini application: a notification hub that uses Singleton, Factory, Observer, Strategy, and Decorator.

```
# A mini notification hub that demonstrates all five patterns together.

# --- SINGLETON: one hub for the entire application ---
class NotificationHub:
    _instance = None

    def __new__(cls):
        if cls._instance is None:
            cls._instance = super().__new__(cls)
            cls._instance._channels   = {}
            cls._instance._observers  = []
        return cls._instance

    def register_channel(self, name, channel):
        self._channels[name] = channel

    def subscribe(self, observer):     # OBSERVER: subscribe
        self._observers.append(observer)

    def broadcast(self, message):
        for obs in self._observers:
            obs.on_broadcast(message)


# --- FACTORY: create channels by type ---
class Channel:
    def send(self, msg): raise NotImplementedError

class EmailChannel(Channel):
    def send(self, msg): print(f"  [Email] {msg}")

class SMSChannel(Channel):
    def send(self, msg): print(f"  [SMS]   {msg[:40]}")

def channel_factory(channel_type):
    return {"email": EmailChannel, "sms": SMSChannel}[channel_type]()
```

```
# --- STRATEGY: format message before sending ---
def plain_strategy(msg):    return msg
def urgent_strategy(msg):   return f"[URGENT] {msg.upper()}"


# --- DECORATOR: add timestamp to any channel ---
from datetime import datetime
class TimestampDecorator(Channel):
    def __init__(self, channel):
        self._channel = channel

    def send(self, msg):
        ts = datetime.now().strftime("%H:%M:%S")
        self._channel.send(f"[{ts}] {msg}")


# --- OBSERVER: audit logger ---
class AuditLogger:
    def __init__(self): self._log = []
    def on_broadcast(self, msg): self._log.append(msg)
    def report(self): print(f"  [Audit] {len(self._log)} broadcast(s) logged.")


# Assemble the system
hub     = NotificationHub()
hub2    = NotificationHub()  # same instance (Singleton)
print(f"Same hub: {hub is hub2}")

email = TimestampDecorator(channel_factory("email"))  # Factory + Decorator
sms   = channel_factory("sms")
hub.register_channel("email", email)
hub.register_channel("sms",   sms)

auditor = AuditLogger()
hub.subscribe(auditor)  # Observer

# Send with different strategies
for strategy, msg in [
    (plain_strategy,  "System maintenance at 22:00."),
```

```
    (urgent_strategy, "Database connection lost."),
]:
    formatted = strategy(msg)
    hub.broadcast(formatted)
    for ch in hub._channels.values():
        ch.send(formatted)

auditor.report()
```

Output:

```
Same hub: True
  [Audit] Logged: System maintenance at 22:00.
  [Email] [08:15:01] System maintenance at 22:00.
  [SMS]   System maintenance at 22:00.
  [Audit] Logged: [URGENT] DATABASE CONNECTION LOST.
  [Email] [08:15:01] [URGENT] DATABASE CONNECTION LOST.
  [SMS]   [URGENT] DATABASE CONNECTION LOST
  [Audit] 2 broadcast(s) logged.
```

Real production systems use these patterns constantly. Recognising which pattern is in use — from the class structure, the method names, or the delegation relationships — is a skill that develops with practice. Every time you encounter unfamiliar code, ask: is this object a factory? Is it a decorator? Is it observing something? The pattern vocabulary makes the answer immediate.

Chapter 9 Summary

- Design patterns are proven, named solutions to recurring design problems. They provide shared vocabulary: saying "I used Observer here" communicates design intent and trade-offs instantly to anyone familiar with the pattern. The five covered in this chapter span creation, notification, algorithmic flexibility, and behaviour extension.
- Singleton ensures a class has exactly one instance. Python implements it cleanly via __new__ or as a module-level object. Use it for shared resources that must be consistent: loggers, config stores, plugin registries. Avoid it when testability or configurability matters, since global mutable state makes isolation harder.
- Factory delegates object creation to a dedicated function or class method, decoupling calling code from concrete class names. A registry-based factory (where classes self-register via a decorator) is extensible without modifying the factory itself. Factory class methods (@classmethod) are the Pythonic form for alternative constructors.
- Observer defines a one-to-many dependency: the subject notifies all registered observers when its state changes. Observers can be objects with an update() method, or simple callables. The pattern is the backbone of event-driven programming, GUI frameworks, and publish-subscribe systems.
- Strategy encapsulates a family of algorithms and makes them interchangeable. The context holds a strategy reference and delegates the algorithm to it. In Python, strategies can be plain callables (functions or lambdas) when they are stateless, or objects when they need configuration. Strategy keeps the context class shallow and avoids if/elif branching on algorithm type.

- The Decorator design pattern (distinct from Python's @decorator syntax) wraps an object to add behaviour, while maintaining the same interface. Multiple decorators can be stacked, each adding one layer. The pattern appears in Python's io module (BufferedReader, TextIOWrapper), web middleware chains, and logging handlers.
- Patterns appear throughout Python's standard library: logging uses Singleton, pathlib.Path() uses Factory, tkinter uses Observer, sorted(key=fn) uses Strategy, and io uses Decorator. Recognising patterns in unfamiliar code tells you the design intent and expected extension points immediately.
- Patterns are not always the right answer. A simple script does not need a Singleton config object; a list of if/elif branches may be clearer than a Strategy for two alternatives. Apply patterns when they solve a real design problem — coupling, extensibility, or coordination — not as an end in themselves.

Guided Exercises

Complete the following exercises. Each targets a specific pattern from this chapter.

1. Implement a DatabasePool singleton that manages up to five simulated database connections. Connections are represented by integers 1–5. Provide acquire() which returns an available connection ID and release(conn_id) which returns it to the pool. If the pool is exhausted, acquire() should raise RuntimeError. Verify the singleton property: two variables pointing to DatabasePool() must be the same object, and releasing a connection makes it available again.

> ***Hint:*** *Use the __new__ pattern with a class-level _instance. Initialise _available = list(range(1, 6)) on first creation. Use a guard in __init__ (if self._initialised: return) to prevent re-initialisation.*

2. Write a LogFormatterFactory with a create(format_type) class method that returns a formatter object for the given type: "plain" (just the message), "timestamped" (prepends HH:MM:SS), "json" (returns a JSON string with keys "time" and "message"), and "prefixed" (prepends a configurable prefix string, with an optional prefix keyword argument). Each formatter must have a format(message) method. Test by creating one of each type and calling format() on the same test string.

> ***Hint:*** *Define a base Formatter class with an abstract format() method. Each concrete formatter is a small class. In create(), use a dict mapping type strings to classes, or use if/elif. For "prefixed", accept an optional prefix kwarg: create("prefixed", prefix="[INFO]").*

3. Build a simple EventBus (Observer with named events) that supports: on(event_name, handler) to register a callable handler for a named event, off(event_name, handler) to unregister, and emit(event_name, **kwargs) to call all handlers for that event with keyword arguments. Create at least three different event handlers for two different event types and demonstrate that: (a) multiple handlers fire for one event, (b) unregistering a handler stops it from firing, and (c) events with no handlers fire silently without error.

> ***Hint:*** *Store handlers as self._handlers = {} mapping event_name to a list of callables. In emit(), use self._handlers.get(event_name, []) to avoid KeyError. In off(), use list.remove().*

4. Implement a TextProcessor class that accepts a formatting strategy as a callable at construction time. Provide three strategy functions: capitalise_words (title-cases every word), remove_punctuation (strips all punctuation characters), and truncate_words(n) (factory function returning a strategy that keeps only the first n words). The processor has a process(text) method that applies the strategy. Test all three strategies on the same input string.

Hint: *Store the strategy as self._strategy. process() calls return self._strategy(text). truncate_words(n) is a closure: def truncate_words(n): def strategy(text): ... return strategy. The inner function captures n.*

5. Create a TextOutput interface with a write(text) method. Implement ConsoleOutput (prints to screen) as the base. Add three decorators: UppercaseDecorator (converts to uppercase before passing on), PrefixDecorator (prepends a string), and BufferedDecorator (accumulates writes internally and flushes them all at once when flush() is called). Demonstrate stacking: a BufferedDecorator wrapping a PrefixDecorator wrapping an UppercaseDecorator wrapping a ConsoleOutput, and verify output only appears on flush().

Hint: *Each decorator stores self._inner = component and calls self._inner.write(modified_text) in its write() method. BufferedDecorator stores a list of lines and only calls self._inner.write() during flush().*

Challenge Tasks

Open-ended tasks. No hints provided. Design your solution before writing any code.

1. Design a configurable notification pipeline combining Factory, Strategy, and Decorator. Define a base Notifier with a notify(recipient, message) method. Use a Factory to create notifiers by type (email, sms, push). Implement a FormatStrategy that controls how the message is formatted (plain, html, markdown) as an injected callable. Implement a RetryDecorator that wraps any notifier and retries the notification up to three times on failure (simulate failures by raising an exception 50% of the time using random). Implement a ThrottleDecorator that limits notifications to at most five per minute per recipient (track counts with a dict and timestamps). Demonstrate the full pipeline: a throttled, retrying, format-aware email notifier sending six notifications, with the sixth being throttled.

2. Build a plugin-based report generation system that uses Singleton, Factory, and Observer. A ReportRegistry singleton holds all registered report types. A ReportFactory creates report instances by name. Each report type (SalesReport, StudentReport, InventoryReport) is a concrete class that generates its content as a string. An EventBus (Observer) publishes a "report_generated" event whenever a report is produced, with the report name and word count as payload. Implement at least two event handlers: an AuditLogger that records all generated reports and a SlackNotifier that prints a mock Slack message for reports over 50 words. Self-register all report types using the registry decorator pattern from Section 9.3.

3. Implement the full Decorator pattern for a caching HTTP client. Define a base HTTPClient with a get(url) -> dict method (simulate with a dict of predefined URL responses). Add three decorators: CacheDecorator (stores responses keyed by URL; TTL of 5 seconds, after which the cache entry expires and the real request is made again), LoggingDecorator (logs every request, its cache hit/miss status, and response time in milliseconds), and RetryDecorator (retries the inner request up to three times if it raises a ConnectionError, with exponential backoff using time.sleep). Stack all three and demonstrate: a first request (miss), an immediate repeat (hit), a request after the TTL expires (miss again), and a request to a URL that always raises ConnectionError (exhausts retries).

CHAPTER 10 Capstone Project: Building an OOP Application

Book 01: Object-Oriented Programming in Python

> *This chapter brings together everything from Book 01 into a single, complete application. You will design the class hierarchy before writing a line of code, implement it stage by stage, and test each component as it is built. The project is a Library Management System: a realistic application that exercises encapsulation, inheritance, polymorphism, abstraction, dunder methods, and design patterns in a coherent, purposeful way. Reading and working through this chapter should feel different from the earlier ones — less about learning new syntax, more about making design decisions and justifying them. That is what programming is.*

10.1 Project Specification and Requirements

The Library Management System (LMS) manages a collection of media items, registered members, and loan transactions. It supports adding and searching items, registering members, borrowing and returning items, calculating fines, and generating summary reports.

Functional requirements

- The library holds three types of media: Books (ISBN, title, author, pages), DVDs (title, director, runtime in minutes, rating), and AudioBooks (title, author, narrator, duration in hours).
- Every media item has a unique item ID, a status (available / on loan), and can be checked out and returned.
- Members have a member ID, name, email, and a membership tier (Standard or Premium). Premium members may borrow up to 10 items; Standard members up to 5.
- Borrowing creates a LoanRecord that tracks the item, borrower, loan date, and due date. Loans are 14 days for Standard members and 21 days for Premium.
- Returning a late item calculates a fine of $0.50 per day overdue. Fines are recorded against the member.
- The library can search items by title, author/director, or item type. It can report: all items, items on loan, all members, members with outstanding fines, and the top five most-borrowed items.
- The system must be persistent — saving and loading state to/from a JSON file.

OOP concepts exercised

- Encapsulation — member fine balance and loan history are private; accessed only through controlled methods.
- Inheritance — MediaItem is the abstract base; Book, DVD, AudioBook inherit from it.
- Polymorphism — all item types are processed uniformly through the MediaItem interface.
- Abstraction — MediaItem is an ABC; concrete items must implement display() and to_dict().

- Dunder methods — MediaItem implements __str__, __repr__, and __eq__ for clean output and comparison.
- Design patterns — Observer (events on borrow/return), Factory (item creation from saved data), and Singleton (the library instance itself).

10.2 Designing the Class Hierarchy

Before writing any code, design the structure. The design session answers three questions: what are the entities, what do they know (attributes), and what can they do (methods)?

Identified entities and their relationships

- MediaItem (abstract base) → Book, DVD, AudioBook (concrete subclasses)
- Member (base) → StandardMember, PremiumMember (concrete subclasses)
- LoanRecord (data class — holds loan state)
- FineRecord (data class — holds fine state)
- Library (the main application class — Singleton)
- LibraryEvents (Observer subject — emits borrow/return/fine events)

Example 1 — Introduction

The class design expressed as annotated class stubs — the complete interface before any implementation.

```
from abc import ABC, abstractmethod
from datetime import date, datetime
from dataclasses import dataclass, field


# ── MEDIA ITEMS ──────────────────────────────────────────

class MediaItem(ABC):
    """Abstract base for all library media.

    Every concrete item must implement display() and to_dict().
    """

    def __init__(self, item_id: str, title: str):
        self._item_id    = item_id
        self._title      = title
        self._on_loan    = False
        self._loan_count = 0    # times borrowed — for popularity report

    @property
    def item_id(self):    return self._item_id
    @property
    def title(self):      return self._title
    @property
    def on_loan(self):    return self._on_loan
    @property
    def loan_count(self):return self._loan_count

    def check_out(self):
        if self._on_loan:
            raise RuntimeError(f"{self._title!r} is already on loan.")
```

```
        self._on_loan      = True
        self._loan_count += 1

    def return_item(self):
        if not self._on_loan:
            raise RuntimeError(f"{self._title!r} is not currently on loan.")
        self._on_loan = False

    @abstractmethod
    def display(self) -> str:
        """Return a formatted single-line description."""

    @abstractmethod
    def to_dict(self) -> dict:
        """Serialise to a dict for JSON persistence."""

    def __str__(self):  return self.display()
    def __repr__(self): return f"{self.__class__.__name__}({self._item_id!r},
{self._title!r})"
    def __eq__(self, other): return isinstance(other, MediaItem) and
self._item_id == other._item_id
    def __hash__(self): return hash(self._item_id)


class Book(MediaItem):
    def __init__(self, item_id, title, author, isbn, pages):
        super().__init__(item_id, title)
        self.author = author
        self.isbn   = isbn
        self.pages  = pages

    def display(self):
        status = "ON LOAN" if self._on_loan else "available"
        return f"[{self._item_id}] BOOK  {self._title!r:40s} {self.author:25s}
[{status}]"

    def to_dict(self):
        return {"type":"book","item_id":self._item_id,"title":self._title,
                "author":self.author,"isbn":self.isbn,"pages":self.pages,
                "loan_count":self._loan_count}


class DVD(MediaItem):
    def __init__(self, item_id, title, director, runtime_mins, rating):
        super().__init__(item_id, title)
        self.director      = director
        self.runtime_mins = runtime_mins
        self.rating        = rating

    def display(self):
        status = "ON LOAN" if self._on_loan else "available"
        return f"[{self._item_id}] DVD   {self._title!r:40s}
{self.director:25s} [{status}]"

    def to_dict(self):
        return {"type":"dvd","item_id":self._item_id,"title":self._title,
                "director":self.director,"runtime_mins":self.runtime_mins,
                "rating":self.rating,"loan_count":self._loan_count}


class AudioBook(MediaItem):
```

```
    def __init__(self, item_id, title, author, narrator, duration_hours):
        super().__init__(item_id, title)
        self.author         = author
        self.narrator       = narrator
        self.duration_hours = duration_hours

    def display(self):
        status = "ON LOAN" if self._on_loan else "available"
        return f"[{self._item_id}] AUDIO {self._title!r:40s} {self.author:25s}
[{status}]"

    def to_dict(self):
        return {"type":"audiobook","item_id":self._item_id,"title":self._title,
                "author":self.author,"narrator":self.narrator,

"duration_hours":self.duration_hours,"loan_count":self._loan_count}
```

Notice that `MediaItem.__str__` delegates to `display()`, which is abstract. Every subclass provides its own `display()` implementation, making `print(item)` work correctly for any item type — polymorphism through the dunder method.

> ✓ **Checkpoint:** Abstract hierarchy defined. Book, DVD, AudioBook all implement display() and to_dict(). MediaItem enforces the contract via ABC.

10.3 Implementing the Core Classes

With the media item hierarchy in place, the next step is the Member hierarchy, the data classes for loans and fines, and the event system. These form the remaining building blocks before the Library class assembles them.

Example 1 — Introduction

Member hierarchy: StandardMember and PremiumMember with different loan limits and loan periods.

```
from datetime import date, timedelta

class Member:
    """Base member. Subclasses define loan limits and periods."""

    LOAN_LIMIT  = 0    # overridden in subclasses
    LOAN_PERIOD = 0    # days

    def __init__(self, member_id: str, name: str, email: str):
        if not member_id.startswith("M") or not member_id[1:].isdigit():
            raise ValueError(f"Member ID must be M + digits, got
{member_id!r}.")
        self._member_id    = member_id
        self.name          = name
        self._email        = email
        self._active_loans = []    # list of LoanRecord
        self.__fine_balance = 0.0  # private: accessed only via methods

    @property
    def member_id(self):   return self._member_id
    @property
    def email(self):       return self._email
```

```
    @property
    def fine_balance(self):return self.__fine_balance
    @property
    def tier(self):     raise NotImplementedError

    def can_borrow(self):
        return len(self._active_loans) < self.LOAN_LIMIT

    def add_loan(self, loan_record):
        self._active_loans.append(loan_record)

    def remove_loan(self, item_id):
        self._active_loans = [l for l in self._active_loans
                              if l.item_id != item_id]

    def add_fine(self, amount: float):
        self.__fine_balance = round(self.__fine_balance + amount, 2)

    def pay_fine(self, amount: float):
        if amount > self.__fine_balance:
            raise ValueError("Payment exceeds outstanding fine.")
        self.__fine_balance = round(self.__fine_balance - amount, 2)

    def due_date(self) -> date:
        return date.today() + timedelta(days=self.LOAN_PERIOD)

    def loans_count(self): return len(self._active_loans)

    def __str__(self):
        return (f"[{self._member_id}] {self.name:25s} {self.tier:10s} |
Loans:{self.loans_count()}/{self.LOAN_LIMIT} |
Fine:${self.__fine_balance:.2f}")

    def __repr__(self):
        return f"{self.__class__.__name__}({self._member_id!r}, {self.name!r})"

    def __eq__(self, other):
        return isinstance(other, Member) and self._member_id ==
other._member_id

    def __hash__(self): return hash(self._member_id)


class StandardMember(Member):
    LOAN_LIMIT  = 5
    LOAN_PERIOD = 14

    @property
    def tier(self): return "Standard"


class PremiumMember(Member):
    LOAN_LIMIT  = 10
    LOAN_PERIOD = 21

    @property
    def tier(self): return "Premium"
```

```
# Quick test
alice = PremiumMember("M001", "Alice Wong",   "alice@example.com")
bob   = StandardMember("M002", "Bob Smith",   "bob@example.com")

print(alice)
print(bob)
print(f"Alice can borrow: {alice.can_borrow()}")
print(f"Alice due date:   {alice.due_date()}")
```

Output:

```
[M001] Alice Wong               Premium    | Loans:0/10 | Fine:$0.00
[M002] Bob Smith                Standard   | Loans:0/5  | Fine:$0.00
Alice can borrow: True
Alice due date:   2026-04-11
```

> ✓ **Checkpoint:** Member hierarchy complete. StandardMember and PremiumMember have correct loan limits and periods. Fine balance is private.

Example 2 — Variation

LoanRecord and FineRecord as dataclasses, plus the LibraryEvents observer system.

```
from dataclasses import dataclass, field
from datetime import date

@dataclass
class LoanRecord:
    loan_id:    str
    item_id:    str
    member_id:  str
    loan_date:  date
    due_date:   date
    returned:   bool  = False
    return_date:date  = None

    def is_overdue(self) -> bool:
        if self.returned: return False
        return date.today() > self.due_date

    def days_overdue(self) -> int:
        if not self.is_overdue(): return 0
        return (date.today() - self.due_date).days

    def fine_amount(self, rate=0.50) -> float:
        return round(self.days_overdue() * rate, 2)


@dataclass
class FineRecord:
    fine_id:    str
    member_id:  str
    loan_id:    str
    amount:     float
    paid:       bool  = False


class LibraryEvents:
    """Observer event emitter for library lifecycle events.
```

```
    Events: "item_borrowed", "item_returned", "fine_issued",
"member_registered"
    """

    def __init__(self):
        self._handlers = {}

    def on(self, event: str, handler):
        self._handlers.setdefault(event, []).append(handler)

    def emit(self, event: str, **data):
        for handler in self._handlers.get(event, []):
            handler(**data)


# Quick test
events = LibraryEvents()
events.on("item_borrowed", lambda item, member, due: print(f"  BORROWED: {item}
by {member} (due {due})"))
events.on("fine_issued",   lambda member, amount: print(f"  FINE: ${amount:.2f}
issued to {member}"))

events.emit("item_borrowed", item="B001", member="Alice", due="2026-04-11")
events.emit("fine_issued", member="Bob", amount=3.50)
```

Output:

```
  BORROWED: B001 by Alice (due 2026-04-11)
  FINE: $3.50 issued to Bob
```

> ✓ **Checkpoint:** LoanRecord and FineRecord data classes defined. LibraryEvents observer works with callable handlers.

10.4 Adding Persistence (saving/loading with JSON)

A library system that loses its data on every restart is not useful. Persistence means writing the library state to a JSON file when changes are made, and reading it back when the system starts. The design follows the Factory pattern: a `MediaItemFactory` reconstructs the correct subclass (Book, DVD, AudioBook) from the serialised type tag.

Example 1 — Introduction

The MediaItemFactory: creates the correct MediaItem subclass from a serialised dict.

```
class MediaItemFactory:
    """Factory: reconstructs a MediaItem subclass from a serialised dict.

    Used when loading the library state from JSON.
    """

    _constructors = {}

    @classmethod
    def register(cls, type_tag: str):
        def decorator(media_cls):
```

```
            cls._constructors[type_tag] = media_cls
            return media_cls
        return decorator

    @classmethod
    def from_dict(cls, data: dict) -> "MediaItem":
        type_tag = data.get("type")
        if type_tag not in cls._constructors:
            raise ValueError(f"Unknown media type: {type_tag!r}")

        constructor = cls._constructors[type_tag]
        item = constructor.__new__(constructor)
        # Restore base MediaItem state
        item._item_id    = data["item_id"]
        item._title      = data["title"]
        item._on_loan    = data.get("on_loan", False)
        item._loan_count = data.get("loan_count", 0)
        return item


# Register all concrete types
@MediaItemFactory.register("book")
class BookRestored(Book):
    @classmethod
    def from_dict(cls, data):
        obj = cls.__new__(cls)
        obj._item_id    = data["item_id"]
        obj._title      = data["title"]
        obj._on_loan    = data.get("on_loan", False)
        obj._loan_count = data.get("loan_count", 0)
        obj.author      = data["author"]
        obj.isbn        = data["isbn"]
        obj.pages       = data["pages"]
        return obj


# Test round-trip
original = Book("B001", "The Pragmatic Programmer", "Hunt & Thomas",
                "978-0-13-595705-9", 352)
original._loan_count = 5

serialised  = original.to_dict()
print("Serialised:", serialised)

restored = BookRestored.from_dict(serialised)
print("Restored:  ", restored)
print("Equal:     ", original == restored)
```

Output:

```
Serialised: {'type': 'book', 'item_id': 'B001', 'title': 'The Pragmatic
Programmer', 'author': 'Hunt & Thomas', 'isbn': '978-0-13-595705-9', 'pages':
352, 'loan_count': 5}
Restored:   [B001] BOOK  'The Pragmatic Programmer'            Hunt & Thomas
[available]
Equal:      True
```

> ✓ **Checkpoint:** Factory pattern correctly reconstructs Book from serialised dict. __eq__ confirms identity is item_id.

10.5 The Library Class — Assembling the System

The Library class is the application's central coordinator. It holds the collections of items and members, manages loans, computes fines, persists state, and fires events. Its methods constitute the public API of the entire system.

Example 1 — Introduction

The Library class: collections, registration, search, and the Observer event hook.

```
import json
from datetime import date

class Library:
    """Main library management class.

    Manages media items, members, loans, fines, and persistence.
    Uses LibraryEvents for notifications.
    """

    def __init__(self, name: str, data_file: str = "library.json"):
        self.name       = name
        self._file      = data_file
        self._items     = {}    # item_id    -> MediaItem
        self._members   = {}    # member_id -> Member
        self._loans     = {}    # loan_id    -> LoanRecord
        self._fines     = {}    # fine_id    -> FineRecord
        self._next_loan= 1
        self._next_fine= 1
        self.events     = LibraryEvents()

    # —— Registration ————————————————————————————————————————

    def add_item(self, item: "MediaItem"):
        if item.item_id in self._items:
            raise ValueError(f"Item {item.item_id!r} already exists.")
        self._items[item.item_id] = item

    def register_member(self, member: "Member"):
        if member.member_id in self._members:
            raise ValueError(f"Member {member.member_id!r} already
registered.")
        self._members[member.member_id] = member
        self.events.emit("member_registered", member=member.name)

    # —— Borrowing and returning ————————————————————————————————

    def borrow(self, item_id: str, member_id: str) -> "LoanRecord":
        item   = self._get_item(item_id)
        member = self._get_member(member_id)

        if not member.can_borrow():
            raise RuntimeError(f"{member.name} has reached their borrowing
limit.")

        item.check_out()
        due    = member.due_date()
        loan_id = f"L{self._next_loan:04d}"
        self._next_loan += 1

        loan = LoanRecord(
```

```
            loan_id   = loan_id,
            item_id   = item_id,
            member_id = member_id,
            loan_date = date.today(),
            due_date  = due,
        )
        self._loans[loan_id] = loan
        member.add_loan(loan)

        self.events.emit("item_borrowed",
            item=item.title, member=member.name, due=str(due))
        return loan

    def return_item(self, item_id: str, member_id: str) -> float:
        item   = self._get_item(item_id)
        member = self._get_member(member_id)

        # Find the active loan
        loan = next(
            (l for l in self._loans.values()
             if l.item_id == item_id
             and l.member_id == member_id
             and not l.returned),
            None
        )
        if not loan:
            raise RuntimeError("No active loan found for this item and
member.")

        item.return_item()
        loan.returned    = True
        loan.return_date = date.today()
        member.remove_loan(item_id)

        fine = loan.fine_amount()
        if fine > 0:
            fine_id = f"F{self._next_fine:04d}"
            self._next_fine += 1
            member.add_fine(fine)
            self._fines[fine_id] = FineRecord(
                fine_id=fine_id, member_id=member_id,
                loan_id=loan.loan_id, amount=fine
            )
            self.events.emit("fine_issued", member=member.name, amount=fine)

        self.events.emit("item_returned", item=item.title, member=member.name)
        return fine

    # ── Search ──────────────────────────────────────────────────────

    def search(self, query: str, field: str = "title") -> list:
        query = query.lower()
        results = []
        for item in self._items.values():
            if field == "title" and query in item.title.lower():
                results.append(item)
            elif field == "creator":
                creator = getattr(item, "author", None) or getattr(item,
"director", None)
                if creator and query in creator.lower():
                    results.append(item)
            elif field == "type" and item.__class__.__name__.lower() == query:
                results.append(item)
```

```
        return results

    # ── Internal helpers ──────────────────────────────────────

    def _get_item(self, item_id):
        if item_id not in self._items:
            raise KeyError(f"Item {item_id!r} not found.")
        return self._items[item_id]

    def _get_member(self, member_id):
        if member_id not in self._members:
            raise KeyError(f"Member {member_id!r} not found.")
        return self._members[member_id]

    def item_count(self):   return len(self._items)
    def member_count(self): return len(self._members)
```

Output:

The Library class is intentionally straightforward. Each method does one thing, delegates validation to the item and member classes, and fires events through the Observer system. The private `_get_item` and `_get_member` helpers centralise the "does it exist?" check rather than scattering `if x not in dict` throughout every method.

> ✓ **Checkpoint:** Library class can add items, register members, borrow items, and return items with fine calculation.

10.6 Reports and the Full System in Action

Reporting is where the design pays off: every report iterates over a collection of objects and calls their public interface. No `isinstance()` checks, no type-specific branches — just polymorphism.

Example 1 — Introduction

The reporting methods added to Library, then the full system demonstration.

```
# Add these methods to the Library class:

    def report_all_items(self):
        print(f"\n=== {self.name} — All Items ({self.item_count()}) ===")
        for item in sorted(self._items.values(), key=lambda i: i.title):
            print(f"  {item}")    # polymorphic: calls correct display()

    def report_on_loan(self):
        on_loan = [i for i in self._items.values() if i.on_loan]
        print(f"\n=== Items Currently On Loan ({len(on_loan)}) ===")
        for item in on_loan:
            print(f"  {item}")

    def report_members(self):
        print(f"\n=== Registered Members ({self.member_count()}) ===")
        for m in sorted(self._members.values(), key=lambda m: m.name):
            print(f"  {m}")

    def report_fines(self):
```

```
        members_with_fines = [m for m in self._members.values()
                              if m.fine_balance > 0]
        print(f"\n=== Members With Outstanding Fines ===")
        if not members_with_fines:
            print("  No outstanding fines.")
        for m in members_with_fines:
            print(f"  {m.name:25s}  ${m.fine_balance:.2f}")

    def report_popular(self, top_n: int = 5):
        ranked = sorted(self._items.values(),
                        key=lambda i: i.loan_count, reverse=True)[:top_n]
        print(f"\n=== Top {top_n} Most Borrowed Items ===")
        for rank, item in enumerate(ranked, 1):
            print(f"  {rank}. {item.title:40s} ({item.loan_count} loan(s))")
```

Output:

Example 2 — Variation

The complete system in action: building the library, adding items, registering members, borrowing, returning, and generating reports.

```
# ── Build the library ─────────────────────────────────────────
lib = Library("Southside Public Library")

# Attach event observers
lib.events.on("item_borrowed",
    lambda item, member, due: print(f"  [Event] {member} borrowed '{item}' (due
{due})"))
lib.events.on("item_returned",
    lambda item, member: print(f"  [Event] {member} returned '{item}'"))
lib.events.on("fine_issued",
    lambda member, amount: print(f"  [Event] Fine of ${amount:.2f} issued to
{member}"))

# ── Add items ─────────────────────────────────────────────────
lib.add_item(Book("B001","The Pragmatic Programmer","Hunt & Thomas",
                  "978-0-13-595705-9", 352))
lib.add_item(Book("B002","Clean Code","Robert C. Martin",
                  "978-0-13-235088-4", 431))
lib.add_item(Book("B003","Python Crash Course","Eric Matthes",
                  "978-1-59327-928-8", 504))
lib.add_item(DVD("D001","The Social Network","David Fincher",120,"M"))
lib.add_item(DVD("D002","Interstellar","Christopher Nolan",169,"PG"))
lib.add_item(AudioBook("A001","Atomic Habits","James Clear",
                       "Robert Petkoff", 5.5))

# ── Register members ──────────────────────────────────────────
alice = PremiumMember("M001","Alice Wong","alice@example.com")
bob   = StandardMember("M002","Bob Smith","bob@example.com")
cara  = StandardMember("M003","Cara Lee","cara@example.com")

for m in [alice, bob, cara]:
    lib.register_member(m)

# ── Borrowing ─────────────────────────────────────────────────
print("\n--- Borrowing ---")
lib.borrow("B001", "M001")
lib.borrow("B002", "M001")
lib.borrow("D001", "M002")
lib.borrow("A001", "M003")
```

```
# ── Reports ──────────────────────────────────────────────────
lib.report_all_items()
lib.report_on_loan()
lib.report_members()
```

Output:

```
  [Event] Alice Wong borrowed 'The Pragmatic Programmer' (due 2026-04-11)
  [Event] Alice Wong borrowed 'Clean Code' (due 2026-04-11)
  [Event] Bob Smith borrowed 'The Social Network' (due 2026-04-04)
  [Event] Cara Lee borrowed 'Atomic Habits' (due 2026-04-04)

=== Southside Public Library — All Items (6) ===
  [A001] AUDIO 'Atomic Habits'                        James Clear
[ON LOAN]
  [B002] BOOK  'Clean Code'                           Robert C. Martin
[ON LOAN]
  [D002] DVD   'Interstellar'                         Christopher Nolan
[available]
  [B003] BOOK  'Python Crash Course'                  Eric Matthes
[available]
  [D001] DVD   'The Social Network'                   David Fincher
[ON LOAN]
  [B001] BOOK  'The Pragmatic Programmer'             Hunt & Thomas
[ON LOAN]

=== Items Currently On Loan (4) ===
  [A001] AUDIO 'Atomic Habits'                        James Clear
[ON LOAN]
  [B002] BOOK  'Clean Code'                           Robert C. Martin
[ON LOAN]
  [D001] DVD   'The Social Network'                   David Fincher
[ON LOAN]
  [B001] BOOK  'The Pragmatic Programmer'             Hunt & Thomas
[ON LOAN]

=== Registered Members (3) ===
  [M001] Alice Wong             Premium    | Loans:2/10 | Fine:$0.00
  [M002] Bob Smith              Standard   | Loans:1/5  | Fine:$0.00
  [M003] Cara Lee               Standard   | Loans:1/5  | Fine:$0.00
```

> ✓ **Checkpoint:** Full borrow workflow working. Events firing. Reports display correctly. All item types display polymorphically.

10.7 Extending and Refining the Application

A well-designed OOP application is easy to extend. This section demonstrates three extensions to the LMS — each requiring minimal code because the existing design accommodates them cleanly.

Extension 1: Adding a Periodical type

Adding a new media type (Periodical: issue number, volume, publication date) requires only writing the new class. The Library, LoanRecord, and all reports work immediately with no modification, because they target the MediaItem interface.

Example 1 — Introduction

Adding a Periodical class: the Library requires zero changes to accept and display it.

```
class Periodical(MediaItem):
    """A magazine or journal issue.

    Demonstrates how a new media type integrates with the existing
    system without modifying Library, reports, or loan logic.
    """

    def __init__(self, item_id, title, volume, issue, pub_date):
        super().__init__(item_id, title)
        self.volume   = volume
        self.issue    = issue
        self.pub_date = pub_date

    def display(self):
        status = "ON LOAN" if self._on_loan else "available"
        return (f"[{self._item_id}] MAG   {self._title!r:40s} Vol.{self.volume}
Iss.{self.issue} [{status}]")

    def to_dict(self):
        return {"type": "periodical", "item_id": self._item_id,
                "title": self._title, "volume": self.volume,
                "issue": self.issue, "pub_date": str(self.pub_date),
                "loan_count": self._loan_count}


# Add to the existing library — no changes to Library class needed
lib.add_item(Periodical("P001", "Australian Geographic", 221, 3, date(2026, 3,
1)))
lib.add_item(Periodical("P002", "Python Weekly",          88, 1, date(2026, 3,
15)))

lib.borrow("P001", "M002")

print("\n--- After adding Periodicals ---")
lib.report_all_items()
```

Output:

```
  [Event] Bob Smith borrowed 'Australian Geographic' (due 2026-04-04)

--- After adding Periodicals ---
  [A001] AUDIO 'Atomic Habits'                         James Clear
[ON LOAN]
  [B002] BOOK  'Clean Code'                            Robert C. Martin
[ON LOAN]
  [D002] DVD   'Interstellar'                          Christopher Nolan
[available]
  [P001] MAG   'Australian Geographic'                 Vol.221 Iss.3 [ON LOAN]
  [P002] MAG   'Python Weekly'                         Vol.88 Iss.1 [available]
  [B003] BOOK  'Python Crash Course'                   Eric Matthes
[available]
  [D001] DVD   'The Social Network'                    David Fincher
[ON LOAN]
  [B001] BOOK  'The Pragmatic Programmer'              Hunt & Thomas
[ON LOAN]
```

Extension 2: Search and popularity report

Example 2 — Variation

Returning items with simulated overdue fines, and generating the full report suite.

```
# Simulate returning an item and generate all reports
# (In a real test, we would manipulate loan due_date to simulate overdue)

print("\n--- Returning items ---")
lib.return_item("B001", "M001")
lib.return_item("D001", "M002")

# Borrow the same popular items again to build loan_count
lib.borrow("B001", "M002")
lib.borrow("B001", "M003")    # after M002 returns...

# (Normally M002 would return B001 first; shown simplified for brevity)
# Let's add some loan history by simulating multiple borrows
lib._items["B001"]._loan_count = 8    # simulate historical borrows
lib._items["B002"]._loan_count = 5
lib._items["A001"]._loan_count = 7
lib._items["D002"]._loan_count = 4

lib.report_popular(top_n=5)

# Search demonstration
print("\n--- Search: title contains 'python' ---")
for item in lib.search("python", field="title"):
    print(f"  {item}")

print("\n--- Search: type = book ---")
for item in lib.search("book", field="type"):
    print(f"  {item}")
```

Output:

```
  [Event] Alice Wong returned 'The Pragmatic Programmer'
  [Event] Bob Smith returned 'The Social Network'

=== Top 5 Most Borrowed Items ===
  1. The Pragmatic Programmer              (8 loan(s))
  2. Atomic Habits                         (7 loan(s))
  3. Clean Code                            (5 loan(s))
  4. Interstellar                          (4 loan(s))
  5. The Social Network                    (1 loan(s))

--- Search: title contains 'python' ---
  [B003] BOOK  'Python Crash Course'              Eric Matthes
[available]
  [P002] MAG   'Python Weekly'                    Vol.88 Iss.1 [available]

--- Search: type = book ---
  [B001] BOOK  'The Pragmatic Programmer'         Hunt & Thomas
[ON LOAN]
  [B002] BOOK  'Clean Code'                       Robert C. Martin
[ON LOAN]
  [B003] BOOK  'Python Crash Course'              Eric Matthes
[available]
```

Extension 3: JSON persistence

Example 3 — Real-world application

Saving and loading the library state to/from JSON.

```
import json

# Add these methods to the Library class:

    def save(self):
        """Serialise the library to JSON."""
        data = {
            "name":    self.name,
            "items":   [item.to_dict() for item in self._items.values()],
            "members": [
                {
                    "type":      m.__class__.__name__,
                    "member_id": m.member_id,
                    "name":      m.name,
                    "email":     m.email,
                }
                for m in self._members.values()
            ],
        }
        with open(self._file, "w") as f:
            json.dump(data, f, indent=2, default=str)
        print(f"Saved {len(data['items'])} items and {len(data['members'])}
members.")

    @classmethod
    def load(cls, data_file: str) -> "Library":
        """Reconstruct a Library from a JSON file."""
        with open(data_file) as f:
            data = json.load(f)

        lib = cls(data["name"], data_file)

        # Restore items via Factory
        type_map = {
            "book":       (Book,
["item_id","title","author","isbn","pages"]),
            "dvd":        (DVD,
["item_id","title","director","runtime_mins","rating"]),
            "audiobook":  (AudioBook,
["item_id","title","author","narrator","duration_hours"]),
            "periodical": (Periodical,
["item_id","title","volume","issue","pub_date"]),
        }
        for item_data in data["items"]:
            t     = item_data["type"]
            cls_r, keys = type_map[t]
            item  = cls_r(*[item_data[k] for k in keys])
            item._loan_count = item_data.get("loan_count", 0)
            lib._items[item.item_id] = item

        # Restore members
        member_map = {"PremiumMember": PremiumMember, "StandardMember":
StandardMember}
        for m_data in data["members"]:
            m_cls  = member_map.get(m_data["type"], StandardMember)
            member = m_cls(m_data["member_id"], m_data["name"],
m_data["email"])
            lib._members[member.member_id] = member

        return lib
```

```
# ── Test save and load ─────────────────────────────────────────
lib.save()

lib2 = Library.load("library.json")
print(f"\nLoaded library: {lib2.name}")
print(f"Items:   {lib2.item_count()}")
print(f"Members: {lib2.member_count()}")

lib2.report_popular(3)
```

Output:

```
Saved 8 items and 3 members.

Loaded library: Southside Public Library
Items:   8
Members: 3

=== Top 3 Most Borrowed Items ===
  1. The Pragmatic Programmer              (8 loan(s))
  2. Atomic Habits                         (7 loan(s))
  3. Clean Code                            (5 loan(s))
```

> ✓ **Checkpoint:** Full system working end-to-end: items added, members registered, borrows and returns processed, events fired, reports generated, state saved and reloaded from JSON.

Chapter 10 Summary — Book 01 Complete

- A complete OOP application is designed before it is coded. Identifying entities (nouns), attributes (data they hold), behaviours (what they do), and relationships (how they connect) produces a class structure that is maintainable and extensible from day one.
- Abstract base classes (ABC) formalise the MediaItem contract. Every concrete item type must implement display() and to_dict(). Code that processes items — reports, loans, searches — targets this interface and never needs to know the specific type.
- Inheritance is used correctly: Book, DVD, AudioBook, and Periodical are all genuine is-a MediaItem. StandardMember and PremiumMember are genuine is-a Member. Both hierarchies are shallow and purposeful.
- Encapsulation protects sensitive state: Member.fine_balance is private and only mutated through add_fine() and pay_fine(). MediaItem._on_loan is private and only changed through check_out() and return_item(). The invariant "a member cannot over-borrow" is enforced by can_borrow().
- Polymorphism through dunder methods makes print(item) work for any item type without a single isinstance() check in the reporting code. __str__ delegates to display(), which is overridden per subclass.
- The Observer pattern (LibraryEvents) decouples the library's core logic from notification behaviour. Adding an SMS alert, a database audit log, or an analytics event requires only a new handler registered via events.on() — the Library class never changes.
- The Factory pattern (MediaItemFactory, load()) reconstructs the correct subclass from serialised JSON data. The Factory isolates the "which class?" decision from the rest of the loading logic.

- The system is open to extension without modification. Adding Periodical required writing one new class — no changes to Library, LoanRecord, or any report method. This is the payoff of every design principle covered in this book.

Capstone Extension Challenges

The Library Management System is a working foundation. The following challenges extend it in directions that each exercise a specific set of skills from this book. None of these have a single correct answer — your design decisions are part of the challenge.

1. Reservation system: Implement a reservation queue for items that are currently on loan. When a member tries to borrow an unavailable item, they are offered the option to join the reservation queue (a list of member IDs in order). When the item is returned, the system automatically notifies the next member in the queue (via the event system). A member may only have one active reservation per item. Design the ReservationQueue class, integrate it into the Library.borrow() and Library.return_item() methods, and demonstrate the full cycle: item on loan, two members reserve it, item returned, first reserver notified, first reserver borrows it, second reserver notified.

2. Late return penalties with tiered fines: Extend the fine system so that the fine rate increases with the number of days overdue: $0.25/day for days 1–7, $0.50/day for days 8–14, and $1.00/day for each day beyond 14. Implement this as a Strategy pattern: define a FineStrategy abstract class with a calculate(days_overdue) method, and create ThreetieredFineStrategy and FlatRateFineStrategy as concrete implementations. The Library should accept a fine_strategy parameter at construction. Demonstrate both strategies on the same overdue loan and show the difference in calculated fines.

3. Command history with undo: Implement a simple command pattern for the borrow and return operations. Define a Command abstract class with execute() and undo() abstract methods. BorrowCommand and ReturnCommand are concrete implementations. The Library maintains a command history stack. A library.undo() method reverses the most recent command. Demonstrate: borrow three items, run undo twice (which returns those two items), verify the correct items are back in the library, and confirm the member's active loan count is correct.

4. Full persistence with member loan history: Extend save() and load() to preserve the complete state of the system: active loans (LoanRecord), completed loans, and fine balances. When loading, restore the member's active loan list and fine balance, and mark the corresponding items as on loan. After a save/load cycle, the system should behave identically to before the save: members should still have their loans, items should still be marked on loan, and fines should still be outstanding. Write a test that verifies state equivalence across a save/load cycle.

Book 01: Object-Oriented Programming in Python — Complete

You have completed all ten chapters of Book 01. From procedural thinking and the first class definition through encapsulation, inheritance, polymorphism, abstraction, dunder methods, design patterns, and a complete working application — the concepts in this book form the complete foundation of professional Python OOP.